The Entrepreneur's Guide to Running a Business

Strategy and Leadership

The Entrepreneur's Guide

CJ Rhoads, Series Editor

The Entrepreneur's Guide to Running a Business

Strategy and Leadership

CJ Rhoads

 PRAEGER

AN IMPRINT OF ABC-CLIO, LLC
Santa Barbara, California • Denver, Colorado • Oxford, England

Library of Congress Cataloging-in-Publication Data

Rhoads, CJ.
  The entrepreneur's guide to running a business : strategy and leadership / CJ Rhoads.
      pages cm. — (The entrepreneur's guide)
  Includes index.
  ISBN 978-1-4408-2988-8 (hardback) — ISBN 978-1-4408-2989-5 (ebook)
1. Strategic planning.   2. Leadership.   I. Title.
  HD30.28.R477   2014
  658—dc23   2014002966

ISBN: 978-1-4408-2988-8
EISBN: 978-1-4408-2989-5

18   17   16   15   14   1   2   3   4   5

This book is also available on the World Wide Web as an eBook.
Visit www.abc-clio.com for details.

Praeger
An Imprint of ABC-CLIO, LLC

ABC-CLIO, LLC
130 Cremona Drive, P.O. Box 1911
Santa Barbara, California 93116-1911

This book is printed on acid-free paper ∞

Manufactured in the United States of America

Contents

Illustrations

FIGURES

TABLES

Acknowledgments

As I mentioned in the acknowledgments for my first book, those who have their names on the cover of a book know that no book is written solely by the author. A good book cannot exist without an entire team of people, and it is only by convention and convenience (not to mention space) that not all of those names appear on the cover. They are no less responsible for the birth of this book than I. If this book is a success, it will be due to the determined and intelligent assistance of many people, many of them my students, partners, and employees, who helped me with the hard labor of viewing, reviewing, discussing, arguing, revising, and redoing all of the work embedded within these pages.

Obviously, the main thanks go to the authors of the books in the series, without whose wisdom this book would never have been: Dennis Chambers, Robert Everett, Dan Goldberg, Jonathan London, Donald Martin, David Nour, James Ogden, Nanci Raphael, Scott Rarick, Ken Tanner, Theo van Dijk, Anne Wenzel, and David Worrell. The content in this book has been taken and adapted from the 12 books in the series, to create this summary volume.

Those who specifically helped me by supplementing my knowledge with their expertise: Frederick Beste, David Bosler, Redmond Clark, Alan Graham, Reuel Launey, Robert Thomson, Sean Mallon, George McKee, Don Yount, Jane Morris, Carl Forssen, Joe Puglisi, Francois Dumas, and Jim Collins.

My graduate students also helped a great deal. Many were instrumental in identifying important points and clarifying major issues. They are: Ismael Arcelay, Zachary Becker, Ashley Blose, Olga Bocharova, Katie Bowers, Chad Fry, Kevin Cortazzo, Tania Dobronsky, Marcela Ferreira, Jeff Harakal, Nick Harasymczuk, Justin Hayer, David Hughes, William Ingham, Rachel Ingram, Jeffrey Kakaley, Kevin Kensicki, Ken Lytz, Chris Najpauer, Lynn Oberneder, Joao Rodrigues, Tom Schu, Trish Shermot, Drew Skelton,

Michael Stampler, Patrick Tramontaro, Wan-Lin Tsai, Christoph Tschapele, Stacy Villamil, Erte Zhang, Xiao Zheng, Chenkai Zhu, and Tyler Zucchiatti.

Additionally, tops in my book would be Jeff Olson, Brian Romer, and Hilary Claggett, the series of acquisitions editors at Praeger/ABC-CLIO, all who worked tirelessly to make this series a success and who asked me to put a capstone on the series by writing this book, thereby giving me the motivation to do what I really wanted to do anyway.

The following people did the difficult task of reviewing various chapters of the book as it was being written: Frederick Beste, Redmond Clark, Alan Graham, Lila Bellando, Mary Ann Stangil, Polly Beste, Reuel Launey, Robert Thomson, Siobhan Hutchinson, Sean Mallon, Steve Meng, Virginia Breen, George McKee, Don Yount, Mary Sturtevant, Lee Willman, Bill Danylik, John Doran, Anne Adams, Jane Morris, Marcia Gobeil, and Alice Cory.

Many of my previous clients appear in these pages, though few with their real names. In any case, my own knowledge is always expanded greatly by those for whom I served for so many years as a strategic management consultant, for I learn much from them in the course of our activities together. I'd especially like to extend my heartfelt thanks to Lee Baker, Peter Baker, David Bosler, David Dries, Bob Goodman, Michael Guido, Joanne Just, Mary Kendray Gelenser, Conrad Karlson, Andy Klee, Pat Krick, Harriet Layton, Steve and Michelle Moyer, Jane Palmer, Ernie Post, Samantha Reimert, LuAnn Seyler, Patrick Sullivan, Anthony Triano, and Linda Wade.

Additionally, I thank the employees and team members of my business and nonprofit organization: Stella Deeble, George Deeble, Denise Rankin, Justin Roach, Erica Hesselson, Gary Bankston, Joe Reighn, Jack Sol-church, Joe Puglisi, Raymond Melcher, Nancy Magee, Isse Elston-Phillips, Nicole Plank, Bruce La Carrubba, Roger Jahnke, Steve Arbitman, Sally Milbury-Steen, and Luk Jih. All were impacted by my decisions and helped me to do what was best.

Of course, none of this would be possible without my many mentors over the years (in alphabetical order): Fred Beste, David Bosler, Jack Bradt, Tom Casey, Betsy Chapman, David Chen, Martin Cheatle, Jim Collins, Bill Douglas, Vanessa DiMauro, Jonathan Dreazen, Francois Dumas, Marsha Egan, Dale Falcinelli, Roger Jahnke, John Lucht, John MacNamara, Nancy Magee, Ray Melcher, John Morgan, Pete Musser, Maggie Newman, Josephine Painter, Joe Puglisi, Leo Robb, Lee Scheele, Glenn Snelbecker, Steve Sperling, Alan Weiss, Kevin Wren, and Yang Yang. Though the amount of time I spent with each varied, each one has given me a gift that has turned out to be of extreme value in my never-ending quest to improve myself.

No list would be complete without my fabulous family: my mother, Judith Liffick, along with my brothers and sisters, Jeffrey Devlin (and his wife Melissa), T. Max Devlin, Eileen Piccolo, and Denise Rankin. I also received a great deal of help and advice from several of my accomplished aunts and uncles, most of whom are authors in their own right: Tom and Barb Liffick, Blaise and Alana Liffick, Kathy Liffick, Mike Lillich, Charles and Elsie Jane Lorber, and Anita and Gary Young.

For anyone who I have inadvertently left off this list, I am heartily sorry. My own Swiss-cheese brain does the best that it can, but it is far from perfect.

Most important of all, of course, is my patient and loving husband Bob. He is my life and my world, and I am so lucky to have found my soul mate and true love so early in my life. To have spent the past 30 years with a man of his incredible talents would have been a treat to anyone, but to have loved him, and been loved by him, all that time is a pleasure of epic proportion.

Introduction

Almost ten years ago, my then-agent, Jeff Olson, came to me with the idea for a series of books on different topics that would cover the essential skills needed by entrepreneurs and business owners. Practical, useful advice from experienced business owners was very hard to find. Jeff thought the business world needed a book series on the subject.

WHY THE ENTREPRENEUR'S GUIDE TO . . . SERIES

This series covers the full cycle of business ownership, not just the beginning of the effort. The series covers business concepts, analysis, business plan development, and financing options, but then moves on to sales, marketing, operations, and team management. With this capstone book, the series also covers our own personal growth, including leadership development and strategic management.

This series was to be different than any other—not filled with fluff or glorifying the process. Not making promises about how much fun it is to start a business. Not so complex that it takes a Ph.D. in English to decipher.

The existing books designed to inspire, motivate, and encourage dreams are great. But they don't get into the nitty-gritty of actually starting and running a business. Entrepreneurs need meat and vegetables, not just appetizers. Scholarly academic books have their own place too. At the same time, entrepreneurs need authors who will speak to them as equals, sharing the secrets of success they have found as they built their own businesses.

About the Series

The authors in this series were handpicked by myself, or Jeff Olson, or Brian Romer (who eventually took over from Jeff when he moved on to another publisher). They were chosen because they could write in an accessible manner. They were chosen because they are mostly entrepreneurs and business owners. They were chosen because they know their stuff.

This series gets into the muck. We share our knowledge and experiences. We specify what works, and what doesn't. We tell stories about our successes and our mistakes. This series is accessible, scholarly, trustworthy, and fully credible. We do not do fluff.

We talk about *how*. How to write a business plan. How to write a proposal. How to get financing. How to find and hire the best people. How to keep them working together in a team. How to handle crises. How to grow. How to make decisions about information technology. How to do marketing. How to figure out what makes advertising work. How to do the marketing research to know which products and services to provide. How to sell (perhaps the most important of all!). How to find capital. How to understand financial statements. How to handle success. And, how to deal with failure.

About This Book

In order to determine how to write this book, I reread each book in the series (some of which I had edited more than eight years ago, including my own) and cogitated on what I thought was most important. What had changed (if anything) since I had originally read it? What order should an entrepreneur or business owner read them? Where are the overlaps? What sections would be most helpful to resolve which problems? What topics were needed that were not included in the series? I tried to organize the topics in a way that made sense.

The goal of this book is to meet the needs of both newly minted entrepreneurs as well as long-established business owners. As entrepreneurs and business owners, we need to run the gamut from concept, to development, to marketing funnel, to prospect, to pipeline, to fulfillment, to backlog, to collections—which is tough. As leaders, we need to set expectations and create a process to meet those expectations, both for ourselves and for our employees. The scope is enormous.

This book can only touch upon each of the topics. We wanted to include enough depth to become a practical how-to guide, a reference throughout the life of the business. We hope that readers can return to this book, again and again, for help and advice over the years. When additional details are needed for any one of the topics, we hope that the related book in the series can be consulted.

Chapter Contents

After much thought, I decided to add some of the research I personally did on strategies to flourish through a recession, which I cover in Chapter 1.

I also added some of my research on leadership to Chapter 2, along with the highlights from the books in the series that discuss leadership. Chapter 3 talks about writing the business plan from the series, with added updates on some of the newer thinking regarding business models and planning. Chapter 4 focuses on finding and building the team, while Chapter 5 covers the changes in information technology over the past five years. Chapter 6 gets into marketing, while Chapters 7 and 8 delve more deeply into branding, pricing, and proposing—important topics that are often glossed over in entrepreneurial literature. Chapter 9 reveals the secrets of successful salespeople, while Chapter 10 shares the riddle of how successful entrepreneurs use the different financial views of their business to manage operations quickly and efficiently.

Chapter 11 concentrates on identifying sources of capital funding for expansion and growth. While it may seem odd to put this near the end, its position demonstrates the recognition that getting external funding generally requires an existing profitable business. Unless we are already serial entrepreneurs with several successful businesses under our belts, we have to succeed before we can expand. Finally, Chapter 12 talks about my own personal experience—what does success look like and how can we take it forward once we've accomplished our goals.

Both fledgling and experienced business owners will find going through the chapter activities helpful as they expand their businesses through many cycles of growth. This book will help everyone adjust their strategy for this new recession economy and technology-driven world.

Whose Voice Is Whose?

The style of this book, and one you will find throughout the series, is informal, almost folksy, as if we were entrepreneurs sitting together in a room, sharing our lessons with other experienced entrepreneurs (though there might be a few neophytes in the room listening in). Generally, we use the first person plural for what "we entrepreneurs" know we should do rather than the "you should" used by experts preaching from ivory towers.

When an author identified a specific idea in their book original to them, I point out directly which author wrote it when I present the information in this book. When sharing information that is either well known, or presented by multiple authors, I present it simply as advice. Think of the ideas and advice from all the authors in the series as a whole, and not as coming from any one individual person.

Real names are often used to give credit, using both first and last names when first introduced. When an example story is presented with just a first name, the name has been changed. To get the first-person stories of the book authors, I encourage you to read the individual books, which are chock-full of examples, stories, worksheets, demonstrations, and other en-hancements. What I present in this one volume is just the tip of the iceberg of knowledge and experience in entrepreneurship and business owner-ship available in the individual books in the series. Each is well worth the trip on its own.[1]

When I use first person singular, I am talking about myself, CJ Rhoads. In most cases, I relate stories from my own life as a serial entrepreneur that correlate with the lessons shared by the authors, introducing them as *cases*, and they are set off in boxed text.

We hope that by sharing this information, we will enable others like us—entrepreneurs and business people—to become more successful.

HOW AND WHY YOU SHOULD READ THIS BOOK

Although this book is the last in the series, it may be best read first because this book takes the nuggets—the best ideas and the best lessons—from all the other books and puts them together in one place. If you haven't actually started a business yet, this book will give you the taste you need to figure out whether or not you should start one. If you have already started one, then you will reap the benefits of knowing how to avoid our mistakes and profit from our successes.

Our Economy Needs Your Help

With the current economy, government agencies and communities are encouraging small business ownership, more than ever. Many see entre-preneurship as the solution to bring us out of the doldrums of recession with which we have been meandering for the past five years. Small busi-nesses generate the most employment for the most people, far eclipsing large businesses when it comes to ensuring employment overall. In 2008, there were over 30 million businesses in the United States, generating over $35 billion in revenue. Due to the economic crisis, the revenues have de-creased since then. But the *number* of businesses is increasing at a dramatic rate (U.S. Census Bureau 2012).

There are many reasons for this prolific launch of start-ups. Bright en-thusiastic people, freshly downsized with a generous package, are in a good position to start a company. They are no longer working under the yoke of corporate culture, and have lots of pent-up creativity. With their brains, a little bit of saved cash, and hoards of unemployed workers who are getting more desperate as their unemployment insurance runs out, it seems almost obvious they should start a business. Add in the cheaper equipment, and abundant inexpensive office space available, and it seems like a match made in heaven!

Governments and communities are encouraging entrepreneurship through grants, low interest rates, and tax credits. Furthermore, recent new legislation has become law that will allow business owners to obtain capital through crowdsourcing (soliciting investors over the Internet), which may increase business ownership even more.

The economy doesn't need any more failing businesses. They need successful businesses. This book can help new businesses get started on the right track.

You Need Help Dealing with the Economy

This book is helpful for the existing business owner as well as start-ups. During the boom years, it was easy to profit and grow, but now, we may find ourselves struggling to make a profit. Now is the time to pause. With this series, we can take a step back and take a look at where we are going. We may need additional information to succeed. In addition to reiterating the best lessons from the series, this book adds knowledge and experience from current economic times.

Some of the first books in the series were written before the great recession. Additionally, technology has changed to a mobile generation, and there is another technology revolution about to start—for which we business owners should be ready. This book enhances the value of the other books in the series by updating the information wherever necessary.

HOW AND WHY YOU SHOULD READ THE SERIES

After reading this book, you will know which of the other books you might need to read for a fuller, more comprehensive view. In some cases, where you can see that you are already up to speed on the topic, this book will give you just the nudge of a reminder to remember what you already know. In other cases, you might see where the biggest holes in your own knowledge are, where you need to get a deeper understanding in order to be successful.

Some of the information in this series is eye opening. You may encounter new directions and creative solutions to problems with which you've been struggling for a while. This series will help you solve your problems in several ways.

Learn from Those Who Have Succeeded . . . and Failed

Nothing succeeds like success. Shortly after I started my first business, I was taking an entrepreneurship course at Lehigh University, where I met Jack Bradt, a successful business owner. He eventually became my long-term mentor, helping me countless times throughout the years. I credit him for the turnaround success of my first fledgling start-up.

His teaching method was to bring in many entrepreneurs who shared the secrets of their success. For each entrepreneur, the class assignment was to write the equivalent of a five-page paper to answer 10 questions based upon the talk. My classmates complained bitterly about the heavy workload, but because I was actually running a business, I found the practical lessons from each of the entrepreneurs invaluable. Similarly, this series was designed to share what works, and what doesn't, from people who've been there.

Learn Actively, Not Passively

These books are powerful by themselves. But they are even more powerful if you bring your active attention to them. If Jack Bradt had just let us sit back and listen to those entrepreneurs, we would not have learned the lessons. It was only after the words of the entrepreneur were no longer ringing in our heads, after we had a chance to sit down and really think about what they said, as we actually put pen to paper to answer the questions, that the lesson was learned. It takes more than just hearing or reading to make it through the labyrinth of obstacles in our brain. Those ideas needed to find a place to sit, where the lesson would take root so that it could come floating back up from our memory at just the right time in the future.

I encourage you, therefore, to take some time after each chapter to really think about the contents. Don't just skip the summary points, but read them. Focus on them. Think about how they might apply, or not, to your current situation. Think about how they might apply to a future situation you might find yourself in. When given an exercise, don't skip it. Actually do it. Put pen to paper (or fingers to keyboard) and fill out the tables, write up the lists, answer the questions.

Some of the advice in these books may, at first, seem odd. For example, in the chapter on Selling, I talk about when my sales coach told me to give up writing proposals entirely. I laughed in his face and thought he was crazy. But after I tried it, I realized the wisdom of the advice. Now, I understand why it works to stop spending so much time on proposals (and after you read this book, you will understand why as well).

Bob Everett introduced the continuous thinking graphic in his book (Figure I.1). This idea demonstrates the importance of learning lessons, trying them out, assessing the results, reflecting on what works and what doesn't, and making better decisions in the future.

All the books in the series are surprisingly useful for the type of decision making that face entrepreneurs and business owners every day. They tell interesting stories to reinforce the lessons so that we will remember them. They help us understand which past decisions were mistakes, and which ones were going in the right direction. They can help us make our future decisions better.

Figure I.1. Continuous Thinking: Assess Past Decisions to Improve Future Decisions

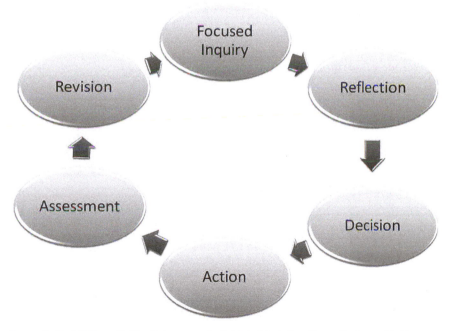

Source: Robert F. Everett, *The Entrepreneur's Guide to Marketing.* Santa Barbara, CA: Praeger, 2008.

1

Strategy: Flourishing in Business during a Recession

In October 2008, out of the blue, I got a phone call from one of the editors for whom I had written a couple dozen articles.

He asked me, "How did you know?"

"Huh?" I had no clue. "How did I know what?" I responded.

"How did you know that there was going to be a horrible financial crisis? How did you know it six months before it happened?"

Turns out he'd been rereading some of my articles, and in March 2008, I had written about the coming credit crunch, the impending financial crisis, and the looming relentless recession that would last for years and years. In my original draft, I had written that the period that was coming was going to be horrific, "the likes of which we hadn't seen since the Depression." The erstwhile editor hadn't believed it at the time. He'd struck out the phrase as being too over-the-top and softened my statements about how bad the coming financial crisis was going to be for publication. However, since he still had the original, he knew that my draft statement was correct. My prediction came true.

My ability to predict the financial crisis in October 2008 was not some great feat. It doesn't mean that I'm any better at predicting the daily stock market than anyone else (much to the chagrin of my spouse, who would love to implement nefarious plans to use my predictive powers for financial gain).

Indeed, I was only one of many who had predicted the financial crisis. But, at the time, it was clear to me that it was going to happen, and going to happen relatively soon. To me, once you looked at the economic indicators, it was pure common sense.[1]

We all know what happened. Popular press dubbed the week of October 6, 2008 as *Black Week*, in reference to *Black Tuesday* (October 29, 1929), which harkened the coming Great Depression and *Black Monday*

(October 19, 1987), when the stock market declined by 25 percent in one day. To most, the current financial crisis is known as *The Great Recession* (Kwoh 2010). The worst economic conditions ensued; five years running so far, and probably many more to go before we see the light at the end of the tunnel. It is far from over.

STARTING A BUSINESS DURING A RECESSION

Which of the following businesses do you think started during a recession: General Motors, General Electric, Disney, Hyatt, iHOP, CNN, Trader Joe's, Burger King, Federal Express, IBM, Microsoft, Google, or Apple?[2] If you guessed before looking at the footnote, did you get it right?

The truth is, during a recession is absolutely the best time ever to start a business. More than half the large successful companies today were started in the midst of a recession of the past (Stangler 2009). It is often the best alternative when jobs are scarce. There are a lot of highly talented people around who are not able to find employment either. And there are great deals to be had as companies go out of business all around you.

People focus every effort, watch every cent, and make "one dollar do the work of two" (as my grandmother used to say) during a recession. People are more satisfied with "just enough" money to survive. Everyone pitches in, and distractions are fewer.

Even more than that, entrepreneurs tend to thrive emotionally when working in their own venture toward the goal of their own eventual success. Entrepreneurs don't have to satisfy the stockholders' need for profits—just their customers' need for products and services. Generally, they work in an industry that they love. This is one of the biggest advantages small start-up companies have over large established businesses during a recession. Passion beats profits.

Starting a business during a recession is not problem-free. When a bad economy hits, banks tighten their controls and cause a credit crunch. Credit is hard to get for anything except for cold hard assets.

In 1990, I borrowed money to expand my business. I discovered that many banks were willing to lend me money to buy the computers, but only one bank was willing to also lend me money to hire people, advertise, and pay for the development of the instructional manuals.[1]

[1] Even that bank wasn't perfect; they just "assumed" that my husband, who had nothing to do with my business, would be the one borrowing the money and signing the paperwork. I had to threaten them with complaints to the regulators to get them to lend me the money in my name alone as a female business owner.

Getting capital is not impossible. All it takes is that one banker who will lend us money, that one angel who will invest, that one venture capitalist who believes. A friend of mine, James Chan, author of *Spare Room Tycoon* (2000), likes to say, "If you kiss enough frogs, eventually one of them will turn into a prince." People who can sustain their efforts during a long, difficult economic downturn will attract capital and thrive.

Recession-Proof Industries

In 2006, I put together a team of students and faculty to research business failure and business success. Before we finished our first research project, the recession hit. The literature often referred to recession-proof industries, so the research team changed our research focus and investigated recession industries in more depth. Are there industries that do better during a recession, industries that perhaps should be the focus during hard times?

We found many lists of recession-proof industries in the literature. Yet, none agreed on *which* industries belonged on those lists. If we look at the different recessions, historically, the "recession-proof" industries were different for each recession. There is no way to tell ahead of time which industries will be okay.

Financial researcher Scott Shane put together a list of high-growth industries (based upon the number of employees) after the 2003 recession. At that time, manufacturing and a new industry called digital printing topped the list (Shane 2005). Our research team took a look at the most recent data: those industries did not fare well in the most recent recession. As can be seen in Table 1.1, education and healthcare topped the list this time (with all of 2 percent growth). They were not even on the radar as high-growth industries in 2003.

We should keep in mind that there are still successes even in industries hardest hit by the recession. Some companies in those industries are making more profits than ever before. Additionally, even within so called recession-proof industries, some companies fail.

Research into Financial Factors of Business Success

The pattern of successes and failures in different industries led the team to this conclusion: There is something different about companies that thrive during a recession. It's not just the luck of the draw. In 2009, we began to investigate the topic.

The first project we completed was to identify factors that impacted business results during a recession. We used a statistic called binary logistical regression analysis, which is a fancy way of saying we let the

Table 1.1. How Different Industries Faired during 2008–2009 Recession

NAICS code	NAICS code description	2009 Paid Employees	2008 Paid Employees	Percent Change # of employees
61	Educational services	3,201	3,141	2%
62	Healthcare and social assistance	17,531	17,217	2%
22	Utilities	642	639	0
55	Management of companies and enterprises	2,853	2,887	-1%
54	Professional, scientific, and technical sectors	7,840	8,033	-2%
71	Arts, entertainment, and recreation	2,010	2,069	-3%
81	Other services (except public administration)	5,264	5,453	-4%
21	Mining, quarrying, and oil and gas extraction	605	629	-4%
72	Accommodations and food services	11,443	11,926	-4%
51	Information	3,288	3,434	-4%
44	Retail Trade	14,803	15,615	-5%
52	Finance and Insurance	6,171	6,512	-6%

Source: HPL Consortium, Inc., copyright 2014, used with permission.

computer compare all of the different combinations of all the factors until it figured out which ones were actually important (Rhoads and Gupta 2012).[3] We started out with 38 objective quantitative factors, and identified which were the most influential for companies that thrived through at least three of the last six recessions (the number of recessions we've had since 1960). Nine of the 38 factors made the cut:[4]

- Fortune Rank
- Relative price-to-book ratio
- Quick ratio
- Total debt-to-total asset ratio
- Three-year total return
- EBITDA margin

- Relative five-year total return compared to S&P sector
- Research and development expense-to-sales ratio and
- Annual retained earnings-to-net income ratio

Companies that thrived during three recessions did better when compared to their industry sector, not just when compared to the average company overall. That eliminated the mitigating factor that some industries do better during a recession than others. These were companies that did better than their peers in the same industry.

We learned many things from this research. First, size does matter. The small fry got eaten, and the large fry just kept on swimming. Second, age before beauty—if a company has been around forever, it takes more than a couple of years of bad times to bring it down.

For companies that started just before a recession, it was a different story. They were the most likely to fail. Paradoxically, the exact opposite was true for companies that started during or just after a recession.

One of the most important influences was how much money the company had retained from earnings over the years. Companies that tended to spend (or give away in dividends) profits made in previous years didn't have a cushion to fall back on when bad times hit. In other words, it's helpful to save for a rainy day. It's essential if it pours.

Quantitative objective factors are a good start, but there is only so much they can tell us in the subjective domain of entrepreneurship and success. So, the team turned to more qualitative research, studying pairs of companies, both successful and unsuccessful.

Factors that Lead to Business Failure

The first question we asked was: *What are the top 10 qualitative factors that lead to bankruptcy in recessionary times?* We identified these factors as most influential in companies that failed:

- Marginal business model
- Uncompetitive value proposition
- Overextended finances
- Overextended management
- Programs/projects too ambitious
- Across-the-board budget cuts
- Treading water mentality
- Failed partnerships

Marginal Business Model

During good economic times, even poor business models can stay afloat. But when the economy stinks, the rubber hits the road, and the basic business model of the company has to be a good one. The customer must still need the product and the company must still be able to deliver the product. Income still has to exceed the expenses.

The most common business model problem is a failure to look at the break-even point. High fixed costs during a recession can kill a business. Running a business with the expectation of 5 million in sales when the volume only comes in at 2 million is a problem. The opposite—running a business with the expectation of 1 million in sales when the volume comes in at 2 million—is generally not as much of a problem (though paradoxically it too can lead to business failure). This doesn't mean that business owners should aim low, but they do need to temper expectations with reality.

Value Proposition of Competition Is Better

Branding and superior customer service add value to the customer transaction, often enough to provide superior gross margins and ensure success—during good economic times. But the influence of branding and customer service changes with poor economic times because the number of potential customers (those who can afford the extra margin) is fewer. Many previous customers no longer have the luxury of being able to pay for the brand. When the economy goes in the toilet, customers flee to cheaper goods and services.

Overextension

A common condition for businesses is that, just before the recession, they may have overextended themselves. There are three ways to overextend: overextended finances, overextended management, and too ambitious programs/projects.

Overextended finances means debt overload. When we start to experience success, we begin to expand—sometimes at exactly the wrong time.

A few years after I started my first business, a technology training and consulting firm, I made the big jump and borrowed money from a bank. When I borrowed the money, interest rates were reasonable, and business was booming. I hired people, purchased more computers, and fitted out a custom-designed computer training lab a block away from our office. The expansion started out wonderfully. Less than a year later, however, the first Gulf War started, and the 1991 recession hit.

Unfortunately for me, interest rates were not kept in check as they were in the most recent recession. My interest payments doubled. People were fearing for their lives because of the war, and no one was interested in technology training. Business dried up.

I weathered the poor times because they lasted less than a year. Soon, training rooms started filling up again. But I spent many sleepless nights during those months contemplating a bleak future, and I nearly lost my business. While no one can predict the future, I should have been more cognizant of the economic indicators, which would have told me to hold off on expansion for a year or two.

Another common problem is overextended management, or stress overload—trying to do too much.

One of my former clients had this problem. The business was a small family company, serving the local community for almost 100 years. The owner, Tom, was the grandson of the founder. He was trying to develop the company into several different businesses. While he justified the expansion as "diversifying," I saw several problems. First, Tom was trying to manage the five different divisions himself. Second, the different divisions were not closely related, and each had a completely different business model. Tom was running himself ragged— getting up at 3:00 A.M. to do a truck run for one business, returning to the office at 7:00 A.M. to see off the field teams in the second business and to manage the retail portion of the third business. Then, he stayed late to complete the paperwork and do the sales and marketing for the fourth and fifth business.

Tom said he was doing fine with this arrangement, but anyone watching him knew that he was not; he was overloaded with the stress of keeping all the balls in the air. The senior management team, doing five times the amount of work, was also feeling the stress. During the first few years, when the economy was strong and business was booming, the added load wasn't too much of a problem. When the primary business started to decline due to the economy, though, all the divisions suffered and the writing was on the wall. (Unfortunately, I was unable to convince the business owner to sell or close any of his businesses. Within two years, the IRS had put liens on his properties because he hadn't paid his taxes and the banks foreclosed because he hadn't kept up his payments.)

Overly ambitious projects are also a problem. Consider Kim, who had spent a year planning the opening of a second and third location for an established 10-year-old retail clothes business. The launch date had been set for January 2009, and all the paperwork was set to be signed in November 2008. Let us imagine that we are Kim, and we hear about the stock market crash in October. What might we think of the situation? That perhaps now is not the right time? That perhaps changes should be made in the scope and timing of the plans? Perhaps if we are smart. But chances are our minds will be paralyzed in fear at the overwhelming thought of the predicted financial devastation of the economy. Our minds will grasp at whatever course will hold off the panic; we will insist that it is not as bad as they say, that the financial impact will be short term and limited to other industries. We will deny the brutal facts and continue on as if there had been no change. We would probably sign the paperwork, and open the two new locations. Two years later, our business will have folded because the new locations could not attract enough business due to the recession to pay off the added cost of capital from the expansion. If we had just stuck with the one store which had been in business for ten years with an already established customer base and no debt, we might have survived (perhaps even thrived) throughout the long recession.

Across-the-Board Budget Cuts

You'd think that cutting the budget when the recession hits would be a good thing, but there is a right way and a wrong way to do it. Companies that flourished were careful about where they cut costs. Cutting the budget across the board may sound fair, but the reality is that it is a big mistake. Companies that cut across the board, or who cut deeply into research, development, or marketing, tended to fail more often.

We need to focus *only* on our most important income stream and ensure dedication to our most profitable customers instead of cutting everything.

Treading Water Mentality

The only thing worse than across-the-board budget cuts is mentally treading water. If the leaders of an organization stick their head in the sand, don't deal with the problem up front, and try to wait out the difficulties, they end up facing the crisis long after it is too late to do anything about it. Sometimes, business owners are paralyzed by indecision. They just keep on keeping on, without making any adjustments or changes. They end up doing nothing at all about the changing conditions.

When a recession hits, if business waits to see what the outcome is, the delay lowers the chance for survival. The more quickly the business makes the necessary adjustments to the new economy, the higher the chances of survival. Even the wrong moves are better than no moves. Doing nothing is like a slow poison, showing a lack of leadership, and ensuring the destruction of the business eventually. However, the right adjustments made quickly enough will allow a business to flourish.

Failed Partnerships

Another poison? Trusting the wrong partner, or not having a contingency plan when strategic partnerships fall by the wayside. Consider my friend, Leslie. After finally reaching an agreement with the technology developer so that work on the new product could begin, Leslie was looking forward to progress. What Leslie didn't know was that the technology developer had just implemented across-the-board budget cuts. Because of the cut in the budget, their star programmer jumped ship to a competitor. The remaining team could not develop the new product without the star programmer. Within six months, the technology developer had gone out of business, leaving Leslie with a huge expense for a product that will never see the light of day and no refund in sight. Leslie might have done everything else right when the recession hit, but had not considered that strategic suppliers also had to do the right thing for the business to survive.

ACTIONS OF FLOURISHING BUSINESSES DURING A RECESSION

Another way to look at the situation is to study factors in flourishing companies to see if the recession made a difference. We put together a list of those factors that were specifically recession related. Businesses that exhibited these behaviors were more profitable than businesses that did not exhibit these factors (even if they both survived) during the recession. Not surprisingly, they mirrored many of the factors we identified as leading to failure during a recession. The factors are:

- Ensure trusted leadership
- Quick response
- Conserve cash
- Strengthen the core
- Eliminate overhead and cut expenses with a scalpel
- Focus on the customer
- Diversify
- Take advantage of downtime
- Maintain innovations
- Think and plan strategically

Ensure Trusted Leadership

When people are scared, they look to people they trust. Believe it or not, recessions can be good for interpersonal development. Dealing effectively with hard times can build relationships in a way that good times never do; shared pain, shared mission, and overcoming obstacles together are a strong key to thriving.

In Reading PA, there is a hardworking gentleman named Al Boscov, who ran the local department store started by his father. He built the business into a chain of 40 stores in five states. He was highly regarded, and well-liked by everyone. He gave back through community projects for the good of everyone in the region. I know from personal experience that there are people in his employment, people who have been touched by his generosity and warmth, who would walk through fire for him.

Al retired about five years prior to the recession. A year into the recession, however, the company that he had built fell on hard times. Boscov's filed for Chapter 11 bankruptcy in 2008. Al Boscov, without a word of incrimination or blame, came out of retirement and returned to the company. People trusted him. People rallied around him. People knew that with his backing, they could do anything. They knew that he would come through, and he did.

Actually, that's a misnomer. He didn't come through; he enabled everyone else to come through. He communicated the difficulties. He outlined possible solutions. He got everyone—his employees, his vendors, the local government, the state government, the customers—he got them all pulling together, rowing in synergy. The company was saved and is stronger than ever. In 2011, it started opening up stores again, and all the vendors had been fully paid. There is no one in the community who does not look to him as one of the most effective leaders they have ever met, including me.

Quick Response

Making hard decisions in the face of difficulty in a timely manner is the hallmark of a trusted leader. People may not like all the decisions made, but they will understand them, and support them, if they have trust in the people who are making them. But the decisions must be made quickly. Delay is not a friend. That's why contingency planning is so important. Strong leaders already have, in their back pocket, a plan B, and a plan C, and a D, E, F, and G. When a crisis hits, there is no time to lose. We can't wait for the problem to be obvious before we start reacting. We also can't wait for the problem to develop the relationships necessary to solve it. Those relationships must already exist.

Conserve Cash

In times of economic crisis, conserving cash is key. As Fred Beste (CEO of Mid-Atlantic Venture Fund, Chair of the Board of the Ben Franklin Technology Partnership, one of my mentors and a good friend) likes to say: Cash is more important than your mother. In a study of 1,300 companies and how they responded during the recession in 2001, companies that did well cut dividends right away—within months of the crisis. Those who waited a year or more to make the change barely survived (Dobbs, Karakolev, and Raj 2007).

Strengthen the Core

Jim Collins (Collins and Porras 1994) calls this core strength the *Hedgehog Concept*. It is what the business does best, better than anyone else, anywhere else. Recognizing one's own hedgehog concept, and understanding how to make the most of that understanding, is an important criterion for prioritizing budgets. Businesses that properly prioritize their budgets are able to flourish during a recession. We can't go wrong by focusing on the core.

> One of my clients, Jessie, had a JD Edwards consulting business with about 30 employees. Just before the recession, the company had expanded into software sales and maintenance. After working with me, and after a more in-depth look, it became obvious that business's forte was training and consulting, not software and maintenance. We cut the entire budget for software and maintenance. (It was especially helpful that much of the expense for software and maintenance is overhead, whereas consulting, typically, has high variable and low fixed costs.) Jessie claims this move saved the business, and it flourished over the next few years by focusing solely on what the company was best at—training and consulting.

Eliminate Overhead and Cut Expenses with a Scalpel

Now is the time to attack the budget with a scalpel and not a machete. Cutting the budget across the board has already been identified as a factor associated with business failure. Not cutting the budget at all is even worse, and cutting the wrong items out of the budget (such as advertising, development, and customer service) is the worst of all. To really flourish, a business must cut the budget—deeply—in many places, but *increase* the budget in other places. The key is understanding the break-even point.[5]

For example, it is usually a mistake to cut the advertising budget during a recession. Customers will have less money to spend in an economic downturn. Competition will get fierce (at least, initially, until our competitors go out of business). Therefore, it is often necessary to increase advertising and marketing costs during a recession. To cut those costs would be like throwing the life rafts off the boat to lighten the load when the ship is sinking.

The place to look for cost cuts is administration. Cut out as much of the administrative support as possible. For example, Jonnie was the owner of an elevator manufacturing company. They were just about to start a major project to automate the back end check processing when the recession hit. As a smart move, Jonnie eliminated the project. As sales dwindled, it was easy to see that the decision was the right one. Cost savings for those types of projects require an increase in volume, not a decrease.

Cancel unnecessary trips and strategic planning weekends in exotic locations. Double up on offices and sublease half the office space. Repurpose all of the secretaries and clerks. No one can afford to be solely a back-office person when there aren't enough sales to keep them busy. Focus should be on sales, sales, and sales.

People who had previously risen to administrative positions can (temporarily) return to frontline operations or sales in order to increase volume and profits without increasing costs. Senior managers can take on the tasks previously done by the people they managed. Another alternative is asking people to work part time instead of full time, or take a small pay cut.

I can hear the ego-driven fears in the response. Many business owners might resist. "But they won't do that!" some business owners will cry. They fear losing their best people. Perhaps. Whether they will or not is much more dependent upon the relationship between the business owner and the employees than anything else, and in how the employees are approached about these various options.

We can put ourselves in the shoes of the employees. If I'm an employee, and I have the ability to save the company by going back and answering phones in addition to managing a division, I'm going to do it *if I like and trust the business owner.*

If I'm going to sacrifice my own position or salary, the change can't be mandated to me. It is best if I am given the opportunity to be part of the brainstorming session, along with my coworkers, in trying to find solutions to the problem of lower sales and spiraling downward profits. I have to volunteer for this change, and feel that I'm doing it to save my own future job.

I have to believe that this is *shared pain*—everyone in the company is sacrificing something, not just a select few. I want to see the owner doing lower level tasks, and working more hours than me. (This is a great time for a business owner to go without an assistant, personal secretary, or receptionist.)

As an employee who is asked to do a lower level task or take a pay cut, I have to trust that the business owner isn't going to take advantage of the situation and keep me down after the crisis is over. The appreciation for my sacrifice from the owner and other team leaders has to be palpable and genuine. It must be made clear to me that I'm not being demoted, or blamed. It must be clear that this action is in not in response to anything that I've done wrong, but is, instead something that I'm doing right, something that reveals my dedicated loyalty to the team. This action must be absolutely necessary. It must be communicated clearly that bankruptcy and job loss is the only alternative to such a drastic action.

In order to trust this fact, I (and all of the employees) must be educated on the numbers. I have to understand the real financial story, and I have to be convinced that my largesse isn't going to end up lining the pocket of the owner.

If I'm an employee who directly supports customers, I'm one of the people on the front lines who make or break the business. If the need were demonstrated to me, I'd probably be willing to take on a larger load of the administration such as filing my own forms and entering my own data. I can probably do that without sacrificing customer service quality. Indeed, in many cases, such activities increase quality because if I'm a sales person, I'm probably much more in tune with the needs of the customer. Satisfying their needs myself streamlines the operations, decreases the opportunities for mistakes and disconnects, and ensures a higher quality customer experience, which leads to more loyal customers who spend more money with us.

The bottom line is that involving the employees in the decision making process of how to cut the budget is essential, and a trusted relationship between the employees and the leadership is a key element in that process.

Focus on the Customer

We also can't go wrong by focusing on the customer. One of the best companies I ever worked for had the words "Think like a customer" stenciled over every single door in every single building. There is no such thing as too much focus on the customer.

Some business owners think this means going out and doing focus groups and asking the existing customers about their customer experience in after-the-service surveys. There is a time and place for both focus groups and surveys, but they cannot be used as the sole point of measurement.

One of my business owner clients insisted that customers wanted the counter to be open all day long. They believed that none of the customers cared whether they could get information about the services through the website. They knew this because they had surveyed their customers. Indeed, the elderly couples who tottered up to the counter every few months to order something would tell you that having the counter service available all day long was important. And they would never order anything on the website.

Of course, you see the problem. Personalized counter service was what the existing customers want. But if this business owner wanted to attract new customers, online ordering, website coupons, or a Facebook page would be more appropriate. If there had been enough current customers to keep the company profitable, no changes would be needed. In this case, the number of customers was getting smaller every year because they were dying of old age. This business needed to attract the next generation of customers if they were going to make a profit.

Diversify

Now, given my current rant on focusing and sticking to your core (your hedgehog concept), you might think I'm antidiversity. Nothing could be farther from the truth. A strong factor of success in a recession is also a diversity of products, services, and/or geography. However, let's be clear about the type of diversity; this isn't the type of diversity where the company searches for more devious ways to part fools from their money, or because it has excess funds it can spend, or because it has become bored with the same old hedgehog concept. Nor is this the type of diversity that requires an entirely new business model, or is far removed from the core business.

Profitable diversity is the result of an intense focus on the customer and the hedgehog concept. Jessie, the client I was telling you about, shut down the software and maintenance portion of the business when the recession hit. But that didn't mean that we didn't diversify. We expanded into training materials. We were able to increase the training business precipitously because of the new customer training materials. Training profits increased as a result—with minimal cost.

Take Advantage of Downtime

When a business is feeding from the fire hose of growing and expanding sales, there is little time for planning, little time for training, little time to think strategically. But when sales slow down due to circumstances beyond the company's control, the employees and management can take advantage of the downtime.

Now is the time to plan. During a recession is the absolutely best time to do process improvement. We may not know when sales will pick up, but we do know for certain that, someday, they will. And when they do, we want to be ready for future demand. Large automation and technology projects are especially important to plan for (not implement) during the lulls, the years when sales are not at their peak. There's plenty of time for meetings and training because demand is not as high.

Since 80 percent of the cost of a technology project is the planning and training, in doing that during the slow years, we are not only getting all of that out of the way, we are also cutting the cost of the whole technology project by 60 percent. When a business tries to get the training and planning done while under the gun of a go-live date, they hire a bevy of consultants to do the work so that their employees can continue to meet the needs of the customers. Instead, we can hire a single consultant to teach the employees to deal with the business requirements and planning. The employees can develop customized training themselves. With the proper guidance, employees can do a much better job than external consultants at a fraction of the cost. They just need enough time to work on it, which they have in abundance if sales are down. The fact that the system might not be implemented for a couple of years does not devalue the time and effort put into the business requirements, planning, and training.

Furthermore, the project that gets implemented will be much more valuable to the organization right out of the gate. Typically, a business must wait two or three years to start getting value from a new system because of the unfamiliar process changes and the learning curve of the employees. A system designed and used by trained employees instead of consultants begins the payback from day 1.[6]

Maintain Innovations

Thriving companies tend to increase research and development costs, or if they do cut the budget, they only cut the budget proportionately, not entirely. They understand that innovation is essential to the future of the organization.

Think and Plan Strategically

Just because we cancelled the luxurious strategic planning retreat in the exotic location with the lavish accommodations does not mean that we shouldn't do strategic planning. During a recession is absolutely the best time to do planning for the future. To reiterate a point, we may not know when sales will pick up, but we do know for certain that someday they will. And when they do, we want to be ready for future demand at a much higher volume and a lower cost.

EASIER SAID THAN DONE; TECHNIQUES TO MAKE IT HAPPEN

We all know how easy it is to say, "Yeah—we'll get right on that." We know that companies *should* be doing these things. But knowing what should be done and actually doing it—well, as my grandmother use to say—"Many a slip twixt the cup and the lip."

> In 2011, I had a client with a $5 million business. The management team—husband and wife—swore up and down that they would do whatever I told them. They nodded yes emphatically when I explained that losing $50,000 a month was not sustainable—especially as they were now over a million dollars in debt, and all their real estate property was overvalued and underwater because they had refinanced in 2006 at the height of the real estate bubble. They agreed that yes—they had to do something. Yes, they had to work on their leadership skills. Yes, they had to cut overhead expenses. Yes, they had to focus on the customer. Yes, they had to think strategically. Yes, they had to figure out their hedgehog concept. But when it came time to actually doing it—well, that was a problem.
>
> They wouldn't, or couldn't, "just do it." All of the plans that we made, all of the items they agreed to focus on were always somehow not important enough. They never got done. They just kept running their business the way they always had—right up until they went out of business.

Executing these ideas is not easy. Here are a few techniques that I've found helpful—both for me and for my clients.

Focus on Leadership

First, I've found that it is helpful to take a really good leadership assessment. Understanding leadership is more difficult than it appears. Many people have a concept of leadership that is not helpful. The wrong kind of leadership is worse than none during a recession.

No one likes to be told they are not a good leader. I know that I resisted that message for years. The problem is that if you don't really know what leadership is, you think you are doing it when you are not. I learned my lesson slowly, a little at a time, and only with the help of several really great executive coaches and mentors. (More on leadership can be found in Chapter 2.)

1 Percent Improvement Every Day

Alan Weiss often speaks of the 1 percent solution—a person only needs to improve 1 percent a day, and in 70 days, they'll be twice as good. Well, it took me a lot longer than 70 days to become a good leader—and I still have a ways to go—but I aim to improve every single day. The bottom line is—you don't have to eat the whole elephant. Just take one bite a day. We can all improve, little by little.

Focus on Sales

I started my first business, Computer Educational Services, in 1986 at a time when businesses were desperate for someone, *anyone,* who could teach them how to use these newfangled machines called computers that were landing on every secretary's and manager's desk. I didn't have to learn to sell—business came, unbidden. All I had to do was to wait for the phone to ring, and for the most part, it did.

When I got involved in my fourth start-up, I went back to technology consulting. But, in 2001—well, the landscape was completely different. Not only weren't clients calling me, but there were thousands of out-of-work technologists who knew more about technology than I did. I had to learn how to sell. I was lucky—I found the best sales coach in the world, a fellow by the name of Dave Bosler. Within one month, I had doubled my business. Within two months, I had tripled it. Within three months, I had quadrupled my business.[7] Learning to sell was one of the hardest things I've ever done, but it was also one of the most valuable lessons I've ever learned. (More on selling can be found in Chapter 9.)

Master the Financials (Especially Break-Even Analysis)

Every business has a break-even point—the point at which all of the fixed costs are covered and the income minus the variable costs of each individual item starts to accrue to the bottom-line profits. You'd be surprised (or maybe if you've been an entrepreneur or working with business owners for a while, you won't be surprised)—at how few people understand break-even analysis concepts.

Even I spent years in blissful ignorance. I thought a break-even analysis was a banal financial calculation—a rarely viewed graph for new products or services that calculated how much profit a business would make based on different levels of sales.

A few years ago, my understanding of how to use the break-even analysis got turned upside down when I took a course called *The Cup and the Gap* at the American Small Business Development Conference in San Antonio, Texas. I was at the conference speaking about online tools for consultants, and the workshop following mine, in the same room, was Carl Forssen from Profit Master. I tried to leave before he started (because I thought I knew what a break-even analysis was, and therefore, didn't need the lesson, or so I thought), but I had been gathering my materials in the center of the room, and the room was so packed (as it had been when I spoke—it was a great conference!) that I couldn't get out without making a huge commotion. I was so glad I stayed. Not only was the workshop fascinating, it turned out that break-even analysis is much more than I thought it was.

Carl demonstrated how the break-even analysis could be used as a framework to discuss the hedgehog concept, and how to strengthen the core, and focus on the customer. The break-even analysis can provide entrepreneurs with a framework to communicate better with their employees. It sure beats saying, "You gotta be profitable, stupid" over and over again. (More on break-even analysis can be found in Chapter 10 on Financials.)

Reduce Overhead by Trading Fixed for Variable Costs

The break-even analysis also lets business owners see how to eliminate overhead—how to trade fixed overhead expenses for variable sales-based expenses. The idea is to turn fixed costs into variable costs so that when sales go down, costs go down. Ask employees to work part time or work as consultants rather than on full time schedules. Renegotiate leases to pay a slightly higher rate for a shorter term or less space, with an option for more space if necessary. Rent equipment instead of buying it. Do things manually instead of automating them. Don't be afraid of paying more for something when the volume of sales doesn't warrant enough savings of a higher level of commitment.

Remain Calm and Just Be There

There are many possible reactions to an unexpected economic crisis. One reaction is to panic. When sales decrease, some people go into hyperdrive. They work more hours, push harder, try to do more, expect the impossible from everyone on the team. The results: stress. The extra effort becomes less and less effective. Eventually, the added stress leads to burnout.

Another reaction is what I call Deer in the Headlight. Without a plan, some people freeze due to fear. Failure is barreling down upon them, and they don't know what to do, so they deny the obvious. Decisions are delayed until too late, and they get barreled over.

Obviously, it's best if we already had a plan in place in the event of an economic downturn. But even if we missed that part, after we demonstrate leadership by facing the brutal facts, we can take a step back to just breathe. Just Breathe. We can invite employees to just breathe deeply with us, being patient while we work on a plan to adjust. This is not to deny and delay. This is getting ourselves into the best mental framework to make the right decisions, calmly.

Here's what breathing does for us, and for our employees. It helps us to remain calm. It gives us space to think more clearly. It gives a stable foundation upon which to act. It gives us flexibility to react appropriately.

Employees need to know that we will be there for them. That we are not planning to take our ball and go home, shutting down the business, just because we might be losing money. Just breathing with them, being with them, letting them see us remain calm and face the issues; these actions will do an incredible amount toward ensuring our team will be there as we face the hard times together.

Make the Tough Decisions in a Timely Manner

Breathing can help us take a few moments, and will calm our minds so that we can think clearly. But these moments of nonaction should not go on for too long. Decisions must be made quickly. Allow the time to be long enough to assess the threat and plan the right response. Decisions, unpopular and difficult decisions, need to be made—and before it is too late. But when the moment of thinking is over, and clarity is achieved on the next steps, the hard decisions must be made and the action must begin.

Understand that We Are in for the Long Haul

It's not enough to just survive during this current financial crisis. We've been in it for a good long time, and it is not yet over. It may even still get worse before it gets better.

Bail outs and stimulus packages have the tendency to dull the sharp pain, but lengthen the effects—like pulling a Band-Aid off slowly, millimeter by millimeter instead of quickly—which would deepen the pain, but shorten how long we feel it. Now, we've got years and years to go before we will see the light at the end of the tunnel. Never again, in our lifetime (unless you happen to be 20-something), will we see the kind of unabashed spending that had been slowly becoming the norm over the last four decades. Welcome to the new reality!

Keep the Faith (Not Optimism, Faith)

You can help your employees stay the course by helping them to understand the difference between hunkering down and adopting a treading water mentality (which is bad), and being patient for the upturn and having faith that it will come (which is good). Jim Collins (2001) tells of the Stockdale Paradox. Jim Stockdale was a prisoner of war—tortured daily, little hope of ever coming out alive. When he did make it through those terrible times, he spoke about those who were optimistic. They would talk about how they'd be home by next Christmas. Then, Christmas would come and go, and they'd still be there. Then, they would talk about getting home by spring. And spring would come and go, and they'd still be there. After a few more hopes and dreams cycles of having their hopes dashed against reality, they would give up.

Viktor Frankl said the same thing in his book, *Man's Search for Meaning* (2006)—about people in the death camps during the Holocaust. Optimistic people—people who were sure the bad times would end soon, that someone would come and save them any day now—were the ones who didn't make it. They would give up and die. However, those who faced the brutal facts—that it would be a long time, much longer than they could imagine—but who kept the faith that eventually the bad times would end, persevered. They lived one day at a time, and not only survived, but thrived.

Lee, the CEO of a credit union of which I was a member, was sure that the recession would end by the next quarter, that interest rates would rise again, that home prices would go back to normal. Every quarter, Lee would provide a forecast that showed 7 percent growth, and a 5 percent interest rate for loans after the next quarter. Though we had sustained heavy losses for years, the future numbers for the coming year were always rosy. After three years, after the numbers refused to turn rosy to match the expectation, Lee gave up entirely—folding the entire organization. If Lee had faced the facts early on, the organization would be thriving today.

Maintain the Vision; Watch for Empirical Evidence of Progress

We help our employees by sharing with them our faith, helping them to see the vision of what it will be like—but emphasizing that the time will come when the time will come. We can watch for objective realistic signs of the economic recovery. For example, we might have a special party after sales rise more than 5 percent three months in a row. Perhaps we could note the first time since the crisis that profits creep past the 10 percent mark. We can pay attention to whichever signs of economic recovery work for us. Faith and hope are not time-specific, but they are powerful motivators while we are traveling the journey to the goal.

SUMMARY OF STRATEGY

The recession has impacted almost everyone all over the world, and it is far from over. It may still get worse before it gets better. But, it will get better. In the meantime, it behooves us to learn from the companies that flourish.

- ☑ The best time to start a business is during a recession.
- ☑ Leadership and trust are important influencers of success, especially during a recession.
- ☑ Making smart choices, quickly and without delay, is important when a recession hits.
- ☑ Facing the brutal facts is essential; the sooner, the better.
- ☑ Focusing on the customer will guide decision making.
- ☑ During slow times is the best time to take the time to plan for enterprise-wide improvements to the processes and procedures.

2

The Many Faces of Leadership

Of all the business topics in the world, the most difficult one to deal with is leadership. As could be seen in Chapter 1, leadership and strategy are inexorably linked with business success.

There are several books in this series about leadership. *The Entrepreneur's Guide to Mastering the Inner World of Business* by Nanci Raphael; *The Entrepreneur's Guide to Managing Growth and Handling Crises* by Theo J. van Dijk; and *The Entrepreneur's Guide to Successful Leadership* by Dan Goldberg and Don Martin are all directly about leadership. Bob Everett's *The Entrepreneur's Guide to Marketing* also has quite a few leadership lessons, as does David Worrell's *The Entrepreneur's Guide to Understanding Financial Statements*.

There is a lot of overlap. My hope is that this chapter on leadership presents a comprehensive whole that does not duplicate information. To start, I will share my own personal journey and views of leadership. Then, I will attempt to share the perspectives on leadership of the authors who wrote on the subject in the series. (Perhaps after you've read it, you can tell me how well I accomplished my goal.)

MY LEADERSHIP JOURNEY

Two executives walk out of a seminar together. One turns to the other and says: "Wow—that leadership course really surprised me." "Really?" said the friend, "How so?" "Well," said the executive, "you know I've been managing my team for about ten years." "Yeah," said the friend. "Well, I always knew that listening was crucial to being a good leader."

"So?" said the friend.

The executive paused a moment.

"But I never realized that I was the one who was supposed to do all the listening."

Case: CJR Story of Leadership

When I started my first business in 1986, I thought I was a good leader and that everyone would listen to me. What I found, instead, was best described by President Bill Clinton: "Running a country is a lot like running a cemetery; you've got a lot of people under you and nobody's listening."

Being young and stupid, I had confused leadership with authority. Authority is what you have when someone calls you their boss. Not worth much (a warm bucket of spit comes to mind). What I learned was that in order to get things done, we don't need authority; we need leadership.

Never was this more apparent to me than during my first executive stint as vice president in corporate America. I had tried, and failed miserably, to get promoted. After a battery of tests and assessments, I was pronounced what they called an "individual contributor"—which largely meant that under no circumstances should I be allowed anywhere near managing other people. Remember—this was *after* I had hired employees, built, and sold my own company. I thought they were wrong.

Then, a few years later at a different company, I received what may have been the worst score of all vice presidents, ever, in the history of all Fortune 500 firms. My bosses, my staff, my peers—they all gave me low scores on leadership characteristics. The only people who scored me highly were my customers—the people for whom I was actually delivering services within the corporation. They were off-the-charts delighted with my performance.

I finally started to get an inkling into my problem—I cared so much about my customers that I was Attila the Hun to everyone else. At the time, I thought that was the right way to be because I thought the needs of the customers trumped the needs of the staff. But I was wrong. Not wrong about the importance of the customer, but wrong about the trumping part. We need to see to the needs of the team as well.

Since I've seen the light regarding leadership, I've seen many entrepreneurs with the same characteristics—competent professionals, highly intelligent, full of integrity, enthusiasm, and capabilities. They do well for their customers. When they deal directly with the customers, their businesses grow. But they don't understand that subtle difference between being in authority and being a leader. They don't know how to transfer their own knowledge, talents, and capabilities to their employees. They don't know how to inspire others. Luckily, contrary to the popular belief that leaders are born and not made, it is absolutely possible to learn to become a leader.

My eventual success proves that no one is a lost cause, no matter how poor a leader they currently are. To learn to lead, I went through many years and many levels of executive coaching and personal revelations. The process was emotionally devastating. The process was psychically painful. But because I went through it, I was able to finally admit the deep, dark, ugly, secret truth:

Hello. My name is CJ Rhoads, and I'm an autocratic dictator.

The process to good leadership starts with admitting the problem—much like the road to recovery for an alcoholic begins with an admission. Being good leaders means fighting internal instincts and ego-based tendencies every day. We have to change our entire attitude and habits to accommodate our newfound knowledge. It is not easy.

And why would anyone go through the potentially painful process of self-actualization that is necessary to become a leader? Because they want to have a better relationship with other people. Because they want to become happier themselves. Because they want to make more money. The research is pretty clear on this point—leaders with real leadership skills are healthier, wealthier, and wiser than everyone else. I'm a classic example.

LEADERSHIP LEADS TO PROFITS

As noted, good leadership skills are not just a "nice to have" quality. They are essential—and at all levels of the organization, not just at the top.

Hard scientific studies have been depicting a real relationship between business profitability and leadership for a long time. A 2001 Manchester study of 100 executives from Fortune 1000 companies found that the average return on investment (ROI) for executive leadership training was 5.7 times the initial investment. The Corporate Leadership Council's study, *Hallmarks of Leadership Success,* revealed that organizations with top-tier leadership teams achieve 10 percent higher total shareholder return than their industry peers. In 2004, MetrixGlobal evaluated a leadership development program designed by the Center for Performance Excellence and given to Booz Allen employees. The results indicated over half (53 percent) made significant improvements. Monetary benefits were validated and rigorously documented. They found over $3 million in increased profits. Four impact areas each produced at least a half million dollars of annualized benefit to the business—improved teamwork ($981,980), quality of consulting ($863,625), retention ($626,456), and team member satisfaction ($541,250). Given that the total, fully loaded cost of the leadership training was $414,310, the ROI was 689 percent (Steinberg; McGovern et al. 2001).

Figure 2.1. Leadership—No Magic Formula

What Is Leadership?

But what, exactly, is leadership? There have been reams of writing and bounties of books on the topic of leadership. The title of the book by Dr. John Stanko (2000) says it all—*So Many Leaders, So Little Leadership.* Dilbert has another take on it (Figure 2.1).

What is amazing is how much research there is on the topic of leadership, and how little understanding there is. The academic research on leadership is prolific, and a short summary of it can be found in Appendix B. But the research is a small part of my own view on leadership. My views are more colored by my experiences, what works, and what doesn't work. There are many who disagree with my views.

At a keynote address at the Academy of Management's 2008 Annual Conference from Indiana University on "Developing Managers Who Build High Performance Cultures: Why It This So Darn Hard?" Timothy Baldwin shared that, despite specific training, 95 percent of the 1,300 MBA students made the wrong choices in a leadership assessment. Perhaps it was because they were just students? No. They assessed 17,000 real-life senior managers too—and their average was 36 percent correct answers. That's 73 percent wrong answers. (No wonder 50 percent of employees rate their bosses as "remarkably bad.")

At a training session on a system called Vleader, which is designed to teach leadership skills, most of the time, the majority of audience members gave the wrong answer. What is worse, when the presenters identified the correct answer, the proper action of a good leader, many in the audience would not believe them and argued about it. People are so used to autocratic dominating leaders that they have a hard time recognizing real leadership, which is often subtle and in the background instead of out in front.

Listening to Collins

Jim Collins is the top management consulting educator who has influenced today's business owners, and he is a pioneer in identifying leadership as the foundation for success. He describes leadership in levels, and *Level 5 Leadership* is the goal to attain.

I first got to know Jim Collins through his book *Built to Last: Successful Habits of Visionary Companies* (Collins and Porras 1994), written with Jerry Porras, which was required reading for vice presidents at the company where I worked. I was impressed, and sought out Collins's first book, *Beyond Entrepreneurship: Turning Your Business into an Enduring Great Company* (Collins and Lazier 1992), as well as his most widely read book, *Good To Great: Why Some Companies Make the Leap and Others Don't* (Collins 2001).

Collins compared companies of similar size and industries to identify what enabled them to maintain success. The factors are:

- Getting the right people on the bus
- Who first, then what
- Facing the brutal facts (and never losing faith that things will eventually get better)
- Focus on the Hedgehog concept
- Recognizing the role of technology as an accelerator
- Spinning the flywheel of continuous improvement (instead of getting on the doom loop of short-term improvement programs)

Since then, he has published *Good to Great and the Social Sectors, How The Mighty Fall: Why Some Companies Never Give In* (Collins 2009), and *Great by Choice: Uncertainty, Chaos, and Luck—Why Some Thrive Despite Them All* with Morten Hansen (Collins and Hansen 2011).

Jim Collins is a different sort of management consultant than Tom Peters, or Michael Hammer, or Michael Porter or any number of other well-known gurus of the day. As I got to know him a little better at conferences and through correspondence, I realized he wasn't a management consultant at all. He was, at heart, an educator. He has created for himself a position like that of full professor with his own endowed chair, where he can do what he likes. Jim likes to work on massive five-year projects, providing real practical value to the business community instead of the typical academic research, which is usually narrowly focused and short term.

Collins has identified the characteristics of the leaders of companies that attain 10 times the normal ROIs (Collins 2005). These leaders exhibit several core behaviors—a central motivating ambition, fanatic discipline, productive paranoia, and empirical creativity, which is constantly checking the results of ideas against the cold hard facts of measurements of reality.

Other Leadership Gurus

Collins provides a great foundation, but there have been many others who have shared views of leadership that coincide with my own.

Marcus Buckingham, author of *The One Thing You Need to Know* (Buckingham 2005) identified the one most important thing for leaders—"Great leaders discover what is universal and capitalize on it." Sam Walton has said, "Outstanding leaders go out of their way to boost the self-esteem of their personnel. If people believe in themselves, it's amazing what they can accomplish." John Maxwell said, "A leader is one who knows the way, goes the way and shows the way."

President Harry S. Truman said, "A Leader is a person who has the ability to get other people to do what they don't want to do, and like it." Similarly, President Dwight D. Eisenhower said, "Leadership is the ability to decide what is to be done, and then to get others to want to do it" (Yihan 2013).

My favorite definition of leadership is Steve Covey's, the author of the self-help bible, *The Seven Habits of Effective People* and *Principle Based Leadership* (Covey 2005). Covey defines leadership as "Communicating to people their worth and potential so clearly that they come to see it in themselves."

Balance

In the final analysis, if you listen closely throughout all the literature, leadership is all about balancing the tasks and the people, the fierce will with the humble stature, the progress ahead with respect for the past, the open communication with the introspective creativity, the big picture with the minutia of process. A leader somehow knows how to walk the fine line that balances the paradox, soothes the conflict, and moves ahead with love and determination. Read on to hear about Nanci's practices, which can help us develop those abilities.

MASTERING THE INNER WORLD OF BUSINESS

Of all the books I've read on leadership, Nanci Raphael's comes closest to what I think of as a how-to manual on what we need to do to get from here to there. Nanci is a specialist in daily practices that lead to leadership abilities. In my journey, I found all of these practices to be extremely helpful.

Leadership Challenges of Entrepreneurs

Leadership is extremely difficult. The most important step in the journey is figuring out how to transform our own minds, our own cultural experience that screams to act differently than we need to as leaders. Furthermore, as entrepreneurs, we have distinctive challenges. We must learn to:

- Deal with our fears
- Remain innovative
- Deal effectively with failure
- Cope with loneliness
- Confront overwhelming "busy-ness"
- Discover the meaning of success
- Climb up from despair
- Know ourselves
- Know our employees

Many think that the challenge of business is getting sales, surpassing the competition, dealing with market forces, managing operations, keeping up with technology, following regulations, and so on. But the reality is that more businesses close down because of leadership challenges, which are only solved by soft skills, what some people might call airy-fairy stuff.

Soft Skills Are Harder than Hard Skills

Nothing is harder than soft skills.[1] Leadership skills development techniques have been used and mastered by some of the most successful people in history. They are, in fact, the basis for the most rigorous lessons in leadership. But we rarely find them in any but the most progressive business schools. They are often the hidden secrets of success.

We're all human. We entrepreneurs are so busy trying to do our business better that we forget to pay attention to the human side of things. Yet, when these human skills are addressed so that we improve the way we think, relate, communicate, and listen, we grow. And when we grow, our business automatically, almost miraculously, grows too.

Growth from these soft skills may begin to happen so fast and so easily that people don't recognize the direct relationship between mastering this aspect of leadership (our own psyche) and our success. It is these softer, more human skill sets that actually hold the ultimate answers for the fulfill-ment of balance in business and in life. When we're energized, happy, and self-confident, we have freedom to vibrantly and courageously lead our business forward and live our lives out loud—with passion and purpose.

Step-by-Step Personal Leadership Development

There are several steps that we can take that will help us on our journey to being true leaders. Detailed examples and many stories can be found in Nanci's book in order to get a more complete picture. Summarized here are the highlights (modified from Nanci's list due to space limitations):

- Take out the trash.
- Go ahead—Discover yourself and dare to be different.
- Be, Do, Have.
- Put your ego to sleep.
- To move mountains, first move people. Listen to them.
- Celebrate the gift of failure.
- Be accountable.
- Build the business you have imagined.
- Remember—The coolest wealth is your health.
- Give yourself a standing ovation.

Take Out the Trash

Taking out the trash does not mean emptying the trashcan in the kitchen. The trash is insidious and it lies inside of us—deep inside our minds. This trash was created from past experiences. It is typically a memory of a feel-ing we had when something happened to us, perhaps even years ago. When we think of a time when we were angry, embarrassed, or hurt, we are thinking of our own trash.

Trash is the type of thinking that can stop us from becoming successful. It can be something painful from the past that still controls our thinking and actions today. Trash can block us from where we want to go and what we want to achieve.

Trash can interfere with a positive state of mind. It clutters our mind with unnecessary thoughts that get in the way and keeps us from think-ing clearly. It usurps our valuable time and energy, taking us away from the tasks at hand. Our patience wears thin. We begin overreacting to situations that we normally handle well. We may second-guess our-selves, rehashing decisions we've already made. This trash, this clutter, becomes a distraction in our day, our business, our leadership skills, and our lives.

In order to run our business, we need clarity—something that trash thwarts. As entrepreneurs, we are typically up to something big—all of the time. We have a vision. Trash makes us hesitate and reconsider. Should we be going for this goal? Doubts get woven into our thoughts. The negativity of trash creates a revolution inside, builds up, becoming a roadblock, a collection of thoughts that need to go. We must be sure that our minds are freed up and clear. The vision is paramount—not the trash.

It's never easy to see our own trash. That's where mind-body exercises such as meditation, tai chi, or yoga come in. These age-old practices have been used by millions of people to improve self-awareness, help solve problems, promote a deep sense of inner peace, reduce stress, slow down aging, and enhance health. These activities trigger the relaxation response, which changes our brain chemistry so that we can think about issues insightfully (Benson and Proctor 2003, p. 26; Walton 2013).

Successful executives in large companies understand the power of these practices. Raytheon, Nortel Networks, Medtronic, Monsanto, McKinsey, Salesforce, Aetna, Google—have had advocates and/or meditation programs for their employees. Bill George from Medtronics says about meditation: "Out of anything, it has had the greatest impact on my career." Michael Stephen from Aetna says it helped transform him "from an impatient, demanding know-it-all into a more effective leader."

The impact of mind-body practices have been under a great deal of study. The physical structure of the brain changes as a consequence of regular practice, resulting in more alpha and gamma brainwaves (typical of calm and insightful behavior) and fewer beta brainwaves (typical of narrow-minded and aggressive behavior).

Dr. Richard Davidson of the University of Wisconsin found that meditation has lasting, beneficial effects that impact the workplace. Four dozen employees met once a week for eight weeks to practice mindfulness meditation for three hours. The result showed that the employees' left prefrontal cortexes were enlarged, just like those of experienced mind-body practitioners. "What we found out is that after a short time meditating, meditation had profound effects not just on how they felt, but on their brains and bodies," notes Davidson (Conlin 2004; Ryan 2007).

Mind-body activities such as meditation, tai chi, and yoga clear the cobwebs and allow us to recognize our own trash so that we can take it out. It is one of the most useful tools in our arsenal.

Go Ahead—Discover Yourself and Dare to Be Different!

Peer pressure is a powerful incentive to follow the crowd and act just like everyone else. Our lemming-like instincts have a basis in survival; going off on our own might be dangerous in a world of saber-tooth tigers.

A friend of ours shows off a new Porsche, we want a new Porsche. Others invite us to their yacht, we want to have our own yacht. What others have, we think we want. We begin to think that keeping up with them is important, valuing what they value is important.

But peer pressure breeds inauthentic behaviors. Inauthenticity is a saboteur—a silent killer of motivation, personal power, and life force. Who are we, really? Where do we stand on issues? Can people count on us to be consistently ourselves? Until we become empowered, until we become an authentic leader true to ourselves—our egos, insecurities, and fears will continue to block both our personal and business growth. Long-lasting success cannot adhere to an inner core of inauthenticity.

There are times when we must push down our fears and move boldly ahead into some unknown task or activity, to *fake it 'till we make it.* But at some point, pretending to be something we are not does a disservice to us and all the people we lead. The mask becomes a sneaky thief, robbing us of our true character and veiling reality.

In order to discover our authentic selves, we need to do three things— assess our strengths and weaknesses, assess our values, and assess our purpose in life.

Most people like their strengths and hide their weaknesses. However, it is right here, at the point of our vulnerability, that we can begin to strip away the façade that keeps us from fully being who we are—limiting our communication, self-confidence, and relating to others.

Knowing our limitations can give us power. We can compensate by rearranging our goals and methods to build on our strengths. Alternatively, we can surround ourselves with people who are more proficient in those areas. For example, sending out invoices doesn't happen to be one of my strengths, so I have an office assistant who takes care of all the paperwork.

To start our strengths and weaknesses assessment, on a piece of paper, we should write down our strengths, at least 20 of them. We should ask peers, employees, business partners, family members, and friends what they consider our strengths. Then—the harder part—we need to list our weaknesses. We should list anything that we believe may limit us. Make this list extensive. Go for at least 20, and 30 is even better. Again, ask peers, employees, business partners, family members, and friends. When they tell us, we need to stifle our reaction. They are not criticizing us; they are helping us succeed by sharing with us what we have a difficult time seeing for ourselves—our weaknesses.

We should look at the lists. Think about how we employ our strengths. How they have benefitted us in the past. Think about how we hide the top weakness. What do we do so others can't see what we aren't good at?

Then, for each strength, we write down a rating for how much of an advantage it is. In other words, number the strengths from 1 to N (the number of strengths we've written down), with 1 being the top strength and N being the bottom strength. Similarly, for each weakness, we rate how much of a problem it is on a scale of 1 to N.

We don't need to do any more than to look at our lists and figure out the best way to take advantage of our strengths. Bob Everett included a way of viewing our strengths and weaknesses in the face of the threats and opportunities that I found helpful (Figure 2.2).

After we are done listing our strengths and weaknesses, we should write down our values. There is no limit to the number. These values are what we live and lead by. There is no compromising on them. Just write down all the things that we think are important in life, what we want. Then, rank them as well. We may value having a great new Porsche or yacht, but do we value them more than a loving spouse or our children? What are our priorities?

Finally, we should write down our purpose in life, the reason we were put on this earth. To discover it, we can ask ourselves several questions:

- What drives me?
- What makes me smile? What brings me joy?
- What makes time fly?
- What makes me feel good about myself?
- Where do I want to go?
- What makes me want to get up in the morning and get going?
- What would I love to do if I didn't have to worry about money?
- What is that burning desire in me that I haven't spoken about because it is so big that I know it is almost impossible to achieve?
- What do I want my life to stand for?

Once we've identified our purpose, it helps to write it down and post it in different places to remind ourselves several times a day. Often, life

Figure 2.2. Threats, Opportunities, Strengths, Weaknesses

	Strengths	Weaknesses
Opportunities	Take Advantage	Build
Threats	Defend	Avoid

Source: Robert F. Everett, *The Entrepreneur's Guide to Marketing.* Santa Barbara, CA: Praeger, 2008.

takes on new meaning when we are constantly reminded of our purpose. We might feel more alive and fulfilled. Mornings will greet us with a sense of excitement. Purpose and passion go hand in hand.

Purpose is not a business mission, it is personal. It does not matter if others don't share our purpose; it is uniquely ours.

Be, Do, Have

Most people work from a Do, Have, Be concept. If you *do* what is needed to reach your goals, then you'll *have* what you want, and then, you'll *be* successful. If you work hard, then you'll get money, and then, you will be rich.

There are several problems with this attitude. It might take decades to achieve your dream. Or, it might be an impossible goal. Focusing solely on achieving the goal might cause you to miss other important happenings in your life that you will later regret.

Instead, it makes more sense to keep your purpose and goals in life in mind, but also take time to enjoy the journey to get there. We need to *Be, Do, Have.*

- *Be* who we want to be,
- *Do* what we need to do in order to . . .
- *Have* what we want to have.

The first step is to identify our goals—specifically. Write them down. Break them down with criteria and timelines. Get crystal clear on what we want to have.

Next, we imagine we've reached our goals. Visualize that we've already done it. Answer these questions:

- What does it look like to have completed the goal?
- What will we do with it? Will it be used for fun or business?
- How will we act? How would we carry ourselves?
- How much more confident would we be?
- How would we treat others?
- How does it feel?

Really imagine it all. The longer we can let the vision endure, the more real our minds will make it.

Most people who want to reach a goal create a to-do list—actions to take in order to realize the goal. This is a good list to create, but it has one problem: If we haven't shifted who we are while going about our to-do list, we're running backwards up the hill. To create less tension and more ease and fun in reaching our goal, we need a *to-be* list—who you want to be each day.

The purpose of this practice is to get us to our goals faster and with less effort. This practice is going to require an internal shift. We're going to have to take a closer look at how we are being. Are we impatient? Do we interrupt others when they're talking to get our point across? Do we think we're always right? Are we judgmental about our own behavior? Judgmental about others' behavior? These types of actions and thoughts are saboteurs that prevent us from *being* who we want to be, and that makes it more difficult to do what we need to do in order to have what we want to have.

Attaining our goals can be difficult or easy. We can choose the difficult ride—one of stress, pressure, and working hard. Or, we can choose the path that is filled with peace by already being who we would be, but *during* the journey instead of only at the end. Basically, in order to accomplish this, we must simply enjoy the ride on the way.

Put Your Ego to Sleep

Admit it. Entrepreneurs have healthy egos. We have to if we're to survive the rocky road we traverse. When Nanci interviewed entrepreneurs for her book, she found an interesting phenomenon occurring. There were those who proudly admitted they had a strong ego and would hold on tight to it. Then there were others who timidly denied that their ego had played a part in their success (could they be the exception to humanity, and not even have one?), but when pressed further, reticently confessed.

A healthy ego can help us win business, stand our ground when confronted by a competitor, or take on the persona of a successful business owner. Our egos want us to be seen as the best, the smartest, the strongest, the most competitive, the most recognized, or the one with the most material gains. Our egos can help us keep going when the going gets tough.

But egos are not cognizant of the greater good, and they are never satisfied. Egos are not good team builders. Our ego will demotivate others and interfere with our relationships. People with out-of-control egos don't listen well, don't take feedback to heart, and have an attitude of a know-it-all. Allowing our egos to run our decision-making unencumbered simply won't cut it.

I'm a good example of this issue. I have a pretty healthy ego. My husband has had occasion to say, "CJ, you need a little more humility," which is true. I found that when I let my ego direct my activities, I often end up working at cross purposes with my actual values, missions, and goals. In the past, when I let my ego lead, I wasted time trying to get back at people who slighted me. I needlessly expended effort on proving other people wrong. I worked on accomplishments that made me look good rather than enabling the team to shine.

Humility is one of the two characteristics that Jim Collins (2005) writes about while analyzing the importance of Level 5 leaders. The seeming juxtaposition of Humility and Fierce Resolve is the distinguishing characteristic of CEOs who took companies from good or very good performance to enduring excellence. Since fierce resolve requires a healthy ego, humility must exist alongside that ego. The key, I believe, is the recognition of the role of others by the leader. Collins writes: "How do Level 5 leaders manifest humility? They routinely credit others, external factors, and good luck for their companies' success. But when results are poor, they blame themselves. They also act quietly, calmly, and determinedly—relying on inspired standards, not inspiring charisma, to motivate" (Collins, 2005).

Big egos want recognition for being the best. Egos are, by their very nature, immature, and don't pay attention to the big picture. We need to find a way to tamp down the impact of our egos when they start to interfere in our future. We need to learn how to gain humility.

Humility wins over followers, builds trust and strong relationships. Without humility, people with strong egos may act as if they achieved all of their accomplishments based upon their own skills and talents, without any help from others. That would be a mistake, not just because it is not true, but because it dissuades others from following them. Once followers realize that they won't get credit for their accomplishments when working with poor leaders, they stop wanting to work with them.

An ego that is too big and out of control doesn't serve anyone. In the long run, it can actually create a breakdown in trust and damage relationships. We can't be a superstar and also build a team.

We can put our egos to sleep in order to build strength in our companies and empower the team of people who trust us. The following activities will help us put our egos to sleep.

Lose on purpose. When we find ourselves in the middle of "fighting the good fight" (or so we think), we should simply stop. If we always pursue winning, no matter what, we'll always lose in the end. Continuously feeding our egos by constantly looking for battles and winning them is not conducive to healthy relationships. But recognizing when losing the battle will enable us to win in the end; that's the sign of a controlled healthy ego.

When employees are struggling to do something, we have several options. We can step in and do it for them (the action I always took in the past, not realizing how damaging that action was). We can tell them how to do it (not much better). We can let them struggle without help (good for them, but often detrimental to the task). Or, we can change the task they are working on (or, even better, define it initially) so that they are doing just part of it—a part they can figure out for themselves after just a little bit of a struggle; challenging, but not impossible. Once they've mastered that part, we can add another part to their responsibility, and then another until they are able to complete the entire task without any help at all. The challenge is to figure out exactly how to divvy up the work and the responsibilities so that all employees are reaching just a little farther than they were able to accomplish before. Over time, they are able to take on entire responsibilities and perform without struggling (too much), and we are able to move on to other employees who need more help.

As we shift from pursuing to win to contributing to the development of winning strategies used by others, we get more victories with less effort while winning and retaining new relationships. When you are used to doing everything yourself, it seems like an unattainable goal to get others to take over. But if we stop trying to win and start trying to coach, the unattainable becomes attainable.

This practice takes discipline. If we become aware of our need to win, gain recognition, and get more stuff, we can notice this while we're right in the middle of doing it. Then, we can just stop. We can find a way to let the other person win. We can tell them they are right, they are the better person at that task. We can recognize them for their capabilities and talents. We can stifle our impulse to show off our capabilities, or prove that we are better than they are. We can ignore our immature ego screaming for us to show how it is done.

At first, this will be hard. We will feel like we're giving up something. But we're not. It is only our ego at work, trying to keep us the victor and the other the loser. Eventually, we will find that when we acknowledge others' capabilities, freely and frequently, we're always the winner. It eventually will come back to us in spades. But first we must stop ourselves from letting our ego control us.

Stop looking for praise and adoration. Everyone loves to be recognized, to be praised for their accomplishments. Our egos want everyone to love us, and sometimes, they go out of bounds in trying to achieve this impossible goal. We should adopt the attitude that it doesn't matter if everyone doesn't love us. We can't control what other people think of us, or what they say about us. What really matters is how we feel about ourselves. Instead of looking for praise and adoration for ourselves, we can get into the habit of looking for opportunities to heap praise and adoration onto others.

Our reaction when someone criticizes us is the other side of this behavior. When we react with anger, it is our ego getting in our own way. When we can detach from the criticisms of others, we can see the areas that we'd like to improve more clearly. We all have weaknesses; it's part of being human. When we can take the criticisms directed at us with lightness, without getting defensive, we'll be able to see more clearly the issues of the criticizer. "Yeah—you're right. I'm working on that" is a much better response to criticism than denial, displacement, rationalization, or any other defense mechanism.

Appreciate what we have. Sometimes, we are so focused on what we want, we forget what we have. Instead, we can change lenses. We can look through the lens of what we do have already and appreciate it. Our egos will constantly tell us that we need more—egos never have enough. If we're always working toward getting more or being better than others, we'll never be happy because it is an uphill battle that never ends. There is always someone with more—more talent, more skills, more money, more stuff. Instead, we can shift our focus to give to others.

Let go of being right, of wanting to hear good things about us from others. As we credit others with their achievements and ignore our own, we'll have more time and more success. As we let go of trying to look better than others, we will be better. As we let go of knowing it all, we will know more. As we let others shine and let go of having to be the superstar, our stardom rises. (If these contradictions sound familiar, you may have read the Taoist text *Tao Te Ching,* attributed to Lao Tsu [which is Chinese for "elder one"]. These statements have a similar feel.)

This will be hard at first—perhaps very hard. We are so used to having to clamber and climb to separate ourselves from the herd in order to gain recognition that we have a hard time figuring out when it is time to stop. The more we practice these behaviors to put our ego to sleep and start accomplishing through the achievements of others, the better we get.

To Move Mountains, First Move People. Listen to Them

After putting our egos to sleep, the next most important step in getting people to move in the same direction is *listening.*

Conscious listening, or active listening, is a real art. It is not something that is taught in the classroom or even at the dinner table. Listening is a learned skill. It takes concentration, intention, clear-headedness, and commitment. As a leader, active listening should be one of the 10 commandments of leadership and should be included in all business school curriculums.

To learn to listen, we can read books on listening, and then, practice with others—our children, our partner or spouse, our coworkers, our employees. To listen consciously, on purpose, we must bring ourselves into the moment. We must listen to what is being said, and to what is not being said. If we are thinking about a problem or something that must be done, we have compromised our listening. We can't have any distractions. We can't interrupt. We can't be thinking about our response. We must simply listen.

The more skilled we become at listening, the more we will learn. As we learn more, we become more empathic. As we become more empathetic, we become better leaders. Keen listening skills will catapult us to unlimited success in areas that are essential to personal and business growth.

Celebrate the Gift of Failure

Successful leaders understand the inevitability of failure. Everyone fails. All the time. It is only through failure that success can be achieved.

Leaders don't lose faith in their ability when they fail; they work on learning what their mistakes were. They figure out how to avoid the same mistakes the next time. They allow themselves the luxury of feeling bad about the failure for a short time.

Oddly enough, this behavior is one of those areas where men and women tend to differ. One researcher asked men and women in the workplace how long they felt bad after making a major mistake—like losing an account worth hundreds of thousands of dollars to a competitor. The men replied; "A long time—2 or 3 days." The women however, would be devastated for months (Tannen 2001). While no one can say how long a person should allow themselves to stay down and lick their wounds, more than a week might be detrimental to the eventual goal, which is to be resilient and return in spades.

During this time, it is often helpful to write about the issues, identify what happened, and figure out what might have been done differently (if anything). Thinking about the issue can help us identify the silver lining, the higher meaning in the event.

Afterwards, it is time to get back up, renewed with refreshed perspective, and start working on that purpose in life again. Good leaders have met with defeat many times and forcefully pushed it behind them. But gifted great leaders do even more: they meet failures, honor them, celebrate them, and know that there is a hidden gift beneath the darkness of defeat.

Be Accountable

Great leaders have practiced accountability and know that by acknowledging their failures or mistakes, they will gain freedom. It is a declaration to themselves and to others that they are not perfect and are willing to take risks, fall down, accept the gift of failure, and move on. Lee, Peterson and Tiedens (2004) did a study that found that companies with leaders who took personal responsibility for a bad year realized up to 19 percent better stock performance the following year than company's whose leaders blamed uncontrollable factors such the recession.

There is an added benefit. As we take ownership for failures (whether we caused them or others have caused them), so will others. We will have opened the door to creating higher standards, the standard in which we acknowledge—and tolerate—each other's weaknesses. With this comes more productivity because people will spend less time complaining and more time doing what they need to do.

Accountability and commitment go hand in hand. Commitment is the giving of our word to someone to do something. When we give our word, we are making a promise or pledge. We are saying, "I will do what I promised." This is powerful. Our word gives us the opportunity to take control of our lives, setting the direction, and then following through, instead of living by happenstance. Making a commitment and then keeping it builds trust. People like working with people they can count on. People remember when you keep your promises. They also remember when you don't.

Build the Business You've Imagined

There are a legion of self-help gurus who have identified the simple power of envisioning a goal—because it works. Here is a list of steps to take:

1. Set your goal.
2. Write it down.
3. Visualize having it.
4. Imagine how it will feel.
5. Read it twice daily.

You might think that you don't need this step—it seems too simple, too easy. Some people dismiss this activity as baseless. Others know the power of this simple step, people such as Rhonda Byrne (2007), author of *The Secret*, the blockbuster self-help book. Rhonda calls it *the law of attraction*. Rhonda notes, "Energy flows where attention goes." By taking the additional action of actually writing down our goals and looking at them every day, we will naturally choose activities that get us closer to that goal, little by little, day by day. Over time, those tiny efforts have a big impact, and we find ourselves arriving at our goal.

Remember—The Coolest Wealth Is Your Health

Many entrepreneurs who experience the stress of running a company know that it takes a toll on their physical and mental health. Stress contributes to weight change, lack of sleep, decreased energy, depression, and irritability.

We all struggle with eating nutritiously, exercising enough, and getting restful sleep. We think we have to sacrifice our health for our business. But we don't. We can prioritize our health.

Ignoring our mental and physical health is a major mistake because our bodies cannot sustain stress and abuse over time. If we let the time demands and stresses of the business interfere in the good nutrition and daily exercise that is required for good health, we will lose in the long run. We will be plagued by chronic illness and disability that zaps our time and energy, wasting our resources and squandering our investments. Health problems are the number one cause of bankruptcy in the United States today.

Nanci recommends that we create the image of a healthy, balanced business person, and then retrain ourselves to actually become that person. For example, instead of going for that extra jumbo muffin made from white flour and white sugar—think. At first, that may be all we do. Think of that healthy person we imagined ourselves to be. Then, if we still want to reach for that muffin, we can go ahead. But perhaps we will eat only half now. Take a taste. Save the half for later. Or better yet, perhaps we will leave it for someone else to eat.

Another way to retrain ourselves is with exercise. As noted, we should be doing some sort of physical activity or exercise daily. We can develop the habit. Even if we don't feel like exercising one day, we would not skip it entirely. We would hold that place with some sort of lighter exercise or activity, such as tai chi or yoga, perhaps just stretches. We can keep the exercise routine going, even when we don't want to. We can make staying fit and healthy a centered way of being, a habit that we barely need to think about, instead of an add-on that requires a lot of effort.

Give Yourself a Standing O

A Standing Ovation (O) is congratulations for a job well done. We, as good leaders, give standing ovations to others all the time. It is how we rouse employees, vendors, and support people to perform well (Herzberg 2008). Praise or acknowledgment for an employee's excellent work is a higher level motivator than money.

Who gives praise and recognition to motivate us, though? As entrepreneurs, we are on top. We rarely give ourselves a "way to go" or standing ovation for a job well done, but we should.

Feeling appreciated is wonderful; inspiring, and quite motivating. We can survey our own accomplishments and recognize the value of what we have done. We can give ourselves a standing O occasionally.

There is a difference between giving ourselves a standing O and ego-stroking. Ego-stroking builds us up *in front of others*. Ego-stroking is out to prove how great we are, perhaps to subconsciously make up for the fact that we feel inferior in some way. Ego-stroking is external.

A Standing O comes from self-appreciation. A Standing O is a generous gesture of self-care. We are taking care of ourselves by acknowledging the work that we've done. It is for us only, nothing that has to be shared. We simply acknowledge and appreciate what we've accomplished.

STILL EVOLVING, NOW IN CRISIS (SENIC)

At the time Jeff Olson first asked me to become the editor for the series, I was working with a client, George, whose business had been successful for about five years, but was having problems. As I read *Managing Growth and Handling Crises,* Theo van Dijk's book, I recognized the descriptions immediately because they were happening in real life in my client's business. As George attempted to expand, diversify, and grow, the issues kept causing trouble.

I also realized, in retrospect, that the same issues had arisen in my own businesses too. If I'd had the opportunity to read Theo's book prior to owning my first business, or even before my second and third businesses, I might have experienced more success earlier.

Here are the most important aspects. To get the full impact, I encourage you to read the stories in the book, which are chock full of solutions to crises that typically beset successful business owners.

Still Evolving

There are lots of books on start-ups. There are lots of books on mature larger businesses. But there are only a few that deal directly with what happens if our initial business survives beyond the first few years, and we face issues that threaten to derail our organizations.

Theo has coined the term SENIC to describe businesses in this stage: Still Evolving, Now In Crisis. Once we recognize the situation, we can seek a way to mitigate the issues to move on to long-term success.

Facing Crises

The initial years of a business are anxiety producing, but exciting; hard work, but exhilarating. Once we've gotten past the initial period, just when we feel like we can relax a bit, take advantage of our success, look forward to a bit of smooth sailing, that is when we are in danger. Before we know it, some crisis or the other has crept up on us and threatens to blow the whole thing apart.

Often, it is our success itself that causes the crisis. When we were still struggling, not making any money, working our tails off, most people (friends and family) tended to ignore us. Either they didn't want to be volunteered to help or they didn't see the point in watching us go down in failure. When we start to become successful, suddenly, people begin to take notice. Friends who wouldn't return our calls before are touching base constantly to see how business is doing. Relatives seem to come out of the woodwork, eager to see if they might get some piece of the pie. "Where there's a will, there's a relative" goes the old Irish saying.

Other times, the crisis is caused by the transition from creative entrepreneurial start-up to an established business with operational processes, procedures, customers, vendors, and employees. This is a tough transition, and many businesses don't make the cut.

Entrepreneur Peculiarities

There is a difference between building and growing. Entrepreneurs tend to be good at the first and want to be good at the latter, but aren't always. The skills necessary for the two phases are completely different. Making something out of nothing is a rare skill, an amazing feat. But being able to take that fledgling something and nurture it carefully, so it can grow and fly away beyond our personal ability to manage, is even more difficult. For entrepreneurs to succeed long term, that is exactly what they must do.

Onset of SENIC

There are several typical scenarios that lead to a crisis point for an on-going business:

- The acquisition of the first really large contract
- The short-lived honeymoon after the first major contract
- When a gifted entrepreneur gets too far ahead of the team
- A too-extreme focus on the truly innovative product (to the exclusion of organizational development)
- A tendency to work harder and harder without a clear strategy
- The sense of invincibility that leads to excessive risk-taking, often spurred on by early success
- Attempting to keep, and please, all customers
- Attempting to diversify the company out of trouble

Getting Out of Crisis Mode

Unfortunately, businesses don't ever really get out of crisis mode. There is always another crisis in the wings. The most we can hope for is longer and longer periods of productivity and fewer and fewer periods of crisis. Van Dijk shares many different stories about getting out of crisis, and several different ideas, but I think the list he provided (p. 113) was the most applicable to most situations:

- Accurately define what we want.
- Prepare for changes by getting support.
- Remember that what goes up must come down.
- Do not forget the system that feeds the system.
- Lead by example.
- Monitor our critical success factors.

This last one, monitoring our critical success factors, overlaps with the performance measurements (the Dashboard and/or the Balanced Scorecard), which is discussed in much more detail in the chapter on Financials.

THE LEADERSHIP MODEL

Don Martin and Dan Goldberg are not just authors in the series; they are personal friends who have often shared their experiences and enthusiastic talents with groups of students in the Entrepreneurially Talented Teen Project, a nonprofit program hosted by the Students in Free Enterprise club at Kutztown University. Their book presents leadership in a Maslow-like pyramid (Figure 2.3).

Entrepreneur's Leadership Model

The model starts with the all-important knowing who we are, and moves on to what our vision and mission are. Using those, we can plan our actions, and then, execute the plans. The next step involved understanding others, empowering others, and continuing on the never-ending path of lifelong learning and change management until finally reaching success. Dan has also devised the seven elements of successful leadership, as shown in Figure 2.4.

Figure 2.3. The Entrepreneur's Leadership Model

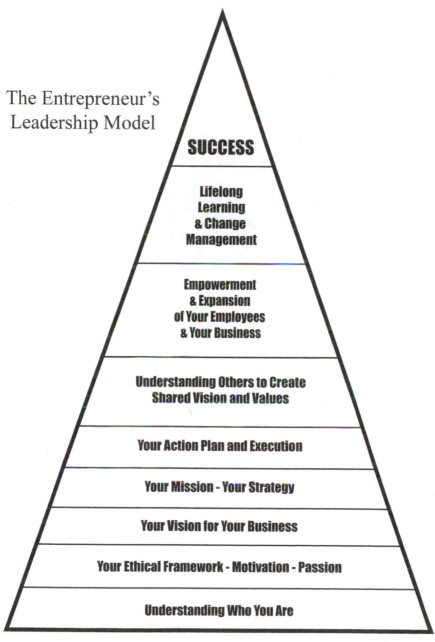

The Entrepreneur's
Leadership Model

SUCCESS

Lifelong
Learning
& Change
Management

Empowerment
& Expansion
of Your Employees
& Your Business

Understanding Others to Create
Shared Vision and Values

Your Action Plan and Execution

Your Mission - Your Strategy

Your Vision for Your Business

Your Ethical Framework - Motivation - Passion

Understanding Who You Are

Source: Dan Goldberg and Don Martin, *The Entrepreneur's Guide to Successful Leadership.*
Santa Barbara, CA: Praeger, 2008.

Figure 2.4. Seven Elements of Leadership

The Seven Elements of Successful Leadership™

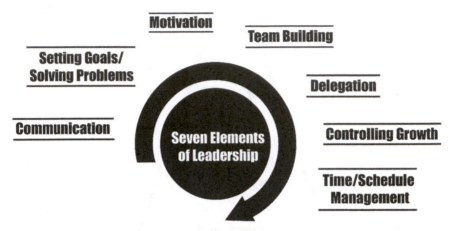

Source: Dan Goldberg and Don Martin, *The Entrepreneur's Guide to Successful Leadership*. Santa Barbara, CA: Praeger, 2008.

Elements of Successful Leadership

Don and Dan's book goes into detail on each one of the levels of the leadership pyramid, and each element of leadership. One of the best parts of the book is the full-paragraph explanation of recommended resources in the appendix of that book.

SUMMARY OF LEADERSHIP

We will touch on many of these aspects of leadership as we focus on the remaining chapters that cover the nitty-gritty of starting, planning, and running our businesses. Here are the top points of the chapter:

- ☑ Leadership is the most challenging aspect of entrepreneurship, but also the most important.
- ☑ Leadership is difficult to define, and many people don't recognize it when they see it (sometimes not even those who are training others in leadership).
- ☑ Mastering leadership often requires a complete change in habits and personality.

- ☑ Mastering leadership will lead to health and prosperity as well as better relationships with others.
- ☑ Understanding yourself, your own strengths and weaknesses is essential to leading effectively.
- ☑ Listening to others is essential to lead effectively.
- ☑ Being a great leader is about encouraging others, coaching others, enabling others.
- ☑ Mind-body practices such as meditation, tai chi and yoga are useful tools to induce the balance needed in order to clarify thinking, recognize different points of view, and remain calm in a crisis.
- ☑ Most businesses, after the initial survival, go through a period of Still Evolving, Now in Crisis.
- ☑ Leadership development is a pyramid of skills starting with understanding ourselves, moving to understanding others, and embarking on a lifelong process of improvement.
- ☑ The elements of leadership is an iterative process that encompasses communication, setting goals and solving problems, motivation, team building, delegation, controlling growth, and time/schedule management.

3

Business Models and Writing Plans

Regardless of whether the business is just a dream at this point, or if we've been struggling in trying to get our company off the ground, or if we've been running it for years now, we need to put the dream, the vision, the goals in writing. The first step in doing that is to generate the business model. Once we've established that, we can write the business plan.

Dennis Chambers wrote the book in the series on writing business plans. Dennis's book covers the traditional descriptions of the different sections of the business plan. Dennis goes even further, and actually gets into the specifics of writing, and how to make the most impact, the most persuasive case, with words. For many entrepreneurs, it has been many years since they've had to do any kind of persuasive writing. Even I, who write more than the average person, found the information helpful, a reminder of the most critical aspects of persuasive writing.

Dennis wrote his book in 2007, before landmark books such as Osterwalder and Pigneur's *Business Model Generation* and Blank's *The Startup Owner's Manual: The Step-By-Step Guide for Building a Great Company* changed the face of business planning. Before we get into the nitty-gritty of business plan writing, we will go over some of the newer thinking on business model and business plan development, including my own experiences with my most recent business in using the new methods for business planning. I received a great deal of help on the newer ideas surrounding business model planning from Scott Schaeffer, Director of the Jump Start Incubator, and Sean Mallon, Senior Investment Director for CIT GAP Funds.

THE BUSINESS MODEL

Business Plan Writing has undergone a drastic change over the past two decades.

Steve Blank (2013, pp. 63–64) describes this recent movement:

> According to the decades-old formula, you write a business plan, pitch it to investors, assemble a team, introduce a product, and start selling as hard as you can. And somewhere in this sequence of events, you'll probably suffer a fatal setback. The odds are not with you: As new research by Harvard Business School's Shikhar Ghosh shows, 75% of all startups fail.
>
> But recently an important countervailing force has emerged, one that can make the process of starting a company less risky. It's a methodology called the "lean start-up", and it favors experimentation over elaborate planning, customer feedback over intuition, and interactive design over traditional "big design up front" development.

The traditional business planning cycle had become a major obstacle to innovation and entrepreneurship. Steve compares the recent lean start-up methods with the agile rapid development methods that prevailed over the long, slow, laborious system development life cycle methods of the 1980s and 1990s. The new method focuses on the business model, which is the rationale of how an organization creates, delivers, and captures value.

I found these processes a very effective method in clarifying my thinking so that my business plan, as I dynamically work on it, is much more focused.

When I started my first business in 1986 and sought out the advice from the Small Business Development Center, SCORE (retired executives who volunteer to help entrepreneurs) and my entrepreneurship teacher at Lehigh University (Jack Bradt). I was told that writing a business plan was the first step. There was no mention of something called a Business Model. I dutifully wrote my business plan.

In 2000, for my third business, I sought venture capital for the first time. I was asked the question: "What is your business model?" I had no idea what that meant, but in context, I got the sense it meant they wanted to know who my customers were and what channels I would use to reach them.

More recently, at the beginning of last year, 2013, I again sought the help of the Small Business Development Center (SBDC). This time, I was prepared with my business plan in hand. They weren't interested in it. The SBDC no longer advocates the long hard journey to do the research, investigate the industry, and write a business plan. Instead, they use shorter-term methods such as Pitch-Then-Plan and the Business Model Canvas.

Why the Change? Blame the Web

Before the World Wide Web, business models were pretty simple. The most common was that a business produced a product or service, and got paid for that product or service by the person or company who purchased and used it. Manufacturing operations required large investments in tangible assets such as equipment and buildings, which then served as collateral for financing. The business model wasn't impacted by the source of funding.

Television and radio (before cable and Sirius) were an exception; those who watched the content were not paying for it; the advertisers who frequently interrupted the content with commercials were paying for it.

Health insurance was also an exception. Businesses paid for health insurance, but employees got the products and services from it. For these types of businesses, the sources of funding were closely related to the type of business model adopted by the industry, but only in those few industries. In either case, the lines were clearly drawn and the models were well known.

During the Internet bubble of the late 1990s, companies in the so-called new economy stretched the concept of business model across the span of many industries. Yahoo, Ebay, Google, Facebook—none of them followed the traditional make-a-product-and-sell-it business model, but were not in the exception industries, such as television or health insurance.

The new business models used were varied. Users of the websites in this new economy often didn't pay for the services available on those websites. Instead, the service was provided for free, and the business model required funding from some alternative income stream. The most successful of these was Google, who eventually was able to sell featured sponsors and ad words in order to pay for the search engines that people used to find information on the World Wide Web.

A business model these days can offer many different choices for how we can make money. For example, if our business is a tai chi studio, our business model might be selling memberships (people who pay monthly for unlimited classes in an ongoing fashion) as our primary revenue. We might also sell products (clothes, health items, DVDs, and books), but not consider the products as our source of revenue. Instead, we might consider them a marketing cost—something we just about give away in order to attract new members who pay for ongoing memberships. That would also be part of our business model description.

A different business model would be to sell the products as our primary revenue. We might consider memberships a marketing cost in order to sell more clothes, DVDs, books, and health items. Alternatively, we might consider the revenue from one-time events or workshops as our primary income, and give away both the memberships and the products. These are all different valid business models. Describing this relationship between all of our activities and offerings, and identifying which is the primary focus that makes us money is our business model.

The most popular business model these days for Internet services is to provide free services, but add premium levels that provide more services. This is the highly successful business model of LinkedIn, where everyone can get a free profile. To send messages to other people on LinkedIn, or to obtain other premium services, members pay a monthly fee. The members who form the largest client base of LinkedIn (and who pay the most to belong, more than 50 percent of the revenue stream) are recruiters who can peruse the profiles of members in order to find just the right skills and talents to match the position for which they are seeking candidates.

In Search of Business Models: Canvas

Because of the variety of business models now available due to the Internet, and the low cost of introducing different ideas to large populations of people due to social media, a business can turn the process around. Instead of establishing the model and then searching for customers, a startup can search for customers and then establish the model. This iterative give-and-take start-up methodology has actually been around forever; it was called trial and error. Jim Collins notes that great businesses were those that tried a lot of different things, kept those that worked, and eliminated those that didn't.

Alexander Osterwalder and Yves Pigneur use a system of putting post-it notes on a canvas or poster board. The post-its are grouped by the key components of the business model—Key Partners, Key Activities, Key Resources, Value Proposition, Customer Relationships, Channels, Customer Segments, Cost Structure, and Revenue Streams. This is called *sketching* our business model. A case compilation of various portions of the business model we sketched for HPL Consortium, Inc., my own business, can be found in Figure 3.1.

Furthermore, the model starts with a bunch of hypothesis. It becomes our task to either prove or disprove each one. We quickly take our ideas to customers and get their feedback and reactions. Based upon what we find, we can go back and rearrange the components. We can continue to add or take away until we find a revenue stream that is profitable.

Pitch Then Plan

In addition to the Business Model Canvas, the Kutztown University Small Business Development Center also uses a presentation template

Figure 3.1. Case Business Model Canvas

called *Pitch Then Plan*[1] to help entrepreneurs quickly identify the most important aspects of their business.

It's the Planning, Not the Plan

As Eisenhower said, "In preparing for battle, I have often found that plans are useless, but planning is indispensable."

When writing a business plan, many entrepreneurs are under the impression that the reader will be as interested in their unique ideas and strategies as they themselves are. Entrepreneurs often go to elaborate trouble to ensure confidentiality and secrecy so that no one else steals their ideas. They may think that the longer the business plan, the better. They may think that getting the numbers as accurate as possible is of primary importance. These would all be misguided thinking.

The truth is bankers and investors are not interested at all in stealing our ideas. They already know that our numbers are inaccurate. They don't have a lot of time to devote to reading long business plans. What they want to know about us and our plan is: *Do we have what it takes to succeed?*

Are we doing those things that they think are essential to building a successful business? Can they make money from our efforts?

In other words, we don't spend countless hours writing business plans in order to share our plans. We spend countless hours on business plans because it helps us. Writing the business plan clarifies our thinking, identifies our assumptions, and demonstrates our ability to prepare for action. We write our business plans to flesh out the business model that we developed, and to codify our operations. We should be writing our business plan because it will help us mold our dreams into something approaching reality.

We spend those hours as entrepreneurs, whether or not we need to share our business plans with bankers, or investors, or just our own team. When we do share our plans with others, they are often just backup to our presentation and executive summary.

It is a mistake to try and outsource the writing of the business plan. If writing the business plan is our preparation for the action of starting, funding, and running our business, then the research that we do prior to the business plan is our preparation to prepare. We are the only ones who can do that.

WRITING THE BUSINESS PLAN

If we do share our plans, however, they need to be professional and persuasive. To do that, we need to know ahead of time with whom we will be sharing the plan. We need to pay attention to good writing practices.

Writing Is All about the Reader

Whether we are writing business plans, proposals, articles, books, or blogs, writing should never be about the writer. Writing is about the reader. In order to make this happen, we must put ourselves in the shoes of the reader, we must envision who the readers are, and imagine what they might be most interested in.

> As I am writing this paragraph now, I'm thinking about you—the person reading it. I'm envisioning people who have already delved a bit into trying to start their own business, and are looking for more success at doing so. Throughout the entire book, I asked myself the question— what do my readers want to know? What do they need to know? As we write our business plan, we should be doing the same thing.

The reader, then, is the focus of the plan. There are several typical readers of business plans—venture capitalists, angel investors, local bankers, employees, friends and family (potential investors), and government organizations such as the Small Business Administration (SBA).

Our first step should be to find out what our reader would like to see. To do that, we can invite questions from the people who will be reading the plan. Dennis describes an excellent interview technique to do that, called FIND—Facts, Issues, Needs, Dreams. By starting with the facts of the situation, and then moving on to potential issues, the needs of the reader, and then the hopes and dreams of the reader, we can find out exactly what we need to know. Incidentally, we will also be able to tell, before we go to the trouble of writing it down, whether or not our plans will fit into the facts, issues, needs, and dreams of the potential reader of our plans. (The dreams of which we speak here are the dreams of the *reader*, not our dreams.)

Obviously, if the facts, issues, needs, and dreams of our potential reader isn't met by our plans, we can save everyone a lot of time by moving on to another reader.

Order of Sections

The optimum business plan should have the following sections:

- Title Page
- Table of Contents
- Executive Summary (1–3 pages)
- Financials (depending upon business stage)
- Company and Opportunity
- Background and Landscape
- Market
- Competition
- Personnel
- Sales and Promotion
- Financials (depending upon business stage)
- Appendix

Successful business plans start with a defining mission, or, ala Jim Collins, our hedgehog concept (that which we do better than anyone else). Dennis was not the only author in our series who identified the mission statement as a foundational concept for businesses; out of the 12 books in the series, seven had sections on mission statements (and the other four referred to them indirectly as goals, purposes, or hedgehog concepts). The mission statement identifies who we really are. The best have six characteristics. They are:

- True
- Easily memorized
- Inspiring
- Defining
- Exclusive
- Regularly recited

The mission statement is at the heart of the business plan, and should be included at the earliest possible opportunity in the business plan.

If you've reviewed other business plan contents, you might note that, typically, a business plan organization starts with the background and ends with the financials. We've put financials in two alternative places, based upon the purpose of the business plan and stage of the business. Sean Mallon explained why he believes the financials should be relegated to the end (in a personal e-mail to me in July of 2013):

> I pay very little attention to out-year projections since in most cases they are 100% speculative. I value $100k revenue in the bank much more highly than I value the prospect of $30 million in revenue 5 years from now. Because financial projections are not important to me (as an early-stage investor), I suggest to entrepreneurs that they include them (and speak to them only very briefly) at the tail end. I suggest keeping the financial forecast very simple: for each of the next 5 years (use 2014, 2015, etc., not Year 1, Year 2, etc.) give estimates for revenue, EBITDA, and # of employees. These numbers should be supported by a more complete "bottoms-up" financial model, but don't go nuts on complexity. Most investors will only ask to see the detailed financial model if they already like the other aspects of the investment opportunity. . . . [Alternatively], I have seen (and been impressed by) entrepreneurs who put the "ask" in one of the opening slides, along the lines of: "We're here to tell your about our business and get you excited about participating in our $750k seed round."

At times, however, it is best to start with the financials. If the reader has a tendancy to turn to the back of the business plan and review the financials first anyway, we might as well give them what they want first. Our financial section should include the proposed (pro forma) profit and loss statement, balance sheet, cash flow statement, sales forecast, advertising plan, and the break-even analysis.

Throughout the business plan, we will be touching on various points that are likely to be top of mind for the reader. Our optimum business plan will answer the following questions:

- What is our hedgehog concept, our vision, our mission, our goal? What makes our company special?
- What problem are we trying to solve?
- How are we solving that problem?
- How big and/or widespread is the problem?
- What does a snapshot of our finances look like now?
- What will a snapshot look like two years from now? Five years from now?
- What do we want this business to become?
- Do we want to stay small? Do we want to get big? How big and how fast?
- Why are we taking such a risk, knowing that most new businesses fail in the first two years?
- Do we have any paying customers yet?
- Who are our best customers and prospects?
- Who is the competition? How do we beat out our competition?
- What is the single most important reason why our customers will come to us rather than go to our competition?
- What is the background of this CEO/management team that will allow them to compete effectively against other well-run and well-funded competitors?
- How is the product/service sold?
- What is the price point and how does that compare to the competition's pricing?
- What about the nature of our business is likely to change in the next five years? How shall we adjust to the change?
- How will we respond if a better, faster, or cheaper way to provide the products or services comes along?
- What can go wrong?
- How much capital is needed before this reaches break-even?
- How much money is the company raising now?
- Does the company have any investments or commitments from other investors?
- Do the owners have a valuation expectation?
- What do we want the reader of our business plan to do?
- What will the reader of our business plan get out of it if they do what we ask?

Our business plans should acknowledge the challenges of today. Running a business is hard. The availability of awe-inspiring technology makes it that much more complex. The Internet makes it possible for any dreamer with a laptop to start a company. It is that much more difficult to break out of the pack and maintain success for the long haul today. Our business plan cannot be so positive and optimistic that it ignores reality. Our plan should face the brutal facts and acknowledge the difficulties while laying out our plan to mitigate any problems we find.

The business plan, as already noted, should be all about the reader. And it should include the next steps for the reader—what specifically we are asking from them.

Avoiding Mistakes

We want to make sure that our business plan avoids the already-well-known mistakes that entrepreneurs are prone to make. When Fred Beste was CEO of Mid-Atlantic Venture Funds, he published an article on the top 25 death traps of entrepreneurs. We've included that essay in its entirety in Appendix C of this book.

THE WRITING PROCESS

Professional writers know how to adjust the tone and style of writing for different purposes, but typically, entrepreneurs are not professional writers. Given that it may have been many years since we've taken any kind of writing instructions, a quick review of persuasive writing techniques might be helpful.

The best business plans use friendly approachable language; short sentences; active voice as opposed to passive voice (We sit on the table rather than describing how the table was sat upon); positive spin on everything; subheadings to make the flow clear; no academic or stilted prose.

Consider the first draft no more than the giant slab of clay that is thrown on the wheel by a sculptor. There is much more work to be done after getting the first complete draft together.

Editing

Typically, we would spend 50 percent of the business plan writing effort on preparation, 20 percent on actually writing the draft, and 30 percent on revising it.

There are many levels to editing. It may be helpful to find others to read the draft and provide some input. It is difficult to edit our own writing; we tend to read what we meant and not what we actually said. Someone else reading it does not have the benefit of what is in our heads, however, so if our thoughts do not make sense to them, we need to edit the writing until it does.

It is easier to edit on hardcopy than electronic. Though I am a consummate technology user, I always print out my final draft and edit it on paper (transferring the edits to my electronic copy before final print out and submission). It is much easier to see mistakes on paper. When I try to edit on the screen, I find I miss a lot.

When we edit, there are several items we can look for:

- Is my structure clear to the reader?
- Do my ideas progress from one to the other logically?
- Do I begin each section with a vigorous explanatory paragraph that makes my point of view clear?
- Is my overall tone appropriate for my reader?
- Are my arguments persuasive?
- Is my plan the appropriate length and in the appropriate format?
- Is my viewpoint consistent, or do I keep shifting from "I" to "you" to "us"?
- Have I made crystal clear for the reader what my product or service is?
- Have I made crystal clear what my plans are for the business?
- If I were the reader, would I invest money in the company described in my plan?
- Are my transitions from one idea to another clear?
- Is the layout visually attractive?
- Does the plan look uncluttered and professional?
- Are there places where I can use graphics rather than prose to make my point sharper or to enhance the reader's understanding?
- Are my sentences short and crisp?
- Are my paragraphs no longer than five typed lines?
- Is my document free of spelling errors or typos?
- Do I write consistently in the active voice?
- Am I specific rather than vague?
- Are my subheads and lists parallel in structure?
- Do I know the rule regarding each punctuation mark I have used?
- Do I use strong verbs with few adjectives?
- Have I eliminated all uses of "very"?[2]
- Is my prose personable, tactful, and respectful?
- Do verbs agree with subjects?
- Do pronouns agree with antecedents?
- Is my writing positive at all times?
- Have I eliminated all clichés?[3]

Persuasion Techniques Research

Research tells us quite a bit about what works best, especially advertising copy research. For example, research has shown that clichés should be avoided because they do silent damage to our credibility; people reading them won't trust or believe us if we use them. Think about it. What is your own gut-level reaction to someone telling you that their product will "sell like hotcakes"?

We also know that graphics (tables, charts, illustrations) enhance understanding of material and draw the reader into reading the material. Readers can't help themselves; they will almost certainly read all the captions under all the graphics. The graphics should be in context; always refer to the graphic in the text and put a caption under the graphic.

The other item that readers are drawn to read are headlines or subheadings, as well as the P.S. (post script) after the signature in a letter—yet another reason to always use headings and subheadings in your text. You should keep the P.S. in mind when you write letters as well.

Color is also recommended; color improves readership by 50 percent. Another important aspect of writing is that white space is important; it avoids the cluttered look, enhances readability, connotes professionalism, confidence, and skill. Additionally, san serif fonts (such as Ariel, Helvetica, and Calibri) work best as headings and serif fonts (such as Times New Roman, Cambria, and Clearface) work best as body text. Unless our business plan is in an artsy or fashion business where we might be expected to buck the trend, it is best to stick with the tried and tested typefaces, especially if our readers are bankers and investors who are not known for appreciating the avant-garde.

Furthermore, choosing a noncommon font may cause logistical problems. When you send a document electronically, the font must exist on the reader's computer or a substitute font will be used. We cannot control which fonts get substituted. Our beautiful well-chosen font may result in an ugly out-of-kilter font when the document is read by the reader on their system. It is best to stick with the common fonts to avoid this problem.

These guidelines work on any kind of writing, not just business plans. Dennis also wrote a wonderful section in his book on proposals, which I have put in the chapter on pricing and proposing.

PLANNING TO SHARE BUSINESS PLANS

As mentioned earlier, the most common reason to write a business plan is to seek funding, which is covered in Chapter 11. However, while Chapter 11 talks about different sources of funding, I thought here would be the best place to have a discussion on *how* to share the business plan with others.

First, in this era of massive information overload, brevity and clarity is the name of the game. The business plan should function as the backup for the executive summary, which is really the most important part of the plan. Often, a quick glance at the executive summary is all a banker or potential investor needs to know to decide whether or not our business is a good fit for their funding. Often, the executive summary will be the only part that gets read.

Good investors are highly sought after, and thus, very busy. We entrepreneurs may not like it, but chances are a potential investor will only devote a couple of minutes to decide whether to set up an in-person meeting with us. Sending a potential investor a 20- or 30-page business plan un-solicited is the best way to be ignored. Investors don't identify great en-trepreneurs by how they write, but rather by how hardworking, smart, approachable, and passionate they are, which they can't discern until they meet us face-to-face.

If we want to get those all-important 10 minutes of face time with a potential investor, we will heed advice from Fred Beste, Sean Mallon, and Bob Thomson from whom I've heard this phrase dozens of times over the years: *be well introduced.*

The venture industry thrives on relationships and established networks. Trying to beat down the door of an investor is counterproductive, and might inadvertently lock the door on a potential future funding source. Rather than boxing up and sending out dozens of business plans, our best bet is to delve into our own networks and find a connection to the target investor, or attend a networking event which we know they will attend. While it may take more time and resources than we'd like, we need to es-tablish relationships with people on the periphery of a potential investor's network so that we can gain access to the central decision makers. Often, it is the only way. And if our attempts at getting their attention don't move as quickly as we'd like, it is a sign that our approach and presentation are not yet compelling enough, or we have not yet found the perfect match of an investor yet. In either case, getting frustrated with the process doesn't help.

Once the investor asks for an in-person meeting, then the presentation becomes key. We should have a short slide or video presentation that out-lines the main points in the executive summary. Powerpoint presentations are great because we can modify them easily to cater to any specific needs of our audience (e.g., more focus on go-to-market strategy for an angel investor, and more emphasis on cash flows when talking to a banker about a line of credit).

We will discuss more deeply what kind of characteristics will make our business an attractive investment in the chapter on Sources of Capital.

SUMMARY OF BUSINESS MODELS AND WRITING

Business plan writing has changed in recent years.

- ☑ These days, it is important to identify our business model before we write our business plan.
- ☑ Business plans are best written by us, ourselves, and cannot be effec-tively written by a third party.
- ☑ Business plans are all about the reader, not the writer.
- ☑ Business plans are more about the planning process and capabilities of our team and potential of our business than the actual contents.

☑ Business plans written for investors must focus on what the investor will get out of the relationship.

☑ Business plans written for bankers must focus on the numbers and reliability and stability of the business.

☑ We can use an interview technique to ensure we understand what readers are expecting. The interview elicits the facts, issues, needs, and dreams of the reader.

☑ Mission statements are at the heart of business plans.

☑ The majority of time spent on writing a business plan should be on preparation.

☑ Our writing must be clear, concise, convincing, professional, friendly, and engaging.

☑ Persuasive writing is direct, specific, strong, grammatically pristine, and free of clichés.

☑ Headings, graphic illustrations, color, choice of font, and use of white space are all important elements of presentation.

☑ The key points of the business plan should be in the executive summary, and in a slide presentation.

☑ The best way to get our business plan reviewed is to be well introduced.

Teamwork and Finding Resources

Ken Tanner wrote a fabulous book for the series, *The Entrepreneur's Guide to Hiring and Building the Team*. He describes the process of setting up our business environment so that we can find, recruit, and attract top employees. He shares the best ways to welcome them into the company, establish a positive corporate culture, and retain good employees. I'll summarize the lessons Ken Tanner presents in the book on this topic in the series.

We will also talk a bit about how the concept of team and hiring has changed since the Internet and its impact on the business environment. Business teams these days extend beyond the traditional employees in our offices in our buildings. I'll be adding specific points about the logistics of virtual rather than physical teams. This will be helpful no matter in which stage of team building we are.

WHO IS ON THE TEAM

One of the most-often asked questions is how many employees do we have. Obviously, businesses can run the gamut in size from hundreds of thousands of employees to Units of One (individual sole proprietorships without formal employees). But even Units of One have teams of people because it takes more than one person to run a business, no matter how small. There are always others; vendors, suppliers, contractors, helpers. There is always a team.

Some team members are formal employees—people we hire and pay a salary, necessitating payment of payroll taxes, social security, worker's compensation insurance, and Medicare, all documented on a W-2 form each year. Other team members are consultants—people to whom we pay a fee, documented on a 1099 form each year. Others are employees of vendors, and yet others might be volunteers (family or friends). When I answer the question about employees in my own business, I include all of these different categories.

The government, for tax purposes, clearly differentiates between employees and consultants, however. The rules are strict. Consultants use their own tools, while employees use tools that we provide. Consultants determine their own working hours and location, while employees must work the hours we tell them to work and in the location we provide for them. Intellectual property work done by employees belongs to our company. Intellectual property work done by consultants belongs to them unless specified otherwise in our agreement with them.

The government is particular about this differentiation, and some companies (such as Microsoft) have gotten in trouble and ended up paying huge fines because they treated 1099 employees the same as W-2 employees by providing them work space and equipment, telling them what to do when, and assuming ownership of their work products without a separate licensing or purchase agreement.

But for purposes of our business, as long as we understand the legal difference, we don't need to count only the W-2 members of the team. We can ignore the bureaucratic differences for team building development, and use the term *employee* or *team member* whether we mean 1099 or W-2, vendor, or volunteer. Selecting and leading the team is the most important task we have as entrepreneurs, and includes all of those who contribute toward the goal of the business.

ATTRACTING EMPLOYEES IN AN ENTREPRENEURIAL CULTURE

Why work for us? The first point Ken makes is that a top candidate, someone who could have a pick of jobs at a larger company for a great salary, might *want* to come and work for a smaller entrepreneurial business such as ours. We should be looking for top candidates. If we understand their motivations, we will be less inclined to settle for less qualified employees just because we are smaller with lower salaries and benefits. There are several potential reasons high-quality people would prefer to work for our business. The candidate might wish to have:

- More opportunities to feel special and needed
- More control over their work environment
- More influence over the business itself
- A better culture
- A healthier atmosphere
- Greater chance for sharing and understanding the vision
- A better communication flow

- Less bureaucracy
- More flexible qualification requirements
- More hats
- Better mentoring
- More opportunity to move up

More qualified does not necessarily mean more degrees or a more highly polished resume. One of the reasons we may be able to find and attract top candidates who would do the job better than anyone else is because we can look beyond the standard templates and cookie-cutter job qualifications. Large corporations often have several layers, which constitutes a gauntlet for top candidates, necessitating inflexible qualification requirements. We, however, can look beyond the surface requirements and find the exact right candidate for the job.

Starting the Search

The most important part of a successful outcome is finding the optimum match between our culture, the existing team, the job requirements, and the candidate. Fully understanding the company culture, working with the existing team, and completely recognizing all aspects of the job description (both what it is and what it is not) constitute the all-important first step of hiring a new person into our company.

We might be tempted to minimize or ignore this step, assuming that it would all be worked out as we talk to potential candidates. Big mistake. We must work through this process, especially the business culture and job description with our existing employees, before finding a candidate. Otherwise, each employee will have, in their minds (and we, as business owners will have in our minds) an idea of what the perfect candidate would be like—but we might not be in agreement on what the criteria are, and we wouldn't even know it. As we recruit, interview, and hire, the vision would keep changing. There is no easier way to sabotage a new employee than to have differing ideas about what the job of the new employee should be.

At one point in my career, I interviewed, and got hired as a Chief Information Officer for a distributor. The owner was originally looking for a programmer, but after talking with me, he decided he needed someone who could take charge and streamline operations. He explained to me that he wanted to enable the business to double or triple without running into the same technical problems that had dogged the company for the last several years.

He introduced me to his senior team, the VP of Operations and the VP of Technology, describing the new path of prosperity we were shooting for. He told them of his plans for us, and what role he expected me to play. Then, he left.

And by left, I mean didn't show up again at the business for seven days. During this time, I attempted to get settled in and start on the plans, but it was difficult without getting any guidance from him. Especially since the VP of Operations and VP of Technology both viewed me, despite what the owner had said, as a programmer. They kept asking me when I would start writing code for the obsolete, difficult-to-manage mess they called a financial system (which had been customized so thoroughly that the base system could not be upgraded, hence the need for a programmer). Obviously, I had no intention of delving into that morass. When the owner showed up for work (finally) on the eighth day, I had an excellent conversation with him on the first steps, and had started to prepare for the launch meeting of the project to replace the system. However, later that day, the VPs both went to him to complain that I was not doing my job. I was fired the next day—not by the owner, but by the VP of Operations.[1] The problem was that the VPs and the owner had widely disparate views of what job they were hiring for.

---

[1] There were other issues—in actuality, I was still recovering from my car accident and was not physically able to work a full day, eight hours in a row. I would have left shortly even if I had not been fired because I really couldn't do the job.

How to Find Recruits

Hiring a recruiting firm is one way, albeit an expensive way, to find candidates. Generally, I think entrepreneurs and small business owners should stay away from recruiters. The CEO of a start-up used a recruiter to find me, and he ended up paying the recruiter more money than I ever received! (Recruiters are typically paid 20–30 percent of the starting salary.)

The CEO who hired me had big dreams, and offered me a six-figure salary. It was only after I accepted the job that I discovered there was no salary until we attracted startup funding and then, when we did, I did not take a salary because we needed the funds for development of the technologies and to apply for a patent on them. In the end, we all lost, except for the recruiter who was paid based on the hoped-for salary. (Lesson learned.)

We are better off recruiting through referrals. We can ask employees, suppliers, trade organizations, community and government organizations, colleges and universities in the area. Often, the best sources are the colleges; the faculty know which students are good (and which are not). Students are generally young enough that they don't have extremely high expectations for their salary. They are also more trainable than someone who has decades of experience. Additionally, colleges and universities often have career fairs and internship programs that allow us to "try before we buy" without the cost of recruiting fees. (Be prepared, however, to go through several interns before finding a good one. The quality is variable.)

There is also a powerful referral network online. LinkedIn, Facebook, and dozens of other websites enable us to share our needs with our connections, who share those needs with their connections. Before we know it, we've received dozens of referrals for people with just the skills for which we are looking.

As an entrepreneur, however, we often need to go beyond the obvious. I've also found it helpful to search for bloggers, discussion groups, and online articles on the skills for which we are searching; people with a passion or a talent at something often volunteer their time on discussion boards, and they are easily searchable.

Other methods of finding people—a sign in the window, friends, and family. For small entrepreneurial businesses, nepotism can be a lifesaver. We must be careful, however, not to allow unqualified or marginal employees to continue to work just because they are friends or family. We risk losing the trust of the other, more qualified and harder working employees if we play favorites.

In some cases (depending upon the job), we can also look at retired workers, employees who might have some mental or physical disability, as well as nonviolent ex-convicts. Because they are often prevented from getting jobs in a more structured larger company, smaller companies like ours can take advantage of highly talented people who might have been convicted of an unrelated crime.

Identifying the Best Candidate

Once we've recruited a suitably large pool of people from which to choose, we need to identify which ones might have the best chance of thriving in our company. Ken recommends a three-step process to identify these candidates out of those we have recruited:

- Resume review
- Phone screening
- Face-to-face in-person conversation

The resume review is to eliminate obviously unqualified candidates. Keep in mind that we are able to be more flexible than larger companies, but not so flexible that we waste our time with someone who would not ever be a good fit for the job. When in doubt, we can leave them in, but pay strict attention in the next two phases.

For the recruits who are left, a phone call may well provide quite a bit of information that will enable us to either eliminate or move forward—without wasting the extra time in travel. During the phone call, we should go over the job description (which we've written down) and ask obvious questions, such as:

- Do you have any experience with this type of job? Tell me about it.
- Why did you leave XXX and take a job with YYYY?
- Why did you choose that major? What attracted you to that topic?
- It says here that you (*pick an item from their resume*). Can you tell me more about that?
- I'm concerned about (*pick an item from their resume*). Can you tell me more about what that was all about?
- What was your total compensation last year?
- If you were to come to work with my company, what would probably be the reason?

No trick questions, no asking about what type of animal they might be, no psychological analytics. We also need to keep in mind that a telephone does not convey as much information because we are missing eye contact, gestures, and posture. But the time spent on the phone is generally a good indication of whether or not we should pursue this candidate. If we do, we should set up a time to meet right away, while we are still on the phone with them. We don't want to delay following through and making a final decision.

We also want to make a special note of that last question, about the reason they might come work for our company. Later on, we'll talk about how this information might be useful.

After the in-person meeting time is set, we should send a recruiting package. At this point, we want the candidate to feel wanted, to know that we are serious, and that they might want to start getting excited about the possibility of coming to work for us.

When the candidate arrives for the interview, our goal should be to have a conversation with them. Questions imbedded in our conversation should be behavioral questions. Human resources experts have found that behavioral questions tend to provide the most information regarding the candidate's ability to match the job requirements. A behavioral question will set up a real or hypothetical situation, and then ask the candidate what they would do or how they would handle it. We are not looking for a right or wrong answer; we are looking for their thought process in choosing what they would do and why they would do it that way. We are also looking for patterns in their answers that would reveal personality characteristics so that we can evaluate their fit within our company culture and with our existing employees.

Additionally, we don't want to wallow in a love-fest. We should make a concerted effort to go negative, identify the weaknesses of the company, ask again about the motivations, the reasons behind the person wanting to come and work for us. Now is our best chance to ensure that this recruit is the best candidate for the job.

Hiring Decision

Deciding to move forward to hire a person does not mean that the judgment process is over. There are many ways to tell if a person is a good fit for a job, and most of them cannot take place within an interview. Personality assessments and skill tests are helpful in determining whether a new employee is a good fit. While it is possible to administer assessments and tests during the interview process, the best ones have a cost to them, and therefore, should not be given until we are sure the candidate is the right one. Additionally, most assessments and tests are not appropriate for hiring decisions; they tend to be better-suited to match candidates to job descriptions once we have established they are right for our company.

Reference checking should be reserved for the time period after we've made our initial decision. We should check the who, what, when, where items on the resume. But we also want to dig a bit deeper at this point—talk to people from the previous company who were not listed as references, network around to see if we know anyone who knows anyone who knows the candidate and will provide some context for them. Depending upon the type of position, this would be the time for criminal background check, credit report, drug testing, and so on.

Once all the data has been gathered, we should go off to a quiet spot and dig in to ask ourselves questions about how well the candidate would fit. This step serves to decrease the influence of several common situations that might cause us to choose the wrong candidate, including: 1) the halo effect (allowing one or two positives to outweigh any other negatives), 2) too quick judgment (making up our minds in the first two minutes and ignoring additional information), and 3) grading on a curve (accepting employees who are not the right fit just because they are the only candidates available).

One truth we must recognize early on is that this process takes time—something we do not have in abundance. But short circuiting the process short circuits the success. If we don't invest the time to find the right people, we will find the wrong people. It is better not to hire anyone at all than to hire the wrong person (Collins and Porras 1994).

Once we've made our final determination, it is time to make the offer. This is a place where our flexibility can snag great employees away from larger companies with better benefits and higher salaries. This is where the answer to those questions, asked back in the phone interview, becomes so important. We can tailor our offer to their specific needs, what they are looking for in a new job.

How we present the offer is almost as important as the offer itself. The salary offer should be up front, but it should be closely followed by all the nonsalary financial benefits, such as health insurance, vacation time, educational assistance, sick pay, and so on. The dollar benefit to the employee should be enumerated—even if we don't pay anything out of pocket for the benefit. For example, credit union membership might be worth several hundred dollars a year to someone who gets a lower interest rate on their car loan. The cost of tuition reimbursement can reach thousands of dollars even if the employee doesn't use it to go back to school.

More importantly, however, are the nonfinancial benefits, such as a prestigious title, an exciting challenge, greater responsibility, increased authority, the chance to make an impact, and the opportunity to be appreciated. This information should be presented to the candidate in person and in writing in the letter. This information should reiterate the answer they gave to the question as to the reason they would work for our company. Our final communication to them should ask the question, *Will you join us?*

The candidate may negotiate for a few things. But we should wrap it up as quickly as possible and not stretch out this phase beyond the meeting. We should already know what, if anything, we are willing to negotiate and what we are not. If the candidate needs further time for a final decision (such as time to talk it over with a spouse), we would request a date by which we can expect an answer.

If the candidate says no, we might want to dig a bit deeper to find out exactly why; the reason might be simple and easily adjusted, such as start time, vacation time, and so on.

Another problem is that many prospective employees change their minds after they have said Yes. There are several things that we can do to prevent cold feet from interfering with a new hire:

- Discuss the possibility of a counter offer from the current employer, and prepare them for the situation.
- Have the employee immediately come in and sign the paperwork.

- Bring in the spouse for a discussion of the family benefits and a tour of the facilities.
- Treat the candidate as an employee right away. Get them settled in an office, set up the computer, get them involved in meetings.

Onboarding

Onboarding is another name for the process commonly known as new employee orientation. Preparing for new employees is something that entrepreneurs tend to do poorly. Since we ourselves are independent, resourceful go-getters, we assume others are too. We don't think they need much help beyond being introduced to a few people who happen to be around in the office on the day they arrive. Our assumption would lead us astray; much more is needed.

The first day of a new employee is telling. The contrast can be demonstrated by my two experiences on my first day as an employee as a vice president at two different Fortune 500 financial firms.

My first day at Firm #1, I arrived and was shown my office and given my log on for the computer right away. I was taken around and introduced to everyone in the department—even if it meant breaking into a meeting for a quick hello. The next day, I was shepherded into a two-week orientation course that provided the history, the background, an introduction into the terminology and culture of the company, an in-depth description of what my job was, and what I was expected to accomplish. The orientation process boded well for my tenure at this company. It is still one of the best places I ever worked.

Contrast that experience with Firm #2. I arrived and was walked by the security guard up to my new boss, who was in the middle of a meeting. I waited for hours, sitting in the common area or wandering around on my own, getting funny looks from people who didn't know who I was or why I was there. It took me three days to be assigned my office (which was taken away from three other employees who had previously cubicled there, and then redesigned for one person—me). It took four days for my computer to arrive, and when it did, there were so many problems that I learned just how well (or how poorly, in this case) the help desk worked.[1] It was two weeks before I had a working computer with a working corporate account and security authorizations. It wasn't that long before I discovered that members of my team were resentful and angry because one of them had expected to be promoted into the position for which I was hired. The lack of focus on process was endemic to the whole company, I soon found. In retrospect, I regretted making the change; the bump in salary was not worth the aggravation. (Lesson learned.)

As business owners, it behooves us to pay attention to onboarding. Small entrepreneurial firms can't afford a two-week orientation, but they certainly can provide a description of the history and vision of the company, a review of the expectations of the employee, an explanation of office routines. At minimum, new employees should be assigned a mentor, introduced to all the coworkers, and their work space and supplies should be ready to go—when they arrive the first day.

BUILDING THE TEAM

Developing a disparate and diverse set of people into a working team is as much art as it is science. In addition to the leadership lessons discussed in previous chapters, there are many tools and resources that can help us become more successful at this task.

Personality Assessments

There are many different personality assessments available that are commonly used to help deal with team dynamics. The most common I've seen are DISC and Myers-Briggs type indicator.

DISC

DISC assesses each person on four characteristics. The characteristic's names depend upon which testing service is used, but are often: Dominance/Drive, Influential/Inducement, Steadiness/Submission, Conscientious/Compliance. Forceful, bold, independent people would have a high D; social people with many friends and a large network would have a high I. Hardworking, dependable, rule-following people would be considered a high S, and detail-oriented, data-dependent people would be classified as a high C. The most common personality type among the general population is a high S or C. The least common is a high D. High Ds, however, are most often CEOs or entrepreneurs. The DISC personality profiles are often used to assess leadership styles, to match personality characteristics to team roles, and to help salespeople assess their prospective customers. More details on DISC's role in sales are covered in Chapter 9.

Myers-Briggs

Myers-Briggs type indicators are used more often to describe personality types to enable team members to be better at getting along with each other, and are less role dependent. The Myers-Briggs indicators also assesses four characteristics, but instead of high-low scores, each has a

Figure 4.1. Myers-Briggs Dichotomies

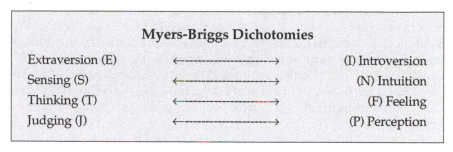

Source: Jonathan London, *The Entrepreneur's Guide to Selling.* Santa Barbara, CA: Praeger, 2009.

dichotomy (as seen in Figure 4.1) (Müller and Gappisch 2005; Henderson and Nutt 1980).

Ken Tanner's Styles, and Why Assessments Are Useful

Ken introduces a personality assessment based upon how each person deals with the issue of control in his book. The four styles in this system are Creator, Cogitator, Connector, and Commander. Do they control others? Are they controlled by others?

The reasons for assessing personality types, styles, and profiles are so that we can understand motivations and internal values. The golden rule is not to treat others as you would want to be treated, but rather to treat others as *they* would want to be treated. Treating all employees the same would only work if each employee was the same; it is our job to treat each employee differently, matching the needs and responsibilities of the jobs to the styles and profiles of the employees. We also need to understand personality types so that we don't make the fatal mistake of hiring too many people of the same type.

Every team needs a diversity of people; every team needs someone of each type. Together, they can form bonds. Gaps in strengths and weaknesses of individuals are plugged by others in the team. If everyone has the same profile, everyone has the same weaknesses. Those gaping holes can take any progress made and reduce it to rubble.

Creating Culture

Cultures that are left to themselves to develop often become negative, gossipy, and spiteful. That first financial firm for which I worked took great pains to structure, build, enforce, and encourage a positive, customer-oriented, productive place to work. The stories that circulated were about how employees went above and beyond for the customers. The senior leaders were portrayed and talked about as if they were geniuses who orchestrated the best company at the right time with the right team. Employees were encouraged to feel like family, to know that they would be taken care of by the company. Everyone knew the story of the founding of the company in an abandoned grocery store, the mission statement, the week's goal (and whether or not the company had reached that goal). Everyone wore their lapel pins every day (the only excuse allowed was that you accidentally left your pin on your pajamas). Awards and rewards were abundant.

The second firm took a laissez-faire attitude, and it showed. Teamwork was nonexistent; it was every employee for himself or herself. The stories that circulated among employees were biting, sarcastic, or humorous tales of the misadventures of the senior leaders. No one knew what the weekly, monthly, or even annual goals were. Some of us knew that we were losing 378,000 customers every month, and that no one—not customers, not employees, not senior leaders—no one was happy.[2]

We want our companies to be more like the former and less like the latter. Research shows that companies with strong company cultures flourish during both good times and bad, and that employees of strong corporate culture companies are more satisfied with their jobs (Collins and Porras 1994). That doesn't necessarily mean that strong cultures are for everyone. People who chafe under the yoke of authority tend to be unwilling to give in to the shared spirit of the company. One's own personal ego must be invested in the success of the organization, and some people are not able to relinquish that control.

But when done right, a strong culture can provide the solid bonds that enable real teamwork to flourish. It can provide an environment where independent decision making is enhanced because the culture will tell the employees which decision is the right one. Disney's cast members[3] still talk about WWWD (What Would Walt Do?). There are many good examples of positive company culture characteristics out there:

- Larry Page at Google allows employees to select projects of their choice to work on for 20 percent of their time.
- Tony Hseish at Zappos gives new hires four weeks of intensive training, and then offers them a week's salary plus $2,000 if they choose to leave. Ninety-seven percent of them stay.
- Howard Schultz at Starbucks spends more on training than he spends on advertising.

How do we establish this culture? There are many ways:

- Make the decision to establish the culture.
- Set a precedent of consistently high standards and fairness.

- Pay attention to interaction.
- Focus on branding: names, symbols, images.
- Tell stories that demonstrate behavior we want to encourage.
- Establish jargon—the insider's language.
- Tell inside jokes.
- Hold ceremonies and frequent methods of reward.
- Establish dress codes (either formal or informal) for attire.
- Demonstrate pride in accomplishments.
- Honor the company heritage through models, pictures, monuments, scrapbooks, and so on.

Team Dynamics

There is more that we can do, beyond hiring right and establishing the corporate culture, to enable diverse groups to work together and accomplish a lot.

- Show how each team member would benefit personally from team success.
- Treat the team as a team.
- Communicate to the whole team, not to individual members independently.
- State goals and objectives from a team perspective.
- Connect compensation such as bonuses and incentives to team performance.
- Establish competition against benchmarks, not by pitting team members against each other for exclusive rewards.
- Do not rank order team members, but encourage evaluation based upon the team roles.

Teams need time to coalesce, and every team goes through a common set of stages. The most well-known names for the stages were introduced by Bruce Tuckman in 1965—Forming, Storming, Norming, and Performing (Johnson et al. 2002). The team leader typically coaches the members through these phases until they reach a point of productivity. We can also look to the team members themselves to tell us what would enable them to come together more effectively as a team.

At one point, I was the Chief Technology Officer for an e-commerce software development company about to move to a new location. I was prepared to provide private offices for each of the programmers, feeling that a private office with a window would be a great reward for a job well done.

It was a good thing that I spoke to the programmers about my plan before ordering the reconstruction of the new space. While I had been conditioned from my years in corporate America to value a private office with a window, these young techies could think of no greater hell than to be by themselves in an office with window glare obscuring their computer screens. They preferred a single large room without windows, with short cubicles that allowed them to easily converse constantly.

I have often succeeded in taking formerly uncooperative, divisive people from different departments and setting up the right conditions for them to coalesce into a productive real team (Katzenbach 1998; Katzenbach and Smith 1994). The process, though time consuming, is not easy, but also not too difficult.

The team of programmers was a great example of a productive team. Watching them work in concert together was like watching a basketball game with the code serving as the ball. Typically, they would all be working on the same website, each taking care of their particular piece of it—inserting and testing the code in turn.

"I'm ready for the popup screen now, Joe."

"It's there, now, Al. Mary, could you test it with your module?"

"Yup. It works. You can insert the graphics now, Kim."

"I'm trying, but I need a new CSS variable added to the style sheet. Al, can you take care of it?"

"Got it. Try it now, Kim."

I marveled at their ability to work together as a team, especially since programmers can be reclusive. I can't take credit for this particular team. I hadn't been at the company long. I credit the person who managed them for many years prior to my arrival, Jim Darlington. But it was still distressing to watch the disintegration of the team shortly before I left the company.

In this case, the destructive dynamics were introduced by a new CEO who didn't understand technology team dynamics. Within two months, the productivity of the team was gone.

The beginning of the end started when he instituted a "suits only" dress code (for programmers!). Then, he gave the two most productive programmers large salary increases. Then, he fired the programmer he considered "least productive" (without recognizing the important role that programmer played in documenting the code changes). Then, he started taking individuals off the project to work on other unrelated projects, causing a complete halt to progress on company-critical priorities.[1]

---

[1] When I insisted these changes be reversed, I was fired. Shortly thereafter, the CEO himself was fired, and the company was out of business within a year.

It is not easy to establish the dynamics that allow a team to coalesce, but it is frighteningly easy to introduce dynamics that break a team apart.

There are many ways to foster productive team dynamics. First, we have to give them the authority to match their responsibilities (what my grandfather called *authoribility*). To expect a team to accomplish a goal without giving them the authority necessary to be fully responsible for the outcome is a sure way to sabotage a team's efforts. We also should provide clear communications about the boundaries for their responsibilities, and explain the expectations.

We must also provide them with the tools they need to be successful. Sometimes, resources aren't abundant (and rarely as abundant as the team members would like), but knowing which resources are available, and which are not available, is important for all the team members.

We must also let them make mistakes. If we try to prevent them from going down the wrong path, they will feel micromanaged, and will not take any responsibility. After correcting their mistakes, the next time, they will simply wait for us to tell them what to do. Why should they do anything if we are just going to second guess them?

However, we must deal with conflict (and not by ignoring it). Conflict is healthy and normal. Using the personality assessments is a great way to help a team deal with those annoying differences, and help them become more tolerant of each others' behaviors. The team can get through conflicts if they constantly search for common ground, focus on points of agreements instead of disagreements. People are willing to set aside differences to work on a common goal if each is respected for their differing opinions. Teams should consider each other like functional family rather than like friends. Friends get together because they like each other and have common interests. Functional families get together because they are family. Functional family members tolerate each other because they have no other choice. Colleagues don't have to like each other, they don't have to be friends, but they do have to get along and work together effectively. Encouraging this culture will improve the effectiveness of the team.

Additionally, teams should be encouraged toward peer leadership. The leadership of real teams is constantly changing, based upon the needed role at any one time. Like the constantly shifting basketball (i.e., the current set of code) passed from person to person on the programming team, leadership can be constantly passed around from person to person, based upon the area of expertise that requires a decision at any particular time. The official leader of the team is actually the coordinator of the leadership rather than the person in charge. All the members of the team are expected to demonstrate leadership and support the other team members.

Virtual Teams

The general rules of building good teams are essential whether the team is physically present or virtually present. Today, working from home is a common reality, and an entire industry has arisen that provides virtual assistants and freelance help (Ferriss 2007).

But virtual teams have special challenges that physically present teams do not face. Physically present teams, for example, are able to communicate with all modalities—including tone of voice, facial expression, and body language.

Virtual teams are virtual either because the members are located in different geographies, or are 1099 employees, which means they are probably each working out of their own offices instead of together in the same building. Physically present teams are more likely to be W-2 employees, which provides a bit more control over the members.

In my experience, it is slightly easier to get productivity out of a physically present team than a virtual team, but that doesn't mean virtual teams can't be productive. They can be. But it takes more effort, more communication, more structure, and more time.

Trust

One of the most important ingredients for virtual teams is trust. While it is possible to utilize technology to monitor the online behaviors of the team members, it is a mistake to do so. How productive would a physically present employee be if their boss was sitting inside their cubicle every hour of every day, all day long? Monitoring a virtual team member's every move throughout the day is virtually the same thing. Just like with physically present team members, the measurement needs to be the deliverables and output, not the work process. People need the freedom to work on their own time in their own way. If our team members need to be watched to accomplish their tasks, there is something wrong with the process.

Instead, roles, deliverables, and tasks should be clearly identified, along with priorities (that don't change constantly) and deadlines, along with lag time. Lag time is the amount a deadline can stretch without doing damage to the schedule or throwing someone else off their deadline. We can think of them as the preferred date and the drop dead date for deliverables. The key is clear expectations that are mutually understood by all team members.

Virtual Team Technology

If members of a team are in different geographies, but all work for the same company, they can be provided with a single technology in order to communicate. There are several companies providing virtual team tools for a fee, and some of the best ones can be found in the list of web resources in Appendix C.[4]

There are several essential tools that a virtual team needs that physically present teams don't always think about:

- A list of names, addresses, phone numbers, and e-mails for all team members
- Recognition of who plays what role on the team
- An easily accessible location for all team files (a virtual filing cabinet)
- An easily accessible work plan or list of tasks, along with who is responsible for the tasks
- A team coordinator who communicates with all team members (This may be the leader, an agent of the leader, or an independent person.)
- A meeting method

Teams can meet face to face through technology such as that currently available through Google Hangouts, WebEx, Skype, GoToMeeting, FaceTime, Lync, Meeting Burner, Uberconference, or Vidyo. But unless we already have a large corporation that can afford high quality videoconferencing to everyone's location, I don't advise it—yet.

At the present time (May 2014), virtual meeting video software is just now working out all the bugs. More details on the technical aspects of the coming video revolution can be found in Chapter 5.

Until the technology is perfected, the video technology interferes more with team communication than it helps, especially if not everyone on the team is highly familiar with video technology. I believe it is best to stick with easy screen sharing software (such as Join.me or screenleap.com) and a teleconference call (such as FreeConference.com).

Because of my entrepreneurial experience with CommerceLinks.net (when we developed a patentable technology for live video customer service), I am deeply cognizant of the limitations of the current infrastructure to seamlessly provide high quality, full video, face to face. For the present time, it is best to stick with simple, free, and easily available tools for voice and slides.[1]

---

[1] Internet virtual meeting software currently is a high venture capital target industry and growing at a rapid rate. Unfortunately, there's no way to know which platforms are going to win the technology war, and the technology itself is changing almost weekly. There will be a consolidation within a few years, and standardization, so that instead of the hundreds of choices there are right now, there will be a handful. However, since we can't be sure which platform will be around in a couple of years, we shouldn't invest in any of them yet.

Virtual teams work best when everyone on the team has gotten a chance to meet in person at least once. So, whenever possible, we should arrange for a physical launch meeting of all team members. In-person meetings, complemented by a community-binding meal, do a lot to enable team members to work together more effectively.

Virtual teams need a central repository for all the work products of the team. Google Drive can serve, or Dropbox, or any other website that enables people to upload and share files among team members. Even a simple FTP site with an easy-to-use front end such as Mollify can easily and cheaply serve as a location for everyone's work files.

If we think that we do not have the funds to sponsor the travel for team members to meet, or specify an online repository for their work, consider the cost of having a nonproductive team on our payroll. It does not make sense for us to put together a team, and then withhold the tools they need to function properly.

Virtual Team Communication

Communication must be more directed in a virtual team. Meeting agendas and minutes always enhance team productivity. However, physically present teams can get along without them, so they are not absolutely necessary. But with a virtual team, there is no substitute for writing down what was discussed and covered in a meeting. The agenda and minutes become the lifeline for each member; it tells them what concerns them (and what does not). It tells them what they are supposed to do (if anything) and what they already did. In the absence of face-to-face meetings and over-the-cubicle discussions, the written agenda and minutes track the progress of the interactions.

In a virtual team, the typical body language used to assess roles in a physically present team is not available. Therefore, roles should not be assumed; they must be directly and openly identified. As always, tasks need to be delineated as to who will be doing them and when, but with a virtual team, there needs to be an added reminder before each team meeting. To Do Items discussed in a meeting, if not written down, are completely forgotten.

Most important of all is contact information. People who meet in the same building do not worry about how to find each other. But unless one person specifically gathers all the contact information and makes it available to everyone, virtual team members may have no idea how to contact the other team members outside of scheduled online meetings. Make sure all the e-mail addresses, phone numbers, and physical locations of everyone can be found in one place, and is kept updated for all members of the team.

Synchronous or Asynchronous

A synchronous conversation takes place live, in real time. An asynchronous conversation takes place in a stored format, such as e-mail, or voice mail, or a discussion group. One of the advantages of virtual teams is that they can take advantage of both relatively easily. It's important to realize the importance of synchronous, however. I've seen managers make the mistake of thinking that they can direct team members via voice mails and e-mails. People cannot be directed that way. There is a role for asynchronous communication in progress updates, posting upon completion, and sharing work materials. But it cannot take the place of a live synchronous meeting either on the phone as a conference call, or in text format such as a live chat.

KEEPING THE TEAM: RETENTION

There are some industries where employees are expected, perhaps even encouraged, to come and go—migrant workers, fast food workers, multi-level marketing companies. But not many. Any seasoned business owner knows, that the power of their organization is not in the equipment, the office space, not even in the process and procedures. A business is only as good as the people who are in. The longer the same people are in it, the more value they bring.

The Value of Retention

Many entrepreneurs discount the value of retention. Large companies do the same, treating employees like interchangeable pieces on a chessboard. People, however, are not their roles; each has unique skills, talents, interests, and dreams. The value any single employee brings to an organization goes far beyond the actual job they perform, and the cost to replace someone who is good may surprise us.

One of my clients was a manufacturer who had decided they wanted to fire their network manager, Tracy, due to a disrespectful attitude. They were afraid of what Tracy might do to their computer systems. My task was to obtain all the networking codes and passwords under the guise of doing a security analysis, and help the company prepare to recruit and hire someone to replace the network manager.

It would have been a simple project except for what I found when I started investigating. Tracy—the network manager—was a star. Without any formal degree, Tracy had managed to master, at the highest technical levels, not only computer hardware, application software design, and programming, but also networking and internetworking, including enterprise network management. The attitude problem? The disrespect showed? Tracy refused, even when directly ordered by the owners of the company, to compromise security. Tracy would not upgrade to an incompatible operating system. Tracy would not stop focusing on patching what needed to be patched. Tracy insisted on keeping track of all the equipment so that they were well maintained. The technically illiterate senior management team kept asking Tracy to do things that they would have regretted shortly thereafter. Tracy knew better.

Tracy was not always tactful to the sometimes-boneheaded requests and commands from the owners of the company. Nonetheless, Tracy had managed, with few resources and little support, to cobble together a surprisingly robust, well-designed, well-documented, smoothly working network system for the company.

In a larger city or a larger company, this genius would be making a six-figure salary. Instead Tracy was making less than half that and doing a spectacular job.

I had to return to the owners after a few days of working with Tracy to let them know that they would be crazy to let Tracy go. I also informed them that for me to help them recruit a replacement was going to take three or four times what they were currently paying because we would need to hire three or four people. I shared with them the typical problems I find at other manufacturers of their size, and described in detail (in language they could understand) exactly what this network manager did to ensure that these were not problems that they would see. I calculated the cost of those problems, as well. The owners had enough integrity to recognize when they were wrong, luckily. Instead of firing Tracy, they hired a coach to help with more effective communication with the senior management team. Tracy still works there today, keeping the systems running smoothly, at a fraction of the cost most manufacturers pay.

That's not to say that we need to always keep all our employees, but we do need to think long and hard before we fire them or encourage them to leave. We need to face the fact that if someone wants to leave, it may be our fault, not theirs. Ken tells of a restaurant owner who was always short staffed, complaining that it was difficult to hire enough people. After looking at the 100+ people who had been hired at the restaurant in the last year (most of whom had quit), Ken looked the owner straight in the eye and enlightened him that the issue was not a hiring problem, it was a retention problem.

A good way to find out if people are leaving either because of unreasonable expectations, a bullying boss, or a poor work environment is a closed-door, confidential exit interview. Most people who quit jobs don't want to quit. Most simply need to have the problem fixed.

Before I started my first business, I was a special education teacher. There is a law (Public Law 94–142), enacted in 1975, which set out the requirements for teaching children with disabilities. In 1985, I transferred to a middle school to take over a "mixed category" class (which means children of all different types of disabilities were enrolled). What I found was a horrendous situation. Twenty-five children of all different types of disabilities in the same classroom at the same time—without any kind of aide. I tried to get help, and found a complete lack of support from the principal of the school, and an incompetent supervisor who didn't understand the PL 94–142 requirements. When I quit at the end of the school year, I notified the state of the issues, and the next year, they replaced me with two full-time teachers and two full-time aides. It cost my employer almost three times my salary to replace me (not even considering the cost of recruiting). If my requests for a single part-time aide at that school had been fulfilled, I might not have left teaching at all, and they would have saved a bundle.

Once we know why people are leaving, we can work to fix the problem so that people don't leave. Prevention is much easier and less costly than recruitment. We need to consider all the costs involved:

- Recruitment expenses
- New employee salary, including bonus, benefits, and so on
- Training costs
- New equipment and supplies
- Decreased productivity
- Loss of expertise and intellectual resources
- Effect on coworkers, including increased vulnerability to headhunters
- Focus away from customers to deal with turnover
- Diminished product or service quality
- Diminished reputation
- Sales loss

The Center for Economic Policy Research has developed a turnover calculator to help business owners calculate how much they save by reducing turnover (http://www.cepr.net/calculators/turnover_calc.html). For a typical start-up with 10 employees, the loss of two employees a year can cost over $25,000 in recruiting and lost productivity, in addition to the replacement salaries of the employees.

The Four Pillars of Retention

In order to ensure that we can keep the valued employees we have, we can incorporate Ken's four pillars of retention:

- Find a need and fill it
- Match the employee with the right job
- Provide a good boss
- Develop a culture of retention

Find a Need and Fill It

Employees have needs. Not the same needs, but differing needs. As discussed before, we want to do unto them as they would want done, not do unto them as we would want done. Instead of trying to guess, it might be a good idea to ask them what they want and need. A good question would be: "If you were to leave this company and go to work elsewhere, what do you suppose might probably be the reason you would leave?" Interpreting the answer to this question, and being able to plan for the current *and future* needs of the employees will go far toward enabling us to keep our experienced employees working for us.

Match the Employee with the Right Job

Sometimes, to increase retention, we need to be more flexible regarding roles within our organization. At the good culture company I worked for, it was well known that few people quit or got fired. Part of the reason was that the company invested quite a bit of money and time into finding just the right people. If they did, perchance, hire someone who didn't quite fit into the role for which they were hired, they were moved into a different role until they found one that matched their abilities and talents.

Provide a Good Boss

Less than 38 percent of Americans were blessed with what they consider a great boss. There are many more examples of bad bosses than good—bosses who don't care, don't nurture employees, are rude and autocratic. Over 70 percent of employees say that a bad boss can interfere with their own health. A bad boss is the top reason people leave employment (Conner 2012; Kiisel 2012).

The Peter Principle illustrates one reason why there are so many bad bosses; people tend to get promoted based upon technical or operational expertise rather than management skills. A management degree doesn't help either. Being on the faculty in a business college, I would love to say that students learn how to become leaders in school, but I can't. As I've noted before, learning to lead takes time, personal development, and hands-on coaching. We can't learn to lead in a classroom.

When we put people in charge of others, we need to ensure that they are good at that part of the job. We should find a way to reward people who are good at other parts of the job without promoting them to manage others unless they are willing to learn how to do it correctly. It is the role of the business owner to ensure that people managing others within the organization are approachable, can be trusted, and inspire loyalty. Not an easy task, but essential.

It should also be clearly obvious that an employee needs to have one, and only one, boss. Matrixed organizations are a bad idea. An employee in a matrixed organization reports to more than one person or group at the same time. This method was common in the late 1990s but, thankfully, seems to be falling out of favor. While I'm sure, on paper, a matrix allows the flexibility needed to bring together and disband project teams easily, in actuality, a matrixed organization tends to cause good employees to resign. Marginal employees may like the situation; they never have to do anything because they simply tell each boss that they are too busy with their other responsibilities to work on anything for them. But conscientious employees get frustrated; they get caught in the crossfire between feuding bosses who each want more of their time. With multiple bosses, the employee is assigned more work than is possible to complete in the given time frame. They cannot do a good job, no matter how hard they try, and they end up quitting.[5]

Develop a Culture of Retention

If we develop the mindset that turnover is completely unacceptable in our organization, it will go a long way toward ensuring that we retain employees instead of losing them. Mistakes in hiring and poor cultural fits need to be recognized so that they can be prevented. There are a few reasons for losing an employee over which we have no control—death, the transfer of a spouse, a personal growth or salary opportunity for the employee that go beyond what our organization can provide. But, for the most part, we should look upon any loss of employees as an opportunity for us to make the changes necessary to prevent such losses ever again.

SUMMARY OF TEAM BUILDING

Being good at hiring and building teams is an essential task for a business leader.

- ☑ Entrepreneurial businesses are often attractive to top candidates.
- ☑ We are often able to be more flexible than larger companies with many layers, and can therefore find highly talented people who closely match our job requirements.
- ☑ We should work with our employees and ensure that everyone agrees on the job description and recognizes the company culture issues.
- ☑ Phone screening is an important step in identifying the best candidate.
- ☑ If we listen to the candidate about why they would consider working for our company, we can understand their key points and motivations.
- ☑ Behavioral questions provide the most useful information to assess whether a candidate is a good fit for the culture and the job.
- ☑ Once the candidate has been hired, we should act to ensure they do not change their mind.
- ☑ A candidate's first day is often telling, and we should pay close attention to the onboarding process.
- ☑ A strongly directed company culture can support teamwork and positive associations with employees.
- ☑ Team dynamics and virtual team development are important influences in a company's success.
- ☑ Losing good employees is expensive and wasteful, so we need to develop a culture of retention.

5

Keeping Up with Information Technology

As with the other chapters, I will summarize the most important points from the book. However, unlike sales, or finance, or marketing, information technology changes drastically very quickly. Therefore, the bulk of this chapter will share what has changed the most from the original book I wrote in 2006–07 and published in 2008. As expected, information technology is a whole new world now.

SWEET SPOT AUDIENCE FOR MANAGING IT BOOKS

Managing IT (Information Technology) has been a problem since its inception, but even more so now that IT is more often than not central to the strategy for a business. Over the years, business owners have gone from viewing IT as a necessary evil expense to an opportunity-driven investment. But making the wrong IT decisions can derail a business. Making the right one is essential. *The Entrepreneur's Guide to Managing Information Technology* goes into detail about how to develop an internal technology map, how to work more effectively with vendors, and how to avoid the typical pitfalls of many who wasted their IT investment.

After my book was published, I wasn't really sure how it would be received by the target audience, non-IT business owners, or by IT vendors and IT managers. I heard first from several IT vendors who were not happy about how they were portrayed (or the secrets I revealed). IT managers were not super-thrilled either since they often disagreed with my advice regarding the importance of smooth, unchanging, computing environments. But then, out of the blue, I received this e-mail (slightly edited and shortened for space) from Donald Leung:

> I found out about your book at the public library. Your Guide to Managing IT is superb. I have been tricked, swindled and scammed by IT to the point I am hostile and paranoid to new programs. Now that I learned about creating an IT map, I can confide in my own decisions rather than live in perpetual hype.
>
> You are my hero. I read a lot of books, and most of them are not worth reading. Ms. Rhoads, I have found your book superior to all other books simply because you deliver value by the boat load. Simply incredible. Your book is the best. There's no two ways about it. It's just so immaculate at every level. As a teacher, business owner, and salesman your book just drips of power, intelligence, and beauty. It helped me see what I didn't know. I just fell in love with your work after reading the introduction. I knew I had to find out more. I have never read anything so beautiful, organized, and loaded with tools and wisdom acquired through the ages.

I knew then that I had done the right thing by publishing the book. To hear from people who benefited from my insights was a breath of fresh air, and to read such over-the-top-praise made my year. Unfortunately, space will not allow me to share all those important lessons again. Here, I can only summarize and update. Therefore, to really understand how to make great IT decisions, I encourage you to read the original book.

THE VALUE OF INFORMATION TECHNOLOGY

There are few who doubt the importance and value of IT to businesses today. Businesses all need IT. To start this conversation, however, we need a definition.

Definition of IT

Information Technology is what used to be called EDP (Electronic Data Processing) or IS (Information Systems). When most people hear the term, they often think "computers," but the reality is that IT is not about computers. IT is the people, the processes, the software, and the hardware that make up the information flow in the operations of an organization.

You can't separate the computers or the systems from the people or the processes. IT is intertwined in every aspect of the business—from product design, service development, marketing, sales, order processing and fulfillment. Like finance and human resources, there is no part of the business that does not rely upon IT.

The difficulty is that, unlike finance and human resources, IT is relatively new. Because it is new, it is constantly changing, evolving, and improving. IT is also constantly breaking, crashing, and costing unexpected dollars.

Do You Remember When . . .

Remember when televisions (TV) first came out? They took forever to warm up, we had to go up on the roof and mess with the antennae to get a good signal (which always degraded the moment we got off the roof), the picture was often snowy, the programming was in black and white, and TV repair shops were in every town because they constantly broke down. Eventually, though, the technology evolved until TV repair shops went out of business because TV's simply *worked!* We hooked them up to the cable, turned them on, and changed the channel. Once the hardware was stable, content proliferated, and we went from three channels on 12 hours a day to hundreds to thousands of channels on 24 hours a day.

Multiply this process by the thousands of different intertwined hardware and software systems and you can understand why, over the past three decades, it seemed that some parts of IT broke down constantly.

Calculating the Risk

Just like with early TVs, the problems with IT have not prevented us from using it, even relying upon it. The downside to relying upon technology is that every technology decision we make means that we are taking a risk. We have no choice in using technology, of course, but we can decide whether to use technology that is more prone to breaking down, or better known as being stable and reliable. The cost to the decision is the time invested in understanding the technology so that we can determine the risk.

When we calculate the cost of losing data, of losing business, or losing good employees because we made the wrong IT decision, we might understand the importance of investing the time. When we calculate the opportunity cost of not having the right technology, of not maintaining a strategic advantage over our competitors, we might understand the importance of making the right decision. We cannot delegate this decision to others. This is a decision which we, as business owners and entrepreneurs, must completely own and control. It is up to us to learn what we need to learn in order to make the right decision—or face the consequences.

The Technology Map Concept

To mitigate the risks, especially for someone who must make management decisions about IT without being one of the 5 percent of the population who actually understands IT, we need a technology map.

A technology map is a mental map of how IT works. IT is like an onion—each layer represents a whole technology onto itself that is working in concert with all the other layers. Those layers include the computers, of course, but also the networking underneath, and the software, processes, and people on top. The overview can be found in Figure 5.1.

How the Technology Map Helps Decision Makers

As noted, the technology map is based upon the idea of layers and encapsulation, both of which are common themes in IT. The concept is to take all the different tasks, break them up into manageable parts, encapsulate each within a shell, defining only the points at which the different layers must communicate some information of some type. Each encapsulated item or object has attributes or characteristics that define what the object can do (or cannot do).

Technologists use the concept of technology map to diagnose problems by mentally encapsulating different parts, and then layering them in a

Figure 5.1. The Technology Map Overview

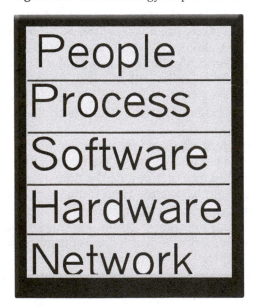

hierarchy. They hypothesize what layer the problem is on, and then conduct tests to determine if they were right or wrong. If they were wrong, they hypothesize another layer and conduct other tests until they finally figure out which layer the problem is on (or, if all the layers have been found to be working correctly, test the interfaces between the layers until the problematic interface is found). Although the layers change frequently, a typical review of the layers and sub layers, as well as the categories associated with them, can be found in Table 5.1.

Table 5.1. Technology Map Categories

Major	Minor	Categories
People	Ability	High Ability, Low Experience
		Low Ability, High Experience
	Experience	High Ability, High Experience
		Low Ability, Low Experience
Process	Who (Role)	Flowcharts and process documentation—often obtained by watching people and what they do as well as asking them
	What (Task)	
	When (Prompt or Time)	
Software	Collaboration	E-mail
		Groupware
		Community Webs
		Social Media
		Search
	Application	Word processing
		Spreadsheet
		Database
		Presentation
		Graphics and Publishing
		Music Managers
		Video

(Continued)

Table 5.1. (*Continued*)

Major	Minor	Categories
	Specialized	Financial
		CAD/CAM (Computer-Aided Design/Manufacturing)
		Vertical Market
	Development	Languages
		Workbenches and Middleware
	Utilities	Backup; Antivirus; Enterprise Network Management
	Operating System	Single User
		Multi User
Hard-ware	Main	CPU, Hard Drive, RAM, ROM, BIOS
	Peripherals	Mouse, Keyboard, Monitor, Scanner, Camera, Printer, Flash Drive, etc.
Net-work	Network Applications	Client Browser
		Application servers; Web servers
	Communication Protocols	TCP/IP, IPX/SPX, UPC, NetBIOS
	Network Interface	Hubs, Routers, Switches, and Network Interface Cards. Connection Type: Point-to-point leased line (T1, T3), Frame Relay, Satellite, FiOS, DSL, Cable Modem, Dial-up

Source: CJ Rhoads, *The Entrepreneur's Guide to Managing Information Technology.* Santa Barbara, CA: Praeger, 2008.

TIMING IS CRITICAL

One of the most important aspects of making the right decision is to understand when the optimum time is for switching over to a new technology. Because technology is changing so quickly, and because IT proponents have repeated the fallacy so often over the decades, many entrepreneurs think that they should keep all their information technology systems up to date all the time. They think that being the first one to use a technology means a competitive advantage. They have been convinced that technology is constantly evolving, and to keep up, they must constantly evolve as well.

I do not agree. One of the overarching themes in my book is that, except under certain circumstances, we need to stay off the bleeding edge of technology. Maximum productivity with information technology comes from maximizing the amount of time the people, process, hardware, and software are stable and unchanging, and minimizing the amount of time the system is changing.

Along with maximum productivity, IT gains the most value when the potential features and functions of IT are carefully examined against the hedgehog concept of the business introduced in Chapter 2. Jim Collins calls IT an accelerator, and it can accelerate us to bankruptcy as easily as it can accelerate us to success (Collins 2001).[1] The difference is not IT; the difference is how IT is applied to the hedgehog concept of the business.

Therefore, with the help of our technology map, we should learn enough about IT to be able to make good decisions regarding use of it. We should sit on the sidelines and watch how others use the technology. Just as a panther sits on a tree and watches prey pass by below, we too must wait. At just the right moment, when our hedgehog concept and the capabilities of already-proven IT match up, we should pounce like a panther. At that point, we would change all of our IT (including processes, hardware, and software) to get a competitive advantage. Then, we allow it to stabilize again, not making any changes, if at all possible, in order to get the most value from our existing IT. We go back into waiting mode until the time is right again for pouncing.

WHAT'S CHANGED IN IT

When I wrote the book originally, I talked about many problems and difficulties that typical businesses encountered in trying to utilize IT. Some of those problems are not really issues anymore, including Internet infrastructure and networking, Enterprise Resource Planning (ERP) implementations, stages of Internet strategy, and e-commerce. Instead, other newer issues have arisen that are dogging us with indecision and doubt. This includes mobile devices, social media, cloud computing, and video revolution.

Internet Infrastructure

In the year 2006, the Internet was still barely a dirt road compared to the highway that it is today. Looking at the chart in Figure 5.2 from USTelecom Association,[2] we can see that broadband adoption, the most common method to access the Internet in the United States, was still growing at a tremendous pace. It did not start to level off until 2009.

Figure 5.2. History of Broadband Adoption

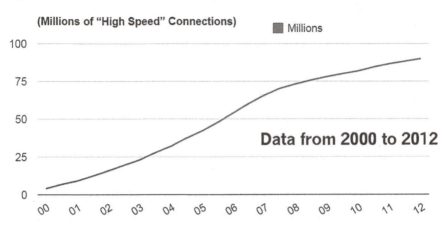

Source: Graph can be found on http://www.ustelecom.org/broadband-industry/broad band-industry-stats/connections/us-fixed-broadband-connections. Used with permission of USTelecom.

There are still issues with trying to use the Internet for high-bandwidth services such as videoconferencing or video streaming that require a feature called QOS (Quality of Service) installed on all the routing devices between the communication nodes (i.e., the computer or mobile devices), but for the most part, the Internet is a relatively robust roadway for communication.

Before broadband was generally available, businesses would have to lease a line from the phone company. That was a point-to-point line from one location to another, and involved very high-cost monthly fees. The terms T-1 line or Frame Relay were used to describe the lines. A T-1 line allowed traffic to travel at 1.55 megabits per second, and a frame relay was typically a fraction of that (156 kilobits per second or 512 kilobits per second). The speed, however, was slow compared to what is available today.[3]

In 2008, I did a research project to determine whether a Digital Subscriber Line (DSL) or cable modem[4] would provide the fastest and most reliable connection to the Internet. At the time, there were many technical issues regarding the cabling, the protocols, and the devices. But today, both DSL and cable modems are reliable; getting them to work is not even an issue anymore. They just work. DSL is available from phone companies such as Verizon. Cable modems are available from cable companies such as Comcast.

Both have been trounced, technically, by a better alternative, if you can get it. The best option these days is Fiber Optic Service (FiOS). Alas, where

I live, FiOS will probably not be available for another 20 years, so I'm still stuck with DSL. But if FiOS is available in your neighborhood, you should go for it.

Not everyone has the choice. Fifteen percent of the homes in various geographic areas of the United States (mostly in poor rural areas) still, in 2014, have no access to high speed broadband and cannot access the Internet easily. We don't tend to think of this as a problem until we hire someone to work from home who lives in Clinton, Pennsylvania, where there is only dialup access to the Internet. Dialup (just using plain old phone lines) is slow and unable to handle modern web pages. Faster wireless options from cellular phone providers is finally becoming more of an option for these rural areas, but the speeds are still much slower than available in more urban areas where there are many options at high speeds.

Another positive note is how easy it is to connect to the Internet. In 2008, it might have taken hours of configuration and many calls to technical support to set up a wireless router at home so a laptop would work in any room and access the Internet. Now—buy it at the store, plug it in, and it works. All the configuration is now usually done by the Internet service provider automatically when the device connects. Hotels, coffee shops, bookstores, airports; most of them provide access to their WiFi network (increasingly, for a fee, unfortunately). Our computers and devices now have an easy-to-use module that constantly looks for wireless networks and gives us a dialog box to enter the passcode when they are encountered.

There are continuing issues regarding security, however. The Internet was developed without any built-in security. This was by design. Any type of security would slow down Internet traffic and make it more difficult to connect. But now that we are utilizing the network so extensively, the lack of security is often a problem.

Virtual Private Networks (VPN) are neither virtual, nor private, and are not even networks. But VPN is a technology that can be installed on both ends of an Internet communication that can encapsulate the Internet packets so that they cannot be read over the open airways. The problem is that a VPN slows down the communication and can be costly to set up. Furthermore, a VPN is point to point connection; a new connection must be established between any two devices, and they cannot be installed on the fly.

Websites do have the option of utilizing a special encapsulation called Secure Sockets Layer (SSL) to transfer sensitive data such as credit card information that doesn't require special setup on the client device. Most shopping carts already incorporate SSL, which is why we often must pay extra for them.

Securing data during transfer from one system to another is just a small part of the security issue. The second portion, a much larger portion, is securing the data stored on the server that is connected to the Internet. Without server security, the data would be available for any hacker to reveal. The danger here is no different than a restaurant employee stealing your credit card information, but the scope is much larger. Stealing credit card data one person at a time is very different than stealing credit card data from thousands or hundreds of thousands customers.

We often are willing to take the risk of an unsecure network and an open lack of privacy. People know that their texts, e-mails, even phone calls can be tracked by the NSA, but they are unwilling to give up the convenience of these communications methods and return to the days when communication was always face to face, in person.

Utilizing the convenience of mobile banking or purchasing items over the Internet involves some risk, but most people continue taking advantage of the convenience because after weighing the options, convenience wins out. We like the benefits, so we put up with the risks.

As a business owner, we need to ensure that we are doing all that we can to ensure that our customers' data is as safe as we can possibly make it, while making it as easy as possible for our customers to access that data. It will always be a balancing act.

ERP implementations

In 2006, there were still plenty of horror stories about companies that tried, and failed, to implement an ERP System to replace dozens of previously unintegrated systems. Problems included customer hiccups, operational issues, and financial losses. Generally, those same ERP systems are now functioning smoothly on a daily basis. There are still a lot of complaints because ERP systems are not friendly and easy to use. More and more these days, though, ERP systems are hiding behind easier-to-use graphical interfaces that are available on mobile devices, which makes up somewhat for the difficulties.

ERP consultants also got smarter about how to implement large systems, too. Now, they get buy-in from the staff before taking away their individual systems. The obvious advantages (of having data stored electronically in a single system, available from anywhere in the company instead of paper forms stored in rooms full of filing cabinets in a single location), have gotten through to everyone at all levels, and the resistance has decreased.

One of the major issues that I wrote about in 2006 had been the consolidation of finance system vendors. One example was Oracle. After acquiring dozens of smaller financial system vendors, most notably JD Edwards and People Soft, Oracle pushed to get all of their customers to adopt a new financial system called Fusion. The attempt didn't work. Now, in 2014, 11 years after the acquisitions, Oracle has only convinced 11 percent of the customer base to switch to Fusion. JD Edwards and People Soft systems are still going strong, being forced by the customer base to be fully and continually supported by Oracle. The fact is, once a business has adopted a financial system, it is cost prohibitive to switch to another.

The consolidation in the field of financial systems has calmed a bit, perhaps even reversing a bit as formerly acquired ERP systems are being spun off again.[5] A handful of financial software publishing companies are holding their own.[6]

Stages of Internet Strategy

When Computerworld first published my article on the phases of Internet Strategy on March 4, 2001, the topic was such a hit that my assistant found it translated into dozens of languages and placed on dozens of websites. I recently reread that article, and I realized those phases are useless now.

First, being on the web is now a given. It doesn't make any sense not to have a website, no matter how large or small our business. Second, when I wrote that, there was no such thing as social media and only large companies could do e-commerce. Then, I called these "advanced stages" of Internet strategies. Now, all the stages are consolidated into one. Facebook and LinkedIn provide the equivalent of a community site without paying for the private infrastructure. E-commerce is almost easy to implement. The Internet has become just another channel for businesses to sell products and services. While many decisions still have to be made, they are much easier than before.

E-commerce

A sharp eye might have noticed the disclaiming word "almost" in the previous section when talking about the ease of e-commerce. E-commerce has gotten easier, but there is still a lot of room for a shakeout regarding which e-commerce platform and which credit card authentication company will dominate. There are still far too many from which to choose, and too many components which have to seamlessly work together. Every e-commerce site includes a backend merchant account, an online credit card authenticating site, a secure connection software, a shopping cart, and a web store front.

Furthermore, setting up an e-commerce site is still a bit too expensive. Though not the hundreds of thousands of dollars it was in 2001, it is still several thousand dollars to get started. For large companies, a few thousand is no big deal, but for the smaller organization, the budget often can't handle the start-up costs.

Social Media

We may no longer need an Internet strategy, but now we need a social media strategy.

Social media is a phrase made up to refer to all those new uses of the World Wide Web that have been made available through such sites as LinkedIn, Facebook, and Twitter. The key to the definition of social media is user-generated content in an online community.

Today's Social Media Is Different

Truth be told, the idea of an online community was not new. CompuServe, Prodigy, and AOL were online communities available in the 1990s. There are three differences—infrastructure, ease of use, and mobility.

First, because the Internet infrastructure is larger and more stable, people can do more than just post text messages to each other. People can post pictures and videos, and send these multimedia messages instantly. This provides googols[7] of user-generated content. Second, they can do this much more easily than ever before. The capability is built into the software—available at the touch of a button. The ease of posting is immensely important. Even the most computer illiterate grandmothers can get a Facebook account and begin posting interesting items and reading all the interesting items their family and friends are posting. Social media is accessible and far reaching. User-generated content attracts more users, and reaches farther and faster than any business-generated content.

Furthermore, because of mobile devices (discussed in more detail next), people are no longer chained to their computer in order to virtually commune with their online friends. They can keep up with events constantly. Previous to a few years ago, only a very small percentage of the population conversed with friends over online communities. Facebook opened itself to anyone (as opposed to just students) in 2006, when it had just 64 million users. Now it has over a billion users—one out of every seven people alive is on Facebook.

Financial Success of Social Media—Still Undetermined

Note that Facebook went public in May 2012, and for a while, lost much of its value. It has been having a hard time monetizing its popularity as

Facebook users go there to socialize with friends, not to buy stuff. Companies are not flocking to Facebook to pay for advertising, though businesses are now encouraged to create a free Facebook page (whereas previously, a human being could only have one Facebook page and account). In its attempts to make money in the past, Facebook has crossed the privacy line, some believe, and has been forced to rescind profit-friendly policies such as directly selling information about its users to businesses. Others don't believe that Facebook will ever be the profitable juggernaut people hoped, so if we spend a lot of time and energy cultivating a following in Facebook, a few years down the road, that following might disappear. Some people remember that 10 years ago, My Space was all the rage, and many entrepreneurs (mostly in the music business) focused a lot of time and effort to build followings there, only to have them dissipate as the popularity of the site fell and kids (the demographic then) switched over to Facebook. The fast growth and rising profile of Facebook is quite an amazing achievement, but the long-term viability is not yet assured. Nonetheless, Facebook surpassed its IPO value, and seems poised to launch ahead.

LinkedIn has had a bit more financial success because they have focused entirely on the business community. They went public a year earlier, and have posted solid growth to more than 100 percent of its IPO value. As an individual, LinkedIn is the place to post your resume-like information, network with the movers and shakers of a field, and link up with knowledgeable people. As a business, LinkedIn is the place to find people with the exact skills that we are looking for in employees. It is the recruitment tool of the century.

LinkedIn's business model is not just advertising, but also rather, their premium recruiting services to businesses, as well as premium member services. Premium members are able to send a private message to people they don't already know by way of referral from people they do already know.

Twitter is a 140-character text messaging service. The company is still private, so there is no way to know if they are making money. Their business model is to sell access to all of the tweets in real time to companies such as Google (who uses them in their search engine). They also sell promotion tweets so that companies can send press releases, or recommend products and services to everyone signed up on Twitter.

These three, of course, are just the tip of the iceberg—the list of sites that might qualify under the banner of social media number in the thousands. Some of the more well-known ones, which deal with different businesses in different industries, are sites such as Yelp, Angie's List, Pinterest, YouTube (owned by Google), or Google Plus. Undoubtedly, the list will have changed by the time you read this, but the key is that there are many sites that are trying to enable people to provide content that will be of interest to other people.

Six Steps to Developing a Media Strategy

Therein lies the problem: too many social media sites, too many options, all requiring time and energy, which are often in short supply among us busy entrepreneurs. My advice is that we should go through the following steps to determine a social media strategy before we invest too much time:

- Determine how many people in our customer base utilize social media.
- Determine which social media channels our customer base is likely to utilize.
- Identify the best uses of social media (simple profile, sales and featured product promotions, premium customer rewards, etc.) in proportion to customer base use.
- Implement small trials in order to identify the best opportunities and use of resources.
- Monitor and measure outcomes.
- Revise and refine strategy.

Marketing campaigns for social media should be part of our complete marketing strategy, but only in proportion to our customer base's use of social media. Some entrepreneurs are attracted to the idea, and think that putting up a company page on Facebook is cheap. Many think the cost is only the time to do so. Submitting profiles to Google is also only the cost of the time. So is LinkedIn and Twitter and so on. If we spend all of our time doing this, but we don't increase sales, that would be a waste. If the cost of the time were calculated as part of the investment, it could be properly compared to the cost of an advertisement in the newspaper and the proper action determined. We should never discount our time, and need to carefully prioritize based upon the return on our investment. Sometimes, our time is better spent networking with decision makers face to face and in person than building up virtual social media campaigns.

To make sure I tested my theories of the tentative nature of time investment in social media and not just ignorance of how to use it, I took a course from an entrepreneur who wrote a book about successfully marketing with social media in two hours a week. After the course, I counted up the time cost of the advice if we included the initial setup time (which was carefully neglected in the two hour calculation). Over 120 hours was my estimate to (1) complete the analysis, (2) figure out in which social media sites to invest time, (3) compile and upload the information for complete profiles, and (4) determine our promotion campaigns. I don't know about you, but 120 hours is a huge chunk of time, and I need to know ahead of time if I'm gambling or investing. For my business at the time, my major customer demographic was small business owners, few of whom were themselves on social media. Other than investing minimal time in setting up profiles and watching for online comments about my business, I largely spent my promotional time elsewhere.

Beware of Social Media Addiction

The one thing we know about social media is that it can become a major time suck. Social media is fun, and it gives people the feeling they are connected and on top of things.[8]

But I've also noticed something else; these same connected people never get anything done. They are not very productive. Social media is addictive, and often, largely a waste of time. One example—I have a good friend, highly intelligent, who started a business after leaving an executive job at a large international media firm. This friend is all over social media and spends many hours a day at it, but has had a major problem making a living wage since getting involved in it. Second example—there was only one writer with whom we contracted for a book in our series who did not complete the book. He started, but just was unable to meet any deadlines. He was the one deeply involved in social media. I don't think these are coincidences.

I'm prone to this problem myself, and always have been, though I have learned to manage it. In years past, I have spent many hours on a daily basis responding to posts and comments on various discussion boards. Today, I forcibly limit myself so that I don't start perusing posts and comments from the hundreds of virtual connections I have on LinkedIn, Facebook, and Google Plus. Otherwise, I will look up and find that I've wasted all day and accomplished nothing.

Pressure to Join the Fray

There are two types of people who insist that promotions using social media will bring large returns to everyone: 1) those who are in the business of selling social media services, and 2) those who are unemployed, underemployed, or retired. Much like Google Adwords (discussed in the marketing chapter), there are some limited situations where investing the time and money in a social media campaign is warranted. If social media is where our customers are, that's where we need to be.

For some of us, our target market demographic is not spending hours and hours on social media. Decision makers tend to be working, not socializing. We might want to dip our toes in long enough to establish a simple profile at two or three major hubs such as LinkedIn and Facebook, and then move back into the real world. We need to think long and hard before hiring someone to create social media campaigns for us, or paying for any social media promotions, which are, by their nature, short term and fleeting.

Last year, I put weeks of time into getting people to "like" our new Facebook page. I got some pretty impressive numbers (I thought at the time), but soon realized that being liked does not equal increased sales. It is much more effective for us to put that time and energy into personally developing relationships one by one, or ensuring that we have a great website. Unlike a Facebook page, on a website we have much more control over placement, and what we do is more permanent. (Of course, as I write this, I become aware that we still have not yet finished the work on our website. Like the cobbler's children who have no shoes, we find it difficult to find the time to update the site despite insisting to our clients that they must keep their site updated regularly.)[1]

---

[1] I resolve to have the website revision work completed before you read this book, so check it out at http://HPLConsortium.com.

Risk of Social Media

There is also a risk regarding social media. Whether we use it for promotion or not, part of our strategy must be to monitor social media constantly. Unhappy customers or unethical competitors can use the opportunity to hurt our credibility or trustworthiness, so it is important to stay on top of all issues that might arise. We might not want to spend hours and hours posting or promoting using social media, but we need to spend at least a few hours a week checking to see if there are any negative opinions, complaints, or issues regarding our business. Google allows us (for free) to set up searches that would alert us to any mention of our name, our products, or services, or anything else related to us anywhere on the World Wide Web.

If there are, it is a sign that at least some of our customers are using it, and we should consider adding social media to our marketing strategy. We cannot delete or suppress truthful negative comments, but we can encourage our customers to overwhelm the few negatives with hundreds of positive comments. We should also respond with good customer service grace as we would to any complaint, but do so publicly. There is nothing worse than a new potential customer reading a negative review of our products or services, and seeing no response at all to the complaint. Our best bet is to acknowledge the valid feelings of the complainer, provide mea culpas for anything our staff has done that was not in the customer's best interest, and pledge to work toward a mutually acceptable solution. Publicly.

Cloud Computing

The first question usually asked is *What is Cloud Computing?* We might get a bevy of answers which all point to the same thing—cloud computing does not really exist as a thing. It is not something to buy, a product to order, or a service to obtain. It is, instead, the buzz word of the current technology age. It's the marketware, the catchy phrase, the thing which makes decades-old products and services sound like they are new. Cloud computing could be referring to use of online applications, such as Zoho, Office360, Google Drive (formerly called Google Apps or Google Docs). Cloud computing could also mean online file storage such as ADrive, Dropbox, Carbonite, Opendrive, HighTail (formerly YouSendIt), Justcloud, Sugarsync, Mozy, or hundreds of others trying to jump on the cloud service boon. Some people use the term to refer to being able to access any website through either mobile or computer browsers.

Using multiple devices to access information on the Internet has been around for decades now. The one thing that is new is ease of use. Let's take iCloud, for example. iCloud is the branding that Apple gives the behind-the-scenes programming they've imbedded in all their products that seem to magically make all of our pictures, contacts, notes, videos, and files available to us, no matter which device we happen to be on (iPhone, iPad, Mac notebook, or desktop). For us to set up automated connections to a website from each of our devices would be time consuming and laborious, requiring answers to tons of questions about which items we want to be primary and which items we want to be copies. Instead, Apple gives everyone a convenient yes/no option in the settings of each device to use iCloud. Voilà! The programming is installed and the questions answered (in the way that Apple programmers thought best) in moments. Never before in the history of connecting to the Internet has setting up online access to our data from many devices been so easy (as long as all of our devices are Apple, and we do not have too many files).

The origination of the term cloud comes from the picture of the cloud that was used to represent the physical equipment and data lines leased from telephone companies but used by businesses. (You can see an illustration in Figure 5.3.)

The original phrase was used in a business plan in 1996, but cloud computing in the modern context wasn't used until Google CEO Eric Schmitt used the term in a speech at the Search Engine Strategies conference in 2006.[9]

Cloud computing is not yet the panacea we would like it to be. As can be seen by the thousands of different companies, frequent changes in names, and lack of standards, cloud computing is still an insecure, untested,

Figure 5.3. An Enterprise Network Showing the "Cloud"

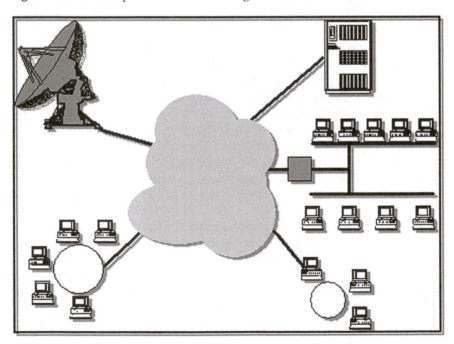

Source: HPL Consortium, Inc., copyright 2014, used with permission.

not-yet-robust capability. Eric Knorr (2013) pointed out some of the dangers of relying on cloud computing in an article "Protect Yourself from the Coming Cloud Crack-Up." He points out that departments are using cloud computing to store department-level data, but there is no coordination or standardization on format or even vendors. If not managed properly, availability of the cloud will result in even more siloed organizational processes—something that businesses have been trying to eliminate for years by using ERPs.

Issues of liability and ownership are unresolved. When we store our data on a remote server, who is responsible for it—us or the owner of the server? What happens if someone steals the information? Or what if it gets lost or corrupted? Certainly, all of those things can happen to our data sitting on our own hard drive or our own servers, but there, the responsibility for (and the control over) the data is clear. The information is clearly owned and controlled by us. We are responsible for backing up our own data. If the hard drive fails, we cannot sue the manufacturer of the hard drive for the loss of our data. But if our information is stored elsewhere on someone else's computer, we cannot easily back it up. If the company were to go bankrupt and close its doors (highly probable at this stage), we would find it difficult to identify the original source of the data.

Furthermore, it is easy to make a mistake and lose all our data. A file deleted from one of the devices disappears from all of the devices. Without offline backups, critical data could be accidentally lost. At minimum, we should implement a well-defined process for moving experimental cloud data to a secured company data server for backup purposes, and only allow non-mission-critical information to be stored on the cloud.

Case in point: Dropbox.[1] For years, I have struggled with trying to keep all the different versions of my files in different locations. I teach in the computer labs at the university. I work in my university office and in my business office. I work on my laptop outside and away from home. I have tried carrying around a 500-gig hard drive (the size of a deck of cards, so not too much of a hassle, but still not optimum especially when I ran out of room for my video files). I have tried a VPN provided by the university to access my network folders from all of the different systems I use. I have tried an FTP account that I set up on my website. All are relatively successful, but still time consuming. There were two major problems with these methods. They don't work with my mobile devices (iPad, iPhone, or Blackberry), and they relied upon me to remember to update the files (always a bad idea because my memory stinks).

Then, I found Dropbox. For almost a year, I've been taking advantage of the free version of Dropbox. It is, by far, the easiest of all the online file storage systems. Conveniently, I could install it on my Blackberry phone, my iPhone, my iPad, my notebook, and my desktop computer. It automatically, without my doing anything, kept all my files up to date. If I modified a file offline from two different devices, the next time it synced the files it would put both files in the folder, putting "CJ's conflicted copy" and the date/time in the file name so that I could easily see that I needed to look at both files and delete the wrong one. Because of an aggressive marketing campaign, Dropbox gave me over 5 gigs of space on their servers for free—far more than the 2 gigs default. Five gigs of space is not enough for all my files (I have over 1.5 terabytes of active files), but enough for the files I need to access frequently from all the different locations. For example, for more than six months, this book file sat in Dropbox, available to me for editing whenever I had the time, no matter where I was physically, no matter which device I had with me. The pièce de résistance—I could access the files using Pages (the word processor on my iPad), or Documents to Go (the word processor on my Blackberry), without destroying the Word formatting. When I got back to my desktop, all my edits were there.

---

[1] The term "dropbox" is used generically to mean any online folder in which we can upload or download files. It is also the branded name of the fast-growing Dropbox corporation, which was founded in 2007 by Drew Houston and Arash Ferdowsi.

Is 10 bucks a month a good price for Dropbox services if we didn't get them for free? Probably not. And I don't think the pricing for the enterprise-team service is realistic. Small groups cannot afford the almost $800 a year for the service, and the $125 per person additional charge is a bit much. Furthermore, like all cloud services, we shouldn't trust them with our only copy of mission-critical files. But Dropbox is definitely a step in the right direction, and the most successful of the individual cloud services.

Mobile Devices

The largest change since I wrote the technology book is the revolution in mobile devices. Mobile devices come in two levels—smart phones and tablets (though recently, a few middle-sized devices being dubbed phaplets have been released).

Smartphone

Apple's iPhone moved the smartphone from a niche business device to an easy-to-use mainstream must-have. It was followed by a slate of competing smartphones, including Samsung's Galaxy, Motorola Droid, Nokia Lumia; HTC Nexus, Sony Xperia, and many others.

The first iPhone was released on June 29, 2007. Akin to my first experience on the Internet in 1992, the first time I used an iPhone, I knew that it was going to completely revolutionize the technology interface landscape. Once we use the intuitive touch screen interface that Apple developed, we are hooked. It's like the difference between using a typewriter and a word processor—we never want to go back.

For those of us who have been trying to use PDA (personal digital assistants) since the days of the Newton, the iPhone was amazing. When it came out, smartphones had been able to browse the World Wide Web for years, but browsing using a stylus or a pointing device is clunky. For the first time, we were able to see the powerful possibilities with having a mobile device that could connect to any resource over the Internet.

The problem in 2007 was apps. There were thousands, but not that many useful ones. There were many that enabled people to take, store, and edit music, photos, and video, but not a lot for business. Furthermore, both the e-mail and the contact management on the iPhone were abysmal.

> In 2009, I purchased both an iPhone and a Blackberry so that I could test the capabilities side by side. I spent more than two weeks going back and forth between the two devices in order to determine which I would use. (The loser was going to be given to my husband.) The Blackberry won the contest, and Bob got the iPhone (which he loved). Though the iPhone was much more fun to use, my main focus was business rather than multimedia.
>
> Two years later, when my Blackberry Bold broke, I again spent two full weeks using the iPhone before deciding which device would replace it. Blackberry had just come out with the Torch, which gave the same touchscreen interface as the iPhone. In the end, however, iPhone still had too many limitations regarding contact management and Blackberry was still great at contact management, so I stuck with Blackberry. Until yesterday. Just as I was doing the final edit of this book, my Blackberry Torch stopped functioning. My next phone won't be a Blackberry.

In January 2013, Blackberry came out with a new device (the Q10), but the lack of apps for it is still a major hindrance. There is some question as to whether or not Blackberry will be able to catch up and regain its former dominance of the smartphone industry. My next phone may just be an Android or iPhone. I would hope that, by then, both the Android and the iPhone figure out the importance of good contact management and create the built-in capabilities that Blackberry has always had. (Of course, one might have thought that by now, they would have figured it out, but alas, they have much to learn.)

Tablets

Tablets have moved the concept of mobile devices one step further because of the larger screen and additional data capabilities that mimic the functions and features of a personal computer. Apple's iPad was released in April 2010.

At first, I did not see the value in iPads. Although it was easier to carry around than a notebook computer, it couldn't take the place of a phone because it couldn't make phone calls, and the screen was too small for real computer work. I just didn't see the need to surf the web that often, and felt the lack of a multiwindow interface would doom the iPad to a small niche device like the iTouch. Since then, I've changed my mind.

It started when I discovered I could use the iPad as a terminal to access my desktop computer (using an amazing piece of software called PocketCloud from WYSE). I can even connect a keyboard. This lets me sit outside on my patio and soak in the sun while I work on the documents stored on my desktop computer using the applications installed on my desktop computer just as if I was sitting in front of it.

I wanted to learn what else I could do with an iPad, so I took a class. I found that many things I thought were limitations of the iPad were not actually limitations; I just didn't know enough about how to use the device. Now I take my iPad everywhere, and leave the laptop computer at home.

The iPad is absolutely great at accessing information while on the road. For $14 a month, the iPad can use a cellular data account to access the Internet, which means we are not limited to areas with WiFi (as we would be with notebook computers). Anywhere that there is a cell phone connection, we can surf the web, access our contacts or calendar on Google, or even work on a simple document. iPads can be used to register people at outdoor events, or to gather mailing list information without having to interpret handwriting or doing data entry.

iPad still cannot replace a PC, however. In 2011, Tony Bradley, a columnist for PC World gave up his computer and tried to use an iPad for everything for 30 days. In the final analysis, Bradley felt that the iPad could be a replacement for users who just wanted to e-mail and surf the net, though at the time, he didn't recommend the iPad as an alternative PC for any kind of heavy-duty technology work (nor for journalists, who need multitasking capabilities that the iPad does not have) (Bradley 2011).

Since Bradley's experiment was two years and several updates ago, I wanted to see if the answer would be different. In May of 2013, I launched what I called "the great mobile experiment." But when I tried to give up my desktop computer for 30 days, I failed. As great as the iPad is, there are still severe limitations and many things that it cannot do, or cannot do well. If I had to pick the most egregious problem, it was that often I could not read e-mail attachments, or fill out forms on websites.

For one thing, though a lot of progress has been made in syncing up contact and calendar information, there are still incompatibilities and limitations. But due to incompatibilities between Outlook's nonstandard and proprietary methodology, the synchronization that can be done is still less than optimum. Many people have been using Outlook for many years. The loss of the specialized contact data sitting in their Outlook folders would be devastating, so switching to any other contact manager is fraught with difficulties. (Outlook has a never-share-the-keyfield mentality, so once you place custom data in Outlook, there doesn't appear to be an easy way for a nonprogrammer to export or synchronize that custom data.) Furthermore, Google places a strict limit on the number of records that can sync with a tablet or smartphone, which means it is not a good place to store records if you use contact management in any serious way.

After many months of trying various things, I ended up with iContacts/Calendar on iPad, Google contacts/calendar on the web, and Outlook on my desktop—but my "source" contact information I keep in an Access Database. I use a third-party application called CompanionLink (highly recommended) to make the synchronization automated and seamless between all four. I have 45 fields of custom data for each contact person, including many fields used for me to send letters and holiday greetings to my contacts. Unfortunately, only a handful of custom fields can be synced with Outlook and Google. Furthermore, I have over 4,000 contacts in my list, but I can only sync 2,000 records with Google, so I had to go through all my contacts and decide which ones would be carried around with me everywhere, and which ones would only appear in my source database.

Despite the current limitations, the tablet has gained the recognition as an essential computing device. Businesses will be moving over to them in a very short timeframe as their IT departments learn to develop customized company-specific applications that will enable them to access corporate data easily from anywhere.

The Future Is Mobile

Although tablets are not yet full replacements for personal computers, and the cloud is not yet the robust platform to store our files the way we want it to be, they are both halfway there. Enabling employees to be mobile while they are being productive is a business game changer. The limitation is no longer the hardware, it's the apps. Businesses have just begun down the long expensive road to making the plethora of corporate data available via mobile technologies. Over the next few years, we will see another huge jump in capabilities. Today, employees can often access corporate data from home or from WiFi hotspots using corporate computers that have been setup specifically to do so. But those capabilities still require a heavy level of technical expertise to configure and maintain. The beauty of the tablet is that corporate IT can set up these mobile devices to work—easily and seamlessly—so that any employee, from anywhere, can access anything they need.

Years ago, I started ordering custom-made suits from an organization based out of Hong Kong. Typically, I would meet the tailor in a hotel room of a large close-by city (in my case, Philadelphia), who would measure me. I'd pick the style, the fabric, and so on from samples strewn around the room. The tailor would write up the order on a multi-part paper form, and every few weeks, would send the orders to Hong Kong to have the suits made. Several months later, the suit would be delivered. I'd try it on, arrange to be measured again so that the suit could be tailored more specifically to fit.

Last year, the organization started to use iPads. The elderly nontechnical tailor ordered the suit right away using the iPad form, and I was e-mailed the receipt instead of being given a carbon copy of the paper form. Instead of getting the suit refitted a second time, the tailor used the iPad to take pictures of me from all angles so that the suit could be made to fit more specifically to begin with. The difference in service and time was amazing.

The built-in videoconferencing capabilities of the iPad is another step in the direction of the next revolution—videoconferencing.

Video Revolution

The next revolution will be around live video technologies. Low-quality videoconferencing has been around for 35 years. Webconferencing has been around for about ten years. Skype, GoToMeeting, WebEx, and countless other websites and browser add-ons can provide the capability for anyone with a camera and a computer to videoconference with others over the Internet.

The end-devices have been around for a while, but there have been several obstacles to videoconferencing. Connectivity for videoconferencing needs to be fast and robust. Otherwise, the quality of the videoconference is poor. Unlike movies being videostreamed, real-time conversations cannot be buffered, which places a much larger strain on the system.

Poor videoconferencing is not a minor problem. Our brains are conditioned to expect that one's words match one's mouth and that movements are smooth instead of jerky. The Internet is bursty (transmits packets of data on different routes in bursts), and therefore, cannot handle the type of traffic generated by a videoconferencing system. Low-quality videoconferencing interferes with communication. It is better to simply talk over a telephone line than to try and speak with people whose mouths don't match their words being spoken, or who blip out every few minutes.

Furthermore, most webconferencing systems can only handle a small videoconferencing window on a PC or mobile device. A smaller-than-real image limits our ability to see emotions and communicate effectively.

While Skype, GotoMeeting, WebEx, Facetime, and other systems are making inroads toward larger screens and higher-quality video, there is still a ways to go.

Infrastructure also has a ways to go. Though we are fast approaching having an infrastructure that can handle high-quality videoconferencing traffic, we are not there yet. The two improvements that are necessary worldwide for live video conferencing are the implementation of IPv6 and QOS. Since the Internet is not owned technology, it can't be upgraded with IPv6 and QOS without everyone agreeing on the upgrades and simultaneously implementing them.[10] When QOS is common, videoconferencing will be as ubiquitous as telephones are today.

Wall-sized videoconferencing systems will have a major impact on businesses and education everywhere. Extremely high-quality videoconferencing called *Telepresence* can effectively substitute in-person meetings. Telepresence is designed to share a full-sized, real-time image so that the people can talk with each other as if they are in the same room.

Consider the impact of this technology. Why worry about getting a corner office with a window when we can display beautiful live views of the Rocky Mountains on our entire wall? Why worry about traveling when we can see our friends and family sitting around a table as clearly as we can see them in person? Add a Wii interface,[11] and we can golf or fish or share a meal with our buddies without ever leaving the room.

Why travel to work to a building in the city when the entire team can meet more efficiently virtually from their homes? What reason would there be for polluting our air with cars once people can connect, in full size, in person, without traveling?

Back in the 1960s, famous author Isaac Asimov wrote a science fiction story about a universe where people never met face to face because they could conduct all their business and do all their socializing through room-sized videoconferencing. (Only married people met in person, occasionally, for sex.) While our world may not become that extreme, once the quality and the infrastructure are there, video telepresence will be everywhere. And it will change the world, again.

SUMMARY OF IT

IT is constantly changing. IT has become an essential element in all businesses.

- ☑ It is essential that we learn enough about IT to make the right IT decisions.
- ☑ Developing a technology map can help non-IT people better understand IT.

☑ Making the wrong IT decisions can accelerate a business to bankruptcy.

☑ Understanding the optimal time to purchase IT will minimize problems and issues.

☑ Maximizing productivity involves focusing on the hedgehog concept, stretching out periods of IT instability, and minimizing periods of IT change.

☑ Several previously difficult IT problems have been solved over the past few years, including getting access to the Internet, implementing ERPs, and doing e-commerce over the World Wide Web.

☑ Several new opportunities/problems facing us now are the rise of mobile devices, social media, cloud computing, and the coming video revolution.

6

Market Research and Marketing

There are two excellent books directly related to marketing in the series—*The Entrepreneur's Guide to Market Research* by Anne Wenzel and *The Entrepreneur's Guide to Marketing* by Robert Everett. Just like with the chapter on leadership, though, there are several other books that had sections that indirectly relate to the topic.

There is a lot of overlap. Market research is what marketing people use to figure out what and how to market. The end result of the market research is the marketing analysis. The market analysis typically includes the demographic profile, as well as the spending and growth trends that will enable us to know our optimum strategy for marketing our products and services.

Even though pricing is generally considered part of marketing, we will not include pricing in this chapter, but rather in Chapter 8, Pricing and Proposing. Here, we will just focus on marketing.

MARKET RESEARCH AND ANALYSIS

Anne did a marvelous job of laying out, step by step, how to conduct the research to gather the competitive intelligence and develop the market analysis needed to create the marketing plan. Most especially helpful is her introduction to online marketing tools available—Google Trends, Google Insights, and the SEC database called EDGAR. All are freely available online.

Properly done market research will help us do the following:

- Identify market needs
- Plan the product or service to meet the market needs
- Analyze the market and the competition
- Refine the product or service features and delivery methods
- Price the product or service

- Reach the market
- Set financial goals for the firm
- Write the market analysis section of the business plan

Primary and Secondary Research

We are able to analyze our market based upon both primary and secondary research. Primary research is data collected by a company for their own use. Primary research includes interviews with customers, field trips or observations, observing store traffic and buying patterns, reviewing company sales data and customer communications, conducting surveys, focus groups, and field trials.

Secondary research uses data from other organizations or companies. Market data and research reports are usually available for a fee from trade associations and research organizations such as Dun & Bradstreet, Hoover's Online, Gartner Group, Boston Group, McKinsey, and so on. Speakers and panelists at conferences, meetings, and expo events may also make their market research available to others.

There are also several sources of free marketing research. The U.S. Census Bureau makes all their data available at a granular level. Trade associations often provide some of their data for free. As noted earlier, the SEC has a database (EDGAR) that publishes all the filings for all the public companies in the United States. One of the newest sources of marketing research data is Google Trends, which enable us to enter up to five topics and see how often they've been searched over time.

Data can be quantitative (numerical and statistically measurable) or qualitative (words and discussions rather than numbers, such as comments made during a focus group or interview). Research can be exploratory, which is unstructured and enables us to go looking for whatever we can find. Alternatively, research can be confirmatory, where we start with a hypothesis and seek to confirm or deny the truth of that hypothesis.

Demographics

Demographics is a qualitative description of a person, group of people, or organizations.

Customer Demographics

In Theo's book on managing crises, one of the most important questions a business owner must ask is "Who is our customer?" One method is to define who we want our customer to be, and then conduct market research to find out how many of them there are and which factors would influence them to purchase our products and services. Another method is to review who is already purchasing the products and services, and identify their demographic characteristics. In any case, demographics can describe customers based upon several different characteristics:

- Age of customer
- Gender
- Marital status
- Presence of children
- Education level
- Income level
- Occupation
- Religion
- Race/ethnic group

The market analysis generally has a section for demographics, market size and growth, market trends, distribution and spending patterns, as well as a detailed discussion of the competition, their strengths and weaknesses. If our company has multiple products and services, the market analysis would need to be conducted separately for each one.

Customer Psychographics

The marketing analysis would also list psychographics. Psychographics are lifestyle characteristics of our customers, for example, whether they are spiritual or scientific, health-oriented or couch potatoes, risk takers or conservative, highly educated or high school dropouts, and so on.

Business-to-Business Demographics

If our customers are organizations or businesses instead of individual people, there are different demographics specific to business, such as the type of industry (retail, wholesale, distribution, manufacturing, service, government, technology, etc.), the sales distribution channels most commonly used, the size of the business, and so on.

Trends

In addition to the demographics and psychographics, we need to understand the trends. A trend is the direction of each demographic or psychographic. Is it stable and not changing? Increasing? Decreasing? If so, how fast? Some free sources of trending data can be found on the websites of many organizations. A list of the most popular ones are found in Table 6.1.

Table 6.1. Market Resources for Trends

Organization	Title/Types of Reports
American Association of Retired Persons (AARP) Research	Research on the needs, interests, and concerns on midlife and older adults
Center for Media Research	Research briefs and links to the original source
ClickZ—Stats and Data	Marketing and advertising news
comScore	Whitepapers and presentations (requires registration)
Institute for the Future	Conducts research on future trends in work and daily life, technology, global business trends, and consumer trends
Kaiser Family Foundation	Health policy analysis and research
Nielsen	Reports accessible from their News and Insights web page (requires registration)
Pew Research Center	Runs seven projects that provide information on "issues, attitudes, and trends shaping America and the world"
Pew Global Attitudes Project	Conducts worldwide public opinion surveys concerning people's own lives and their views on important issues
Pew Hispanic Center	Research to improve understanding of the U.S. Hispanic population and Latinos' growing impact on the nation
Pew Internet & American Life Project	Produces research reports on the impact of the Internet on families, communities, work, and home
Social & Demographic Trends Project	Studies American behaviors and attitudes of family, community, health, finance, work, and leisure
U.S. Bureau of Labor Statistics American Time Use Survey (ATUS)	Released June of each year, data for prior year
U.S. Bureau of Labor Statistics Consumer Expenditure Survey	Provide information on the buying habits of American consumers
U.S. Department of Agriculture Economic Research Service	Focuses on food, farming, natural resources, and rural development

Source: Anne M. Wenzel, *The Entrepreneur's Guide to Market Research.* Santa Barbara, CA: Praeger, 2012.

Another excellent source of trending data, as mentioned earlier, can be found on Google Trends, Google Insights for Search, and Twitter trends. These websites allow us to enter key words, and they will tell us, for whatever time period we'd like, how many people are searching or posting on those topics.[1]

Google Trends and Twitter Trends are newer sources of data, and are powerful, often eclipsing what was previously only available through highly paid specialists in each of the fields in which we might be searching. It makes sense to fully utilize all of these free tools and sources of data *before* spending any dollars on marketing consultants.

Distribution and Spending Patterns

Once we've analyze the demographics/psychographics, and reviewed the trends, we are ready to analyze the distribution (also known as sales channels) and spending patterns of the products and services in our business. To do so, we would consider the following:

- Cost efficiency: Should we market directly to our customers, or through a distributor, wholesaler, or retailer?
- Location: If we serve business or retail clients directly, is it important to our customers that we be easily accessible via foot or automobile? Can we easily and cost effectively relocate to a more desirable location?
- Time: Is there a cost effective way we can deliver our goods or services to customers more quickly?
- What are the standard methods of delivery? If we offer a new or different method of delivery, will we gain or lose more customers?
- How do the different methods of distribution affect the quality of the product, service, or shopping experience for the customer?
- Are there any security considerations we need to consider with the different methods of delivery?
- If we utilize a faster, more secure, or more convenient method of delivery, will it raise operating costs? If so, are customers willing to pay more, or are we willing to operate with lower profit margins?

The objective is to match the demographic and psychographic and trend information that we found to the appropriate distribution channel. For example, if large bookstores are declining and online sales of books rising and our customer base is employed in white-collar positions (and therefore, are computer literate), it would make no sense to choose bookstores as our sales channel. Online sales would be the matching channel for new publishers.

Market Size

We may think market size is simple, but it is not.

Segment the Market

As mentioned in Chapter 4, Fred Beste has published a list of the top 25 death traps for entrepreneurs (Beste 1996), which can be found in Appendix C. The 17th one talks about entrepreneurs who go to venture capitalists with a statement similar to the following: "The market for our product is 3 billion dollars and growing at 20 percent each year. If we just got 3 percent of the market, we'd be successful!" (Said with huge smile on entrepreneur's face.) Fred will tell you that any venture capitalist, angel, or banker will turn around and shut the door at such a statement since it shows an immature understanding of market size.

We need a lot more than one single overarching number for our market. We need to know exactly how many product X items were sold, where they were sold, who bought them, and for what purpose. Fred named this particular death trap "Failure to Segment Market"

> The U.S. tent market is $100 million. You plan to sell high-end back-packing tents and expect to be shipping $5 million worth of them in five years. All you have to get is 5 percent of the tent market, right? No sweat, piece of cake.
>
> Wrong. On closer inspection, one discovers that circus, funeral and special event tents make up 30 percent of the tent market; moreover, the military represents 20 percent and backyard family tents 20 percent. The two largest backpacking retailers, representing 20 percent of the market, own captive suppliers. That leaves 10 percent of the $100 million. The truth is that your falling-off-a-log $5 million sales objective represents 50 percent of the actual, segmented market. (Beste 1996, p. 8)

Our market size, therefore, must be segmented by geography, industry, channel, and customer type. Furthermore, we can only count as part of our market the geography, types, industries, channels, and customer types to which we are marketing.

Phantom Market or New Market

It is important that we define the actual market, not a fantasy market. It is far too easy for a bright-eyed, bushy-tailed entrepreneur to fool themselves (and, consequently, their investors) into thinking that there is more of a market than there actually is. We also need to understand that while we *may* be able to create a new market for some new product or service, the cost of doing so is many times the cost of pilfering market share from competitors in an already-existing market. Educating a product-buying public that our product is better than a competitor's product is a short easy communication. Educating a product-buying public that they need our product, despite the fact that they aren't utilizing anything like our product today—that's a long and often difficult communication. Sometimes impossible.

Consider, for example, the smartphone. Today, the smartphone (iPhones, Androids, etc.) is the fastest growing segment of the cell phone market. But for decades, the precursor of the smart phone, personal digital assistants, were available but were considered a small, very niche market, typically with only a few well-traveled business people as customers. Apple spent more than $100 million on the development of the Newton (shown in Figure 6.1) in 1987 (equivalent to more than $205 million in today's dollars). Nonetheless, Apple could not convince the public that they needed personal digital assistants, and in 1998, Apple dropped the product entirely, admitting what the public already knew; the Newton was a colossal failure.[2]

Figure 6.1. The Apple Newton (1987–1998) and the iPhone (2007–present)

Source: Photo by Blake Patterson. Used by permission.

Apple only spent $150 million on developing the iPhone (which was equivalent to only $81 million in 1987 dollars). This time, Apple succeeded because, by 2007, the public was already familiar with the concept of cell phones, personal digital assistants, and digital music devices (and was getting awfully sick and tired of carrying around three separate devices [five when you counted GPS devices and digital cameras]). The public didn't need to be convinced they needed a cell phone in 2007—they already knew it.[3] They only needed to be convinced that the iPhone was a better phone than the Motorola Razr.

Market Value

The market value (in dollars) is related to the market size (in units or number of customers). Our portion of the market share of the segmented market depends, in part, on how many competitors there are, and how intense the competition is. We might be able to get 30 percent market share of the customers within 50 miles of our store if there are only one or two other established stores in the same neighborhood. If there are already 15, the market may be saturated, and the chances that we can dominate 30 percent of it would be slim to none.

Furthermore, the market value may be impacted by the economy. When economic factors are going down, the market value drops even when the market size is the same because many businesses discount and lower prices. Businesses get more desperate to sell their products and services, and discount even more. Of course, the market size may also drop because now, fewer people can afford to purchase the products or services.

Earlier, we noted that there is no way to tell in advance which industries or subindustries are going to do well during a recession. Similarly, there is no way to tell in advance which industries will fare poorly in a recession. As already noted, healthcare did well during the most recent recession, as did education. In previous recessions, food industries did well, but not this most recent recession (starting in 2008). The food industry did poorly except for organic foods. The value of the subindustry organic foods grew, and is still growing, as people are becoming more aware of the negative health impact of highly processed, chemically enhanced foods.

The music industry, in general, has declined quite a bit in the last decade, but the market value of subindustries such as analog vinyl albums has grown. Fewer albums are sold, but they are sold at much higher prices as collector's items.

Demographics also impact market value. It may be that only 24 percent of seniors (people age 62 to 100+) will be purchasing personal emergency response systems, and that the percentage remains stable. But if the number of people in that age group increase (as it will in the United States as the baby boomers begin to enter their senior years), then the market value will increase.

Analyzing the Competition

There are three types of competition—direct, indirect, and emerging. Direct competitors are other companies in businesses similar to our own. Indirect are products and services that use up the same market dollar, but are not sold by companies or businesses similar to ours. For example, customers can spend their money watching movies in our theater, or in the movie theater across town (our direct competitor). But there are several indirect competitors as well. Customer might travel to a stadium to watch a ball game instead of traveling to the movie theater. Or, they might spend their money on a movie subscription service on their home computers.

Ten years ago, watching a movie on a home computer from a subscription service was unheard of—so it would have been considered an emerging competitor then. But not anymore. Now, the service has been around long enough that it is losing market share to people watching YouTube videos on their mobile device (such as an iPad). That makes the mobile video the emerging competitor. Online movie subscription services would be considered just an indirect competitor.

We should know our competitors (all types—direct, indirect, and emerging) as well as their locations, websites, owners, markets, strengths, weaknesses, and so on. Smart entrepreneurs have a simple grid-based spreadsheet listing all of their competitors, their contact info, their strengths and weaknesses, and any other information about them that might be helpful. On a regular basis (perhaps annually), the list should be revisited and revised as applicable, so that we can keep our finger on the pulse of our market. This information is known at Competitive Intelligence, and can often mean the difference between a winning strategy and a losing strategy.

Anne includes many examples of this type of data in her book, but Dennis's book on writing business plans and Bob's book on marketing also have several examples of competitive intelligence grids. Sources of this type of data can be found in Table 6.2.

Competitive information such as contact information, pricing, location, market characteristics, strengths, and weaknesses is pretty easily entered into a grid on a spreadsheet or word-processing table for direct competitors. But what about indirect competitors? That is a little bit more

Table 6.2. Table of Sources for Competitive Intelligence

Source	Types of Competitive Intelligence
Company website and brochures	Products and services offered, pricing, markets targeted, certifications/licenses, competitive advantage
Internet review sites	Information shared by reviewers, such as pricing, levels of customer service, distribution methods, competitive advantage
Directory listings	General contact, product and service information, link to website.
Trade Associations	General contact information, detailed list of products and services, types of customers served, distribution methods, competitive advantage
Business Source Premiere Regional Business News Gale Directory Library Business and Company Resource Center	These are all online databases, usually available in a local university library. Information provided varies, but can include products and services offered, competitive advantage, methods of distribution, pricing, markets served
General Internet Search	Information varies, as with online data bases. If no information is found, firm is weak competition
Dun & Bradstreet	Fee-based. Sales and employment size, profitability, reliability
Shopping with the competition: Purchase products and services, or request quotes	Pricing, distribution methods, customer service, and competitive advantage information

Source: Anne M. Wenzel, *The Entrepreneur's Guide to Market Research.* Santa Barbara, CA: Praeger, 2012.

difficult. Anne recommends that we conduct the following analytical activity in order to help define our indirect competitors:

1. Identify two or more of the most important needs that we fulfill for our customers. Can we save them time? Improve their health? Enhance their well-being? Provide entertainment?
2. Write down four different ways that our customers can meet those needs. For example, a person seeking improved physical fitness can join a gym, or they can buy fitness videos and work out at home, or they can join a hiking or a cycling club.

3. Pick one of the competing products, services, or technologies above, and below, write down ideas/ways we more effectively meet our customers' needs. Can we meet those needs faster, better, or at a lower cost?
4. Repeat this exercise for each of the significant indirect competition identified.

Analyzing Competitor's Advertising

Analyzing our competitor's advertising is one of the best ways to compile data as part of our competitive intelligence gathering. To accomplish this, answering the following questions will be helpful:

- Who is our direct competition?
- Who is our indirect competition?
- What strengths do our competitors have in terms of advertising and integrated marketing communication?
- What advertising themes have our competitors used over the past five years? Ten years?
- What are the strengths and weaknesses of competitive advertising?
- How successful are our competitors' advertisements and promotional activities?
- Would any of them lend themselves to our advertising or promotion?
- Is there any research that can verify competitive effectiveness?
- What data/information can we get on competitive advertising budgets and spending?
- Are our competitors' geographic area the same as ours?
- Are our competitors' demographic and psychographic data the same as ours?
- How does their sales program and plan compare with ours?

It makes sense to analyze our competitors' advertising to see what works, what doesn't, borrow what does, and avoid what doesn't. Most importantly, we use our knowledge of their advertising to differentiate our products and services.

Competitive Intelligence Ethics

There are ethical issues involved in gathering competitive intelligence. More than a decade ago, I was involved in the development of a certification curriculum of competitive intelligence for Drexel University, which had acquired an excellent reputation for this topic. Until then, I hadn't thought much about the ethics involved in pretending to be a customer, calling up a competitor with a fake name, and (based upon completely bogus requirements) obtaining inside information on the pricing and operations of the company. I'd done that frequently as I built my first business.

Working on the competitive intelligence curriculum made me see competitive intelligence in a new light. The question is—would I want my competitors to do that to me? True, my competitors could misrepresent themselves and gain valuable competitive data. They probably would. That doesn't mean I should do that to them. Since I consider myself a person of integrity, I decided that pretending to be someone else and gathering data was unethical and immoral, and I never did it again.

I feel perfectly fine with obtaining public information about competitors. I see no problem with actually going to a competitor and purchasing their products and services. There is nothing unethical about becoming a customer of our competitors in order to keep tabs on them—as long as we do not misrepresent who we are.

What Do We Do with Competitive Intelligence

Once we have the demographic and psychographic information, we can use it to identify the best geographic locations for our business, the best distribution channels, the best advertising methods to reach our customers, and so on.

How do we figure out how to do that? People tend to have their own methods. For the most part, though, they involve a process described by Bob Everett in the series book on Marketing:

1. THINK.
2. Gather information.
3. THINK.
4. Ask people.
5. THINK.
6. Notice what information we are missing.
7. THINK some more.
8. Make a decision and ACT.

I would replace the "Ask people" step because I consider that part of gathering information, and I would add a few more steps involving organizing and illustrating the information.

One of the reasons we, as business owners and entrepreneurs, should do our own market research (and not hire a firm to do the market research for us) is that organizing the information is the key to understanding it. Marketing researchers tend to understand the data gathering part well. But when they analyze the information, they organize it in a way that is typically academic or exteriorly structured, such as alphabetical. That's not helpful to us. We need to look at, think about, and organize (or reorganize) the information ourselves. As a business owner, I might want to organize competitors based upon their impact on our business, or how closely their product lines match ours. Simply figuring out how to organize the information is a valuable marketing strategy exercise.

The other part is illustrating the data. The information needs to be graphed, charted, dissected in hundreds of different ways. The person who should be doing that is the person who can determine, at a glance, whether the graph, chart, or table reveals useful information. The information provided to us from market research consultants might not be the most salient information to us. Often, it is the most easily graph-able information, which may turn out to be useless to us.

So, in my mind, one of the most important things that entrepreneurs should do is organize all the marketing information, create bunches of graphs from the data, and then just sit and look at it. Think on it. Dwell on it. Review it. Then, think some more.

For example, one of the most useful graphs is a perceptual map. Perceptual maps help us identify what our product or service position actually is as compared to our competitors. An illustration can be found in Figure 6.2.

Figure 6.2. Generic Perceptual Map

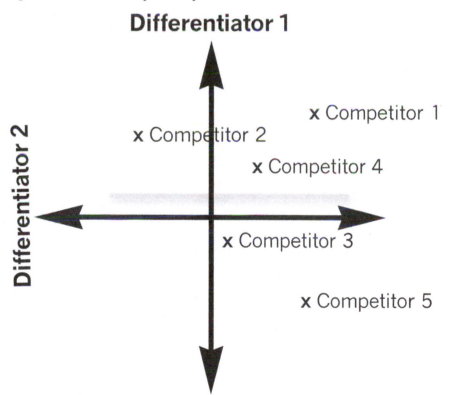

Source: HPL Consortium, Inc., copyright 2014, used with permission.

There are four steps to using the perceptual map.

Step 1: Select two of the key factors that the marketplace uses to differentiate among competitors.
Step 2: Evaluate each of our important competitors along these two dimensions.
Step 3: Display the results in a two-dimensional grid.
Step 4: Look for patterns, especially open spaces in the grid.

This exercise allows us to see where the holes are, where there might be an underserved market that no other product or service is designed to fill. We would do this exercise for each of our products and services, and for all of the differential dimensions we have for each product or service.

After we organize, graph, and illustrate, we should back off. Set the whole thing aside and take a break. Research shows that our minds can work through issues and problems much more effectively when we back off direct cogitation on a topic.

After a bit of time, we should return to the illustrations and listen deeply to whatever insights our brains can elicit from the data. Again, we should think and reflect in order to figure out our best options.

Finally, we should choose the most salient graphs and charts to be included in our marketing plan. We add our supporting reasons for going in whatever direction our insights take us, and we have identified our marketing strategy based upon our market analysis.

MARKETING

As a youthful inexperienced entrepreneur who had only ever been trained to become a teacher (which is what I was when I started my first business), the first time I came across the term "marketing," I didn't even know what the term meant. I asked my brother-in-law (who had a degree in business, this was long before the days of Google.) and he explained that it was the planning for the promotion of a product or service. I knew even less about advertising. Entrepreneurs, especially technology-driven entrepreneurs, are often focused on development, operations, and finance. We are looking for the better mousetrap, not the people to whom we would sell the better mousetrap. The information that Bob shared in his book on marketing is essential, and he provides lots of tables and worksheets to help entrepreneurs complete the activities for effective marketing.

Marketing Is about Relationships

Marketing is not nearly as much about planning as it is about relationships with people. Bob Everett developed a model to help his students understand marketing, and dubbed it SPUR, *Strategic Process for Understanding Relationships.* He makes the following key point (which can help demystify the marketing process):

> If you have any successful relationships anywhere in your life with anyone (including your pet), then you already know how to market. You just need to learn how to apply that knowledge in a business setting.

Six Core Questions for Market Strategy Development

Bob presents six core questions we must answer in order to establish a successful marketing strategy.

1. What do I want?
2. Who can give it to me?
3. What do they want?
4. What can I deliver?
5. Who else can deliver it?
6. What makes me special?

At the core of any of our actions, including relationships, is our motivation. In a personal setting, what we want includes our long-term goals and aspirations as well as our more immediate needs and desires. In a business setting, these are the mission, goals, and short-term objectives of our company.

Relationships cannot work in the long run unless they are win-win. Both sides have to have some important needs met or the relationship ends. Entrepreneurs have to be especially careful. It is extremely easy to think that people "should" want our product. However, the most important thing entrepreneurs need to learn about marketing is that it doesn't matter what we think, it only matters what our customers buy.

Another tough question is whether or not we can actually deliver what they want. We cannot be all things to all people. We have limited funds and limited operational capacity and time. We have to choose what we are going to be excellent at and focus on that. This will require an honest and fearless assessment of our company, our products and services, and ourselves. It requires that we know what we can't deliver even more than knowing what we can deliver.

We have both direct and indirect competition. Knowing our competition and their strengths and weaknesses will help us find our own unique niche in the marketplace.

This unique niche is what makes us special. Finding our place in the market, the place that customers see as uniquely and powerfully ours, can be one of the most exciting parts of the entire entrepreneurship process.

A Six-Step Process for Selecting Target Markets

Bob also presents a six-step process for selecting a target market. The selection of one or more key target markets for our marketing efforts is critical if we are going to use our marketing dollars efficiently. The six steps Bob proposes are:

1. What potential market is there for our products and services?
2. How big is this market?
3. Why would potential customers in this market want our product or service?
4. What competitors would we face in this market?
5. How saturated is this market? (i.e., what percent of the potential customers in this market already have or use a competitive product or service?)
6. In what ways could we be special to the potential customers in this market?

Strategic Marketing

If we have unlimited funds, we could just try everything to see what works and what doesn't. Chances are we do not have billions stashed to gamble away. So, we need to be strategic about where we start with our marketing dollars. Though no one can predict what will work and what will not, we can predict what is more likely to work and what is less likely to work, and that means thinking strategically.

To do that, we go back to the core questions and look closely at two of them. We need to figure out who are our best potential customers. We need to figure out how to reach them. We need to figure out how to enable them to see our products and services as special.

Our Best Customers

We are looking for someone (or some organization) that:

- Needs what we can provide
- Derives value in excess of what our product or service would cost them
- Has the resources to purchase
- Is accessible to our marketing efforts
- Can be adequately supported post-sale

All too often, identifying a good customer is given too little attention. It is easy to get enthusiastic about our own products and services and assume that other people would share that enthusiasm if only they knew about our products or services. Unfortunately, that is not normally the case. The truth is that:

- People will only do business with us if they perceive it to be in their own interests to do so.
- The way people perceive their interests can be complex, and potentially, contradictory.
- People don't make buying decisions logically, but rather, purchase emotionally.
- People are reluctant to change the way they do things, even in the face of information offering a better way.

As a new business, our best customers will be those that are unserved or underserved by our competition and among whom we can establish a clear advantage over those competitors.

Positioning Products and Services

The target market has an iterative circular relationship with products and services. We choose a target market that had a need for our products and services, but we modify our products and services based upon the needs of the target market. Making this iterative cycle move along more quickly is at the heart of lean start-ups discussed in Chapter 4. But the cycle has always been around.

COMPUTER EDUCATIONAL SERVICES: CASE 1

When I started my first company, my goal was to provide a service I thought was desperately needed—computer training for teachers. When I had first become a teacher, green and fresh out of college, in my first position, I was given an Apple IIe computer, and told that I had to take a class on how to use it. I did. I took a class at the local Reading Area Community College in how to use the computer. The problem was that the computers they taught were IBM-PCs, which was like taking a course in sailing to learn how to drive.

My next step was to take a course using Apple IIe from Temple University, where I was getting my master's degree. That was fun, and taught me how to design and program computer-aided tutorials for my students to learn their subjects. Unfortunately, I wanted to keep track of my students' names, parents, addresses, phone numbers, classes, and grades, not design computer-based instruction. The third course I took taught me how to do BASIC programming. That was like trying to build a car to get across town.

It wasn't until my fourth course, the course I took while working on my doctorate at Lehigh University, where I learned about this magical thing called *database*. I also learned about word processing and spreadsheets. What teachers needed, I realized, was how to use office applications (though this was before they were called "office applications") so that they could better manage their students and classes. So, my first business, Computer Educational Services, was started to teach teachers how to use word processing, spreadsheets, and databases.

However, I soon found that despite the fact that teachers really needed this service, school districts were not willing to pay for it. Luckily, I found that businesses were willing to pay for it. I realized a better target market was businesses who wanted their secretaries, clerks, managers, and executives to learn how to use the computer.

As a result of my finding a better market for technology applications training in business, we changed the positioning of our services to meet that need instead. Furthermore, we found that our best customers were those who had just invested in computers. We formed strategic partnerships with local computer stores who were more interested in selling computers than the long, slow process of training people to use them. (This was back in the day when software was difficult to learn. Each software used a different interface, each used the function keys in different ways, each had different menus. There were no icons, graphics, Windows, or mice.)

Once we've found a market position, we can modify our products and services so that they can uniquely serve that market.

What made CES special was that we were more flexible in how we taught people. We could teach in group classes, in private instruction, onsite, or in our own training rooms. Our competitors typically taught using just one of those methods. We were the only one providing all of those choices of training methods for each software. We positioned ourselves to be the training and consulting firm of choice among businesses with many different levels of employees (executives, clerks, managers, etc.) who all needed training on the new software. Typically, we would provide personalized individual training to executives, group offsite training to secretaries and operational folk, and small group onsite training to managers.

Position as a Noun or a Verb

There are two ways to define positioning:

1. How the marketplace actually perceives our products, and
2. How we would like the marketplace to perceive our products

In the first case, "position" is most often used as a noun. The sentence "This is our market position" usually means "This is how the marketplace perceives our products or services."

In the second case, "position" is used as a verb. The sentence "We position our product as the most cost-effective alternative" means "That is how we want the marketplace to perceive our product." Our goal is to determine our position (noun) in the context of the competitive information gathered, evaluate the strength of that position, and, if found wanting, position (verb) our product differently. We know if we've correctly positioned our product or service if our sales volume is profitable. If not, then something is wrong. We may have selected the wrong target market. We may be positioning our products or services within the target market incorrectly.

Our goal is to have a position in the marketplace that will:

- Accurately reflect our actual distinctive competencies and differential advantage
- Focus on unserved or underserved market segments
- Be achievable, given current resources
- Be sustainable over the longer term
- Be defensible in the face of competitive response

While it may seem easy, positioning is actually relatively difficult to do. The most common mistakes are: underpositioning, overpositioning, confused positioning, and doubtful positioning.

Underpositioning means that we have not been clear or specific enough about where our products and services stand. Overpositioning is when we are so well known for one specific thing that we cannot move successfully into other areas. Confused positioning means that our customer isn't sure of what our position is. Perhaps we tried to make our brand mean more than one thing. Doubtful positioning is trying to establish a new market position that is so far from our current position that the marketplace will just not accept it.

Once we've established our marketing plan, which includes our target market and our market strategy, we are ready to deal with the most common method to establish our position—branding and advertising.

SUMMARY OF MARKETING

Marketing is an essential part of our business plan, and an ongoing need for any successful business.

☑ Properly done market research can help us identify needs, analyze the competition, price our products, plan our strategies, reach the market, and forecast sales.

☑ Demographics, psychographics, market size, and market trends are important influences in our marketing plan.

☑ There is an ethical and an unethical way to acquire competitive intelligence. Ethical methods are a better choice in the long run.

☑ Though we can rely upon others to provide supporting data, we entrepreneurs ourselves are the best people to gain the most insight by reviewing, organizing, and thinking about the marketing data.

☑ Marketing is about planning our business's relationship with people.

☑ To establish a marketing strategy, we need to know what we want, who our target market is, what we can give them, and why they would get it from us.

☑ The best types of market to target are those that are underserved by our competition.

7

Branding and Advertising

The Entrepreneur's Guide to Advertising by James Ogden and Scott Rarick covered many of the same marketing topics as the previous chapter, but also delved much more deeply into branding and advertising—essential ingredients of the marketing plan. In addition to summarizing the highlights here, I will add examples from my own business, as well as information about valuing branding as an intangible asset within our company.

BRANDING

Branding is not just a logo and a jingle. Branding is putting a clear, memorable label on our market position. The purpose of a brand is to lock-in our market position in the minds of the customer. The brand will remind people of who we are and what we stand for in a way that is easy to say, easy to spell, easy to read, and easy to remember.

Branding Is a Philosophy

A brand, in its most profound sense, is a way of thinking, a belief system, or a philosophy. When properly delivered to your existing and potential customers, a brand will transform a simple product or service into a staple need of a particular lifestyle, or even a necessity for those who follow similar beliefs.

We should treat our brand as a valuable asset to be developed and nurtured, just like our personal reputation. If we do things well, over time, we will develop brand equity. Since a brand has a positive asset value on the balance sheet when a business gets sold, it is a way for a company to get a return (sometimes, a large return) on the advertising and marketing dollars spent over the years.

Common Mistakes with Branding

Brands only develop slowly, over time, and their value can be eroded. A brand cannot be built, and then left alone. A brand needs to be nurtured and maintained continuously.

Our brand, by itself and apart from the products and services of the company, develops and grows in value because of what it calls forth in the minds of consumers. In order to safeguard this value, we need to exert strategic control over the brand. Common mistakes of entrepreneurs in managing brands are:

- Using the brand on products or services that are too far afield from what people currently think the brand stands for
- Introducing shoddy product or services and eroding the respect our brand has
- Letting others use our brand (e.g., franchising) without tight controls on what they can and cannot do

How Is a Positive Brand Developed?

A brand cannot be bought. It is far more than the box we put our products in, or the color of our buildings. The brand is the emotion, *the memory*, that is elicited every time a person sees the logo or illustration that represents the brand. We may think of the brand as something we own, but the reality is that the brand is owned by our customers. We can exploit the brand, but they hold the value of the brand in their minds, not us.

For consumers, our brand is the promise of a particular experience. We must deliver on that promise through our product attributes, such as quality, cost, and availability. And we must continue to deliver on the promise, again and again, and again.

The most effective brands are the ones that have developed out of the belief system of the organization. The brand is the outward manifestation of the hedgehog concept, the unique selling proposition, the core competency of the company. When everyone in our company feels the same way about our products, and is delivering the same message to the public, our chances of successful brand development are the greatest.

Assessing the Value of a Brand

As mentioned earlier, the true test of a brand is the amount that someone is willing to pay for it. We are not able to place a monetary value on our own brand (no matter how much or little money we've invested in it). Only someone else can place a value on it. According to Interbrand, a brand rating agency, Coke is the No. 1 most recognized, and most valuable, brand in the world, valued at $77,839,000,000. That's almost $78 billion, 43 percent of the shareholder value of the company. Apple is the second most valuable brand in the world at $76,568 million. The last in the list of the top 100 is Gap, valued at $3,731,000,000, only 20 percent of the shareholder value (Frampton 2013).

The only definitive way to assess whether or not our brand is strong or weak, valuable or worthless, is to sell our company and see what someone will pay for it. In the meantime, we can try to evaluate our brand value by doing a self-assessment with these questions:

- What is our brand essence, or the promise of our brand summed up in its simplest terms?
- Do consumers view our brand essence the same way we do?
- Is recognition and recall of our brand by our customers at an acceptable and effective level?
- Is our brand protected, legally? Trademarked?

We could hire someone to do focus groups and surveys to assess our brand equity, or we could just talk to a few customers to see what they think our brand essence is. If we talk to 30 customers, and 28 of them state something similar to what we think of as our brand essence, then our brand is strong. If we talk to 30 customers, and only five of them state something similar to what we think of as our brand essence, then our brand is weak.

Goal of Brand Building

Our goal, when we plan our marketing plan and advertising to support our brand, is to be top-of-mind for all existing and potential customers. We want to be top-of-mind for the product or service within our whole industry or category. Furthermore, we want to convert that brand awareness into brand loyalty. Brand loyalty leads to the longed-for status as a brand leader, which means that our products and services become the one that all of our competitors are trying to beat.

Branding on a Shoestring Budget

As start-up entrepreneurial businesses, we don't have the 123 years it took for Coca Cola to build their brand, nor the billions of dollars that Apple has spent on their brand. We do need to get our name out in our community as quickly as possible, for as long as possible. We shape our brand with every conversation we have. Every form of communication our employees have with every person they encounter builds (or tears down) the brand.

From day one, it is important to pay close attention and actively engage in brand building. To begin building our brand, we can:

- Make sure our website says what we want it to say, gives a good impression, and follows the rules of Jakob's Law for navigation.[1]
- Join the local chamber of commerce. The connection to other businesspeople and community leaders can be invaluable.
- Attend mixers and work to expose other members to our products or services. If we can, we should host a mixer at our location.
- Always include our company tagline and key differentiating point (or single basic benefit) on our business card and in our e-mail signature.
- Create a company page on social networking sites, such as Facebook.com, and establish a Twitter feed to it. Post weekly. (Too often is not good, too rarely also is not good.)
- Invite local media representatives out for a tour or interview. Include the business editor of any local newspapers and business journals, if our area has one.
- Write articles about our business or industry. If we can't get a local newspaper to print them, then post them online through relevant websites and blogs.
- Be sure we are listed in any local directories relevant to our business. For example, if we provide services that would be helpful to someone who has just moved, we should get listed in "new mover" publications and "welcome wagon" directories.
- Set up a Google location so that people searching in our geographic area will get our website listed at a higher priority than others.
- Provide business cards, brochures, and discount offers to people in related businesses who can, in turn, pass them along to new customers.

ADVERTISING

Advertising is usually the main focus of mass marketing. We've done all of the market research, analyzed our target market, and positioned our products and services. But it all means nothing if we don't communicate to the target market the information that would position our products and services. In this section, we will investigate the definition of advertising and how it differs from other aspects of marketing, how and when to hire an advertising firm or consultant, how advertising interacts with branding, and how to know which media to use in advertising.

Branding and Advertising

Branding is not an advertisement method. There is a lot more to branding, including its role in the valuation of our company. Advertising is an important part of the process in developing a brand, however. It is said that public relations and publicity build brands, but advertising sustains them.

Definition of Advertising

Advertising is a tactic that is used by marketers to communicate messages with their customers and other stakeholders. Advertising provides the best possible selling message to the right target audience at the best possible price. Advertising is a bulk communications process. Advertising is placed in various media to reach the correct audiences, usually used to reach large numbers of people with one campaign.

Advertising is paid, unlike public relations or publicity. Therefore, we have full control of the content and media placement of the advertisement. Advertising should be designed to accomplish the following:

- Tell people that our company exists.
- Let our audience know what products and services are available to them.
- Let our customers know where we are located, and provide directions if we're located in an obscure location.
- Tell our audience the reason why they should purchase from us as opposed to opting for other products.
- Share our Unique Selling Proposition (or USP).

Advertising is one of the last marketing tasks undertaken. The marketing communications plan (which includes the advertising) is a logical extension of the company's marketing plan. It describes exactly how the company's objectives, mission, vision, and strategy are shared. Doing any kind of advertising before those essential elements have been fully worked out is a waste of resources.

Advertising Firms and Consultants

Small organizations with small budgets cannot afford to hire most advertising agencies. The reason is not necessarily the cost of the consultants themselves; the reason is because advertising is a mass communication product. It makes no sense to splurge thousands of dollars (or tens of thousands of dollars) on an advertisement that is going to go to a few hundred people who attend a conference. Most advertising agencies don't even bill you hourly; their business model is to reap the rewards from the markup when reselling the media services. So the first question is if we should even hire an advertising agency.

COMPUTER EDUCATIONAL SERVICES: CASE 2

In my early days as a budding young clueless entrepreneur, I went to a marketing workshop being put on by the local Chamber of Commerce. I really liked the workshop facilitator, and I asked him to spend a few hours with me sharing his expertise for his normal fee (which turned out to be $450 for an afternoon of personalized attention, a custom-developed marketing template, and a boatload of know-how). It was probably the best $450[1] I ever spent as a struggling young entrepreneur, but it didn't turn out as I expected.

I had planned on taking about $5,000 and spending it on radio ads. He advised against it. I don't remember everything he told me, but I do remember him saying that little bits and pieces of advertising, produced ad-hoc, do not result in anything, and would be a waste of money. In the world of advertising, $5,000 is barely a drip. In advertising; only a torrent gets results. He said that if I didn't have at least $45,000 to spend on an advertising campaign, I was much better off spending that $5,000 on something else—like folders and mugs to give out to students who come for the classes (which is what we did end up doing).

---

[1] $450 in 1986 dollars is the equivalent of about $1,000 today, 2014.

Should We Hire an Advertising Firm?

How do we know when to hire an advertising agency versus doing it ourselves? Chances are, we don't have the expertise to do the advertising ourselves. If we are planning to spend any significant amount of money on the advertising, we should hire a professional. If we spend $10,000 on a brochure or $45,000 on a commercial, or $5,000 on a website, we will have wasted our investment in advertising if we do an amateurish job. Even worse, we might do damage to our reputation.

There are many issues when considering hiring an advertising agency:

- What types of information is needed to more effectively advertise?
- What role do we want our inside personnel to play in regard to our advertising?
- What is the time frame, or urgency, in getting the advertising completed?
- What is our time frame to undertake our advertising research, development, and design?
- Do we currently exploit any economies of scale for our advertising?
- What is our advertising budget? Is it large enough to make a difference? What are the budget constraints?

Professional help is essential if we don't have the competence and experience necessary to manage all of our advertising functions. If we don't know what we are doing, then someone else can do it better, cheaper, and more effectively than we can. It is often much less expensive to outsource advertising and marketing services than it is to have professionals on our staff to perform those functions. Using professionals frees up capacity that can be better focused on production than marketing.

Advertisers utilize specialized equipment, hardware, and software that would be costly to purchase for infrequent use. Most entrepreneurs and business owners do not have experience with what is involved in the difference between a high resolution photo for print advertising and a low resolution picture that looks fine on a web page. (For example, we cannot download a picture from a web page and put it into a brochure. There are many different reasons spanning technical, ethical, and legal arguments.)

Most people do not understand the graphics rendering process, how to convert vector-based graphics to bit-based graphics, the specifics of the EPS format, or any of the highly precise features and functions of advertising. They might think that white space is wasted space, or that it doesn't matter if the colors don't match exactly. They might be completely unaware of the difference between Pantone, sRGB, RGB, and CMYK.

Advertising and graphics are highly specialized fields (especially these days, when there are so many options at so many levels). It is not a field for amateurs, no matter how easy they make it look.

Professional help is also best when we want to establish credibility for our product, service, or organization. External suppliers seemingly give a third-party endorsement of our business. They can tap into awards and support programs that present our products and services much more effectively than if we were to just spout about our products ourselves. Consider the difference between the impact of two messages. Message #1 is to simply tell all of our customers how great we are. Message #2 is to tell all of our customers about winning a J.D. Power and Associates Award. The J.D. Power endorsement carries much more weight.

Maximizing Our Advertising Dollar

The sad fact is that start-ups and small businesses are in most need of advertising, yet they have the fewest resources. Large, long-established businesses spend the most money on advertising, but have the least need since they already have a large customer base and a well-known brand. Additionally, unlike equipment or other capital costs, advertising is an expense for which it is difficult to get financing. Imagine going to a bank with a wonderful business plan that requires $200,000 to be spent in advertising over the next year in order to reap $1,000,000 in sales the following year. I highly doubt any bank will lend the money. Banks tend to prefer companies and people who have tangible capital for collateral. But there are ways to stretch our advertising dollar.

When we hire professional consultants to design the advertisement or create the logo, it makes sense to listen to them. They are the experts in the process, and know a lot better than we do (often) what will work and what will not.

To maximize our advertising dollar, we can, and should, get a complete set of electronic copies of our logos, ads, campaigns, and visual elements. We want to be able to use them anywhere and not be forced to return to the designer for every incident. We paid for their development, so we own them (unless we signed an agreement stating otherwise with the agency), so we should be sure to obtain a copy of everything in several different formats and sizes. Generally, we can ask for a DVD or CD that contains the ads, logos, elements, and so on in TIFF, JPG, PDF, and EPS format, in tiny, small, medium, and large sizes. We will pay a little extra for the time to convert the graphic elements into all these different formats, but it will be well worth it.

We can obtain the graphical elements to create our own letterhead and flyers, for example. But we should run them by the agency each time we use them. We don't want to modify them from what the designer created, but use them exactly as they were designed to use. Designers are usually picky about things such as fonts, colors, sizes, spacing, graphics, placement, and so on. We can't take what they've done, modify it, and use it without understanding all of the factors that go into the impression being attempted. We can easily ruin our investment by unknowingly compromising the quality of the impression.

After I went through the process of getting a new logo for my company, the graphic designer I worked with was absolutely adamant that I throw away all of my old business cards and letterhead with the less-than-professional logo that a friend of mine had developed. Being the frugal business owner I am, I wanted to use them up before adopting the new logo. (We compromised; we used the old letterhead and business cards for internal communications, and adopted the new professional-looking cards and letterhead for all external communications.)

This same graphic designer had another client who had a hand-drawn, amateurish-looking logo that had been done by an artistically challenged grandfather decades ago for the family business. Even though the client had made the decision to present a more professional appearance to clients, and had approved the new logo after a many-months-long process, the client would not stop using the old logo, despite the pleas of the new logo designer. As a result, the investment made in the new marketing plan, the new logo, and the new strategy for the business was wasted. The negative impact of the old was countermanding the positive impact of the new. (The client, unfortunately, did not do well, and I believe this was one of the major reasons.)

Additional sources of funding or discounts for advertising can be found in co-op dollars, contract and frequency rates, trade agreements, sponsorships, and media buying services.

Co-opetition[2] and complementary business relationships can come in handy for large advertising campaigns. There may be a neighboring business (ideally one with a similar target market, perhaps even a competitor) who would be willing to split the cost of advertising with us, in a cooperative effort. This can be most effective when the creative execution of the ad focuses on the synergy between the benefits of each entity, thus providing an even greater benefit back to the listener, viewer, or reader. For example, a fitness center and tai chi school may split a full page ad in a coupon magazine, each taking a half page. Both aerobic activity and stress reducing exercises are essential to health, so it would be a good fit.

The number one way of stretching advertising dollars are co-op dollars. Co-op dollars are discounts on the products and services we purchase and resell from our suppliers and business partners. For instance, if we are operating a tai chi studio, the manufacturer of our tai chi footwear might offer to pay for a portion of our advertising. Typically, they pay up to 50 percent if we mention their name, or place their logo in our advertising. Trade organizations often offer co-op dollars to help develop general product or service awareness, such as the *Got Milk?* campaign.

COMPUTER EDUCATIONAL
SERVICES: CASE 3

After eight years of building the company, when I sold Computer Educational Services to systems integrator Hi-TECH Connections (a business selling technology networking and equipment), I got an unexpected bonus. One of the advantages I found after the sale was that our advertising budget was immediately doubled because the parent company could get rebates of up to 50 percent of the ad cost just by including the logo of their suppliers in the advertisements of our training schedules.

Types of Advertising Agencies and Support

There are many different levels of advertising support. Full service agencies offer their clients many services necessary to carry out the total marketing function (i.e., planning, ad creation, ad production, media placement, and often, evaluation of the effectiveness of the campaign). Additionally, full-service agencies often offer marketing services such as marketing research, brand reviews, competitive analysis, sales promotion (planning, creation, and execution) and others.

There are also specialty agencies. Certain agencies are experts in one type of marketing or one type of industry. Some firms specialize in just buying and placing media for their clients without a lot of other add-on services. Others provide any services they need, à la carte. For example, these agencies may create just a logo, just a tagline, just weekly newspaper inserts, just radio ads, and so on.

The independent creative boutique agencies specialize in the development and production of creative executions (also known as campaigns) for their clients. Local colleges and universities with marketing programs often offer low-cost or free services by the students, or fee-based professional services from the professors. (Keep in mind some caveats about students; we might find a shining star, but we may go through many duds before we find one who is able to do the job effectively.)

In addition to advertising agencies, there are a number of other providers of service that may be required for the advertising portion of the marketing program. Videos, photographs, and other types of creative assistance are available for a fee from The Carlyle Group (who purchased the popular Getty Images in 2012), Reuters Media, Corbis Corporation, or Agence France-Presse. Some companies offer salespeople as an outsourced service. Most local media (radio, television, web-based) have professionals on staff to assist with our advertising needs. Important and often overlooked sources of service are database management and marketing companies.

Customer Relationship Management (CRM) is the term used for software to manage the contact information for clients and potential clients. CRM has become an increasingly effective tool for low-budget advertisers. There are also agencies and companies that specialize in postal mail advertising that elicits a direct response in the form of a postcard, phone call, or looking up a web page. Agencies often can provide additional help for merchandising and point-of-sale displays to accompany offline and online advertising.

Types of Advertising Support

Our advertising goals determine which types of advertising support we should choose. The choices run the gamut from full service agency to just an image or two from an images company.

We can, for example, choose an advertising agency that will confer upon us some level of prestige. Many firms have high brand equity themselves, and when our stakeholders (customers, investors, bankers, etc.) see that we're using a high-quality agency, we may end up adding equity value to our brand. We might even get a higher quality product or service from a higher-profile advertising agency, but even if we don't, just hiring them is part of the investment and their partnership is the return on the investment.

It also makes sense to look for experience. What past experiences does the provider have? Do they have particular expertise in a given area? What other clients do they have? A single class in marketing cannot compete with someone who has been around with years of practical hands-on experience in advertising.

Also remember to look at the provider's personnel—not just the top dog who made the sale. Oftentimes, rainmakers describe a wonderful outcome, and know how to make the sale, but when it comes to actually providing the advertising services, college kids with no experience are left to do the design and fulfill the contract. Make sure the agency personnel have the right qualifications, skill base, and knowledge.

The bottom line is that we need to select advertising service providers that will generate additional sales. Without significant additional sales, we won't have a return on our advertising investment. The costs must be in line with our expected additional sales from the advertising campaign.

MEDIA

Media is simply the means we employ to deliver our message to our target audience. Sometimes, media is called a vehicle or a channel. Media come in a variety of sizes and shapes, places, and times. Traditional media vehicles include television, radio, newspaper, magazines, and outdoor, or out-of-home. Out-of-home media include billboard, transit, bus shelter.

Whether online advertising is now considered a traditional medium is debatable. The answer at this point is probably industry-specific. If our target audience is young and technically literate, online would probably be considered traditional because the young have been ensconced in the online world for almost a decade. If our target customers are seniors, then the medium is still relatively new. It is only recently that websites such as Medicare.gov have enabled seniors to access services on the web, so they are just now becoming more accustomed to going online.

Media Options

There are several options for our media mix (i.e., the different types of media in our plan and the percentage of spending or expected impressions from each). Print media include newspapers, magazines, periodicals, tabloids, organization publications, directories, playbills. Broadcast media include radio and television. Online media include banner and block ads, video preroll, pay-per-click links, and paid sponsorships.

The pros and cons of each can help us decide which ones should be in our mix.

Newspapers

Newspapers have a good reach, and high circulation. Newspapers have longevity as a trusted tool for information delivery, with high acceptance and credibility. The lead-time for placing and providing advertising can be short, which means that messages can be timely and quickly updated, as quickly as the next day, if necessary.

Newspapers are a good vehicle for couponing and inserts. They are accommodating when it comes to size and shape of advertising, with many new customizable and attention-getting options available. Different sections allow for demographic targeting.

However, newspapers may be viewed as information overload. Sometimes, they appear cluttered. Newspapers offer little in the way of exclusivity, or competitive protection. Many newspapers are struggling with subscription and newsstand sales due to the online presence of similar news content as well as their own electronic versions being available.

Because newspapers are losing market share to online services, rates are increasing for ad space at the same time that the population of newspaper readers is shrinking. Newspaper markets across the United States often have multiple papers servicing the same geographic areas, which creates crossover (and occasionally, complete duplication) for the same population.

Furthermore, newspapers are a passive medium, making it difficult to force the reader to act.

Magazines

Magazines offer a targeted readership, and cater to a special interest or particular demographic. Content can be targeted regionally, even in some national consumer magazines. Good geographic selectivity can be found in larger markets (city-by-city).

Most magazines tend to be high-quality glossy paper, which helps the quality of the advertisement itself. Photos and colors stay crisp and clean. Magazines are ideal for image and branding campaigns. Many magazines have a long shelf-life, and exceptional pass-along value. Some are even collected, or highly coveted.

Now, more than ever, magazines are offering unique advertising spaces and technologies to those advertisers who really want to cut through the clutter, such as post-it note stickers, preprinted inserts, pop-ups, fold-outs, and so on.

Magazine ad space costs are increasing, however. The frequency can be limiting, and the lead time is long. We must wait month to month or longer to change our message.

Magazines tend to reach a relatively low percentage of their overall target market. Furthermore, magazines tend to have a higher ratio of ads to editorial content than newspapers. Some magazines are almost 90 percent advertisements.

Magazine readership is low in comparison to other media. According to research, only an average of 3 percent of people's time is spent reading magazines.

Television

Television is used by more people, and for longer durations of time, than any other medium (approximately 4.2 hours per day)—even in this digital world of the Internet. Television has good reach, and high impact. Given the reach and impact, the cost is relatively low. It is especially good for image and branding ads/campaigns. A story can be told, and multiple variations of a spot can be created, thus different selling messages can also be conveyed.

With television, there are fewer restrictions on creativity. Particular times of the day can be targeted for particular demographics. The number of spots availability tends to be high. There is also a growing presence of the viral aspect of marketing, as more and more television programs and ads get shown online, especially social websites and video-content sites, such as YouTube and Facebook.

However, the total cost for television is higher than other mediums. Production costs are high. Viewer recall of commercials is lower than other formats, so customers require a higher ad frequency than other media. Additionally, watchers may avoid commercials by zipping and zapping, or skipping and surfing instead of watching. Furthermore, television viewing, in general, has a seasonality to it, and tends to drop at certain times of the year, such as during the summer months.

Radio

Radio has a good reach, and frequency is easily maximized. Radio can be somewhat geographically targeted, and the costs are low. Radio advertising is more flexible, and can be changed relatively quickly. The lower cost allows for a longer, more elaborate message to be conveyed. Production can be kept relatively inexpensive. Particular times of the day can be targeted.

However, like television, radio listeners can zap away from a commercial to another station, missing the message entirely. Furthermore, radio is a passive medium, as most listeners are engaged in another activity while listening; thus, some distraction can occur. The modality is only aural—without the enhancements of visual colors or graphics.

Radio stations, while catering to specific types of listeners, overlap significantly with each other within one market, therefore you may find it necessary to buy advertising from multiple stations in order to fully deliver your message.

Outdoor Billboards

Outdoor billboards have a relatively low cost. Billboard advertising tends to be large, and more in-your-face, resulting in greater impact. Geographical targets, down to the specific neighborhoods, are possible.

With billboards, simple ads can be the most effective. Advances in outdoor displays have opened up all sorts of possibilities, from the popular tri-vision or tri-wave boards which change messages in 5- to 8-second intervals, to the extremely attention-getting digital displays, which are as vibrant as most television screens.

However, billboard ad messages must be brief. The effectiveness and total reach are relative to traffic flow and weather, and the image might be impacted negatively by the location's immediate surroundings. Furthermore, recall of billboard advertising tends to be low. In some markets, space or slot availability can be limited. Changing a message or an error in the ad can be costly.

Online Outlets, Google, and Search Engine Optimization

Within a short time since its introduction, online media has grown to be the most widely used type of advertising. The message can be easily changed and the cost of advertising is relatively low.

More people find information online each year, so the target population grows automatically. Demographic, psychographic, and geographic targeting is possible, based on the specific nature of most websites.

However, online advertising growth means that there are millions of websites from which to choose for targeting. Measurability and effectiveness are questionable with online advertising—more so than any other medium—because it is difficult to interpret. What is a hit? What is a click-through? If an automated program (called a search bot or a crawler) reads our web page, should that count or not? Obviously, the organization selling advertising would argue that it counts, whereas the advertiser would prefer to only count human eyeballs, but the measurement system can't tell the difference—a click is a click to a computer. Therefore, while some say that online advertising is more trackable, I say that trackability is more illusionary than real. It is still our responsibility to figure out whether click-throughs and hits turn into the resulting action of a sale.

Many people swear by Google keywords or Ad Words. With Google Ad Words, you bid a certain amount for each word that you choose. For example, if you bid on "tai chi", whenever anyone went to Google and typed in "tai chi," if you bid more than anyone else for that ad word, you become the sponsored ad that appears next to the search result websites on Google. You don't have to pay anything unless someone clicks on your ad, so the promise is that you are only paying for effective advertising.

I believe Google Ad Words can be very useful, but we need to be careful. Guessing which words people might type in when looking for our services is difficult; there are simply too many variations and choices. Furthermore, clicks don't equal sales. I had one client who was spending $400 a day (almost $150,000 a year) on Google Ad Words. He thought that it was the most effective advertising he was doing, and he showed me the statistics that indicated he was getting more than 500 click-throughs a day as a result. Theoretically, it sounds wonderful. We know that millions of people search using Google every hour of every day, so it seems reasonable to think that 500 would search on the words we chose to pay for. But when I followed up with an investigation into exactly how many actual sales that $400 a day investment provided, I discovered that the number was incredibly small.

I suspect that if we were inclined to spend a few thousand dollars investigating further, we would find that, in addition to search bots that mimic human click-throughs, we would find many of those click-throughs were from existing customers. People are lazy. They don't like to type in website names—even when they know them. It is so much easier to go to the Google search bar, type in the first few letters (because the name comes up if you typed it before), and then click on the ad that appears next to the list. Bling! We just paid for a customer who was using Google to get to our website, but who was not a new potential customer searching for our products or services.

While there may be something to be said for making it easier for our customers to find us, the truth is the same process works without our paying for the ad word. We still appear in the list when the customer searches. The only difference is our web page appears under the search box instead of to the right. It is much more effective to simply understand how Google search engine works so that we can get higher on the search list without paying a penny.[3]

Search Engine Optimization (SEO) is the industry that has grown up around getting higher on search engine listings. Many entrepreneurs believe they must pay for SEO services to get listed, but that is not true. I warn all my clients to consider carefully before hiring SEO services. Some SEO services backfire because they try to game the search engine algorithms. What gets us to the top of the list one day may plunge us to the bottom of the list the next, or even worse, blacklisted for trying to game the system.

Google refines their search engine rules all the time. They publish a list of best practices for websites so we can ensure that we have the best chance of getting highest priority on the list.[4] We can increase our chances of getting higher on the list by following the guidelines that they recommend.

First, we should avoid content managers (such as Joomla or Wordpress) because they don't provide content in a format that search engines can read. We should include unique page titles, headings, and meta-keys on each page of our website. (I know—entering page titles and meta-keys is extremely time consuming because we can't automate the process. We also can't count on our web developer to do it. Usually, we must give them the keywords and titles to enter or enter them ourselves.)

Furthermore, we should use text, not graphical, menus. As a matter of fact, more text content and fewer images and videos is better. Additionally, make absolutely sure there are no grammatical errors or misspellings anywhere on our web pages. We may think a single misspelling is unimportant, but the search engines think misspellings are a sign of a spammy site, so they downgrade them.

The longer we have a website and domain name, the better; longevity give us lots of credibility in the eyes of a search engine. That means we shouldn't change our name or domain if at all possible. Furthermore, we should change a percentage of the content on our website frequently (like weekly), but not too frequently (daily is too often). If we change our content too frequently, the search engine thinks we are an aggregator site (sharing content from other sites but not providing our own content) and downgrades us in the listings. If we don't change our content frequently enough, we are downgraded as a nondynamic site.

Finally, we are raised in the listings when other sites link to ours, so it is a good idea to get as many sites as possible to put links on their sites leading to our site (but not so many that we trip the fraud alert and get downgraded).

How Much to Spend on Media

Many businesses follow the rule of thumb that 80 percent of the total marketing budget should be spent on media advertising. However, this is not a universal rule. Much depends on the type of industry, the size of the market, and the longevity of the business.

If we manage our advertising media plan correctly, we can commit to longer time frames or more frequent advertisements at a lower cost. These are known as contract rates or frequency rates. The key is signing a contract outlining the entire buy. The difference in price is significant, which may be one of the reasons ad-hoc advertising doesn't work well.

Additionally, sometimes, publications, television, or radio can offer some editorial coverage surrounding our business, products, or services, especially if it is highly relevant to their readers. News organizations may provide just a bit more coverage to organizations that have committed to long-term partnerships through a contract agreement.

Sometimes, being a new advertiser has its advantages. We might get a premium position in a publication at no additional charge, or gratis spots during overnight times on radio or television.

If we have a product or service that we are willing to offer in exchange for free advertising space or time, we may, at least for a portion of our advertising investment be able to cut our cash costs. Some media, such as radio stations, welcome the idea of getting gift certificates or gift cards that can be used as incentives for their listeners. The added on-air mentions that we receive during the giveaways and promotions can be powerful. Similarly, occasionally, a media company may agree to be a sponsor of an event or activity for which our business is doing a promotional effort, such as an in-store celebrity appearance, a book signing, or a sweepstakes or give-away. In turn, this could result in donated ad space or time in that medium as part of the sponsorship agreement.

We can also cut costs by using an agency with a specialized media-buying service. We may find that savings enjoyed are far greater than the fees charged by these companies, mostly because they are placing larger amounts of advertising, perhaps on their own bulk contracts, through reps with which they have long-standing relationships.

Media Mix

Deciding on the balance of the media mix is a delicate matter. Too little will run the risk of not being seen or heard, and too much may be a waste of our money. It is difficult to know when the market will be saturated with our message. In the graphic illustration in Figure 7.1, we see that under a certain point, our advertising is not effective because we are not spending enough. Over a certain point, any additional dollars we spend are not bringing us any additional business because our target market is saturated. We need to find the sweet spot in the middle.

Generally, it is not a good idea to limit advertising to one media, although we don't necessarily have to utilize all media. To figure out what percent we want to spend on which media, we start with our overall budget. We start with fixed-cost formats such as print, online, and outdoor media. Then, we can look at the more flexible investments of radio and/or television. We will always make adjustments and reshape our media plan over time, trying new things, eliminating media with which we have had little response. Trial and error is normal for any business putting an advertising plan in place for the first time.

It may be helpful to understand the terms that advertising people use, such as reach, frequency, GRPs, and CPM. Reach is the number of individuals (or, in some cases, households) who have seen or heard an advertisement at least one time, expressed as a percentage of the overall population. Reach is also an unduplicated count of the audience.

Frequency is the number of times an individual (or, in some cases, a household) has seen or heard an advertisement, typically expressed in terms of average number of times per month. GRPs, or Gross Rating Points, like reach, shows a calculation of the total number of exposures of individuals to your advertising. But in the case of GRPs, the totals are derived from all exposures, meaning there is audience duplication. The simplest way to arrive at our GRPs is to multiply our average reach times

Figure 7.1. Relationship between Advertising Dollars and Amount of Influence

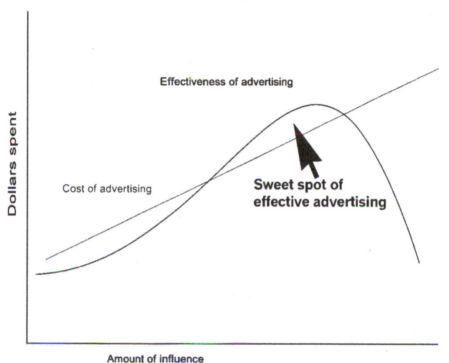

Source: James R. Ogden and Scott Rarick, *The Entrepreneur's Guide to Advertising.* Santa Barbara, CA: Praeger, 2009.

the frequency that each of those individuals sees or hears our ad. Reach times frequency equals GRPs.

CPM (or Cost Per Thousand) is derived from taking our total investment in a medium divided by the number of total viewers or listeners who come in contact with the ad or schedule (in thousands). This calculation gives us a comparable figure for each different media investment based on the cost to reach 1,000 people with each.

Ultimately, it will be up to us to decide what the best reach and frequency are for our advertising. More complicated products and services require more frequency to convey the full message. Simpler products and services may obtain a greater reach with less frequency.

Flight Plan

Advertising campaigns work most effectively as part of an entire multimonth or multiyear plan. Advertisers call this a flight plan, and it typically looks like a Gantt chart for advertising (Figure 7.2).

Figure 7.2. Example Flight Plan

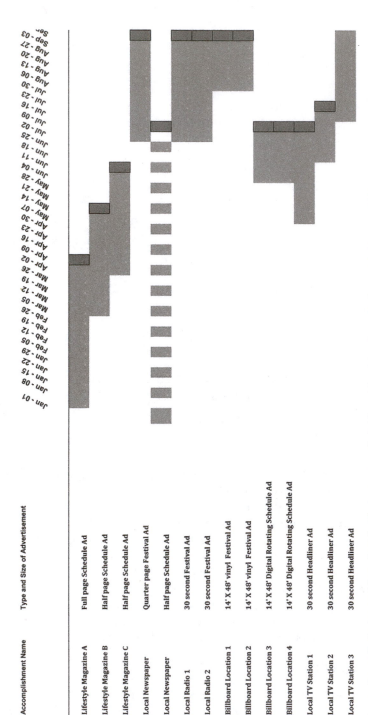

Source: James R. Ogden and Scott Rarick, *The Entrepreneur's Guide to Advertising*. Santa Barbara, CA: Praeger, 2009.

Measuring the Effectiveness of Advertising

Advertising effectiveness should be measured twice—before the plan has been implemented, and again, several months after the plan has been implemented. In the initial phases of the campaign, we want to assess the value of the concept that we've created for our targeted audience (before we've spent all the money on the implementation).

The concept test helps us get a feel for our audience's reaction to our campaign ideas. We can execute the concept test ourselves, or outsource it to an advertising agency. After the advertising campaign is over (or, if a continuously running campaign, after at least four or five months in order to give the campaign time to work), we test again, this time with more actual data such as sales. Methods used to undertake testing include, but are not limited to the following:

- Focus Groups. In a focus group, advertising researchers invite a small group of people in from an overall sample. These six to 12 individuals then give their opinions about advertising
- Delphi Technique. The Delphi Technique is a structured technique that follows certain rules about which questions to ask of how many people on a topic. It is commonly used to ask decision makers what they think about a particular advertising campaign so that sales forecasts can be predicted based upon their responses.
- Rating or Scaling. We often develop scales in research to try and figure out the strength of an advertisement or brand. The scale may read on one side, "totally love the advertisement," and on the other, "totally hate the advertisement." The results of the research are tallied and shared.
- In-depth Personal Interviews. Because we often find that 20 percent of our customers provide us with 80 percent of our revenue, we may wish to speak with the best customers in order to get their opinions on advertising campaigns.
- Opinion Polls or Questionnaires. Questionnaires can be sent to large samples of the target audience in order to assess some item, such as the effectiveness of the advertisement.
- Paired Comparison Tests. In a paired comparison test, respondents are asked to give their opinions about which one of a pair of similar products, services, or objects they like better. This allows advertisers to measure consumer preference based upon competing advertisements.

SUMMARY OF BRANDING AND ADVERTISING

We establish our position in the marketplace through branding and advertising.

☑ Branding is more than a logo; it is our hedgehog concept communicated to our target market.

☑ Brands are intangible, but can add tangible value to our business in many different ways if they are carefully managed.

☑ Advertising is a mass media communication over which we have total control because we pay for it.

☑ Advertising works best when planned in bulk, professionally developed, and frequent enough to make a difference to our future customers.

☑ Each type of media has advantages and disadvantages. We should choose a media mix which has the greatest reach and frequency for the least cost in our target market.

☑ There are several ways to measure advertising and marketing expenditures; it makes sense to follow through to ensure we are maximizing our marketing dollars.

8

Pricing and Proposing

I had a hard time figuring out where to draw the lines with market research, marketing, advertising, pricing, writing proposals, and selling. I rearranged the chapters several times before I finally decided that pricing and writing proposals had to go into a chapter together.

Small entrepreneurial businesses tend to be a lot more flexible in pricing alternatives, especially for service businesses. That makes pricing a much bigger deal than it would be in a large corporation, where the pricing of commodities is pretty cut and dry.

In the books in the series, the little there was about pricing was handled expertly as part of *The Entrepreneur's Guide to Marketing* by Bob Everett. Writing proposals was skillfully handled as part of *The Entrepreneur's Guide to Writing Business Plans and Proposals* by Dennis Chambers.

Nonetheless, I wasn't satisfied that there was enough in any of the books about using a break-even analysis to calculate pricing. Given its importance to entrepreneurs, I added that topic, and included a how-to on the *goal seek* feature of Excel, which I use all the time to calculate optimal pricing and break-even analysis.

PRICING

Once we've done all of the market research, analyzed our target market, and positioned our products and services, it is time to identify the pricing of our products.

Improper pricing is one of those deathtraps, according to Fred Beste (1996). It is important to understand the factors that influence pricing and the strategies that are best utilized by entrepreneurs to ensure proper pricing.

Factors that Influence Pricing

There are several factors that impact our pricing decision: price elasticity, product cost, perceived scarcity, and market demand.

Price Elasticity

Price elasticity is the concept that demand is a function of the price. More people will be able to afford an item at a lower price, and fewer people will be able to afford an item at a high price (but we need fewer people to purchase it to make a profit). The classic comparison is between a Rolex watch ($9,000) or a watch from Timex ($40). Only two people a month might be willing and able to spend $9,000 on a watch, while 450 people a month might be willing to buy a Timex watch. Both have the same gross sales figure of $18,000. In other words, if the price is higher, only the people who will derive benefit greater than the cost increase will buy. If the price is lower, more people may buy because the added value of the product or service is higher than the cost threshold.

Price elasticity is measured as the percentage change in revenue as the result of a percentage change in price. For example, suppose we sell a software program for $200. At that price, we can sell 500 per month. We decide to raise our price to $250—a 25 percent increase. We notice that sales drop to 400 per month. That is a 20 percent drop. The price elasticity, then, would be measured as the change in demand, divided by the change in price. The price elasticity ratio would be calculated as 20/25 or 0.8.

If the price elasticity ratio is less than 1.0, the product or service is considered inelastic. Demand does not drop off as much as the price increases. If demand for our product is inelastic, raising our prices will increase our profit. We could establish a higher, rather than lower, price without hurting sales too much.

However, if demand for our product is elastic (i.e., the price elasticity ratio is greater than 1.0), then sales will increase disproportionately to a price cut. We would lose money by raising prices because fewer people would purchase the item. But we would make more money by cutting our price because more people would purchase the product or service.

Paradoxically, sometimes the sales volume of an item *increases* when the price goes up. Setting a price often instills in the mind of the customer the *value* of the item. A book that is too cheap is easily dismissed. It couldn't possibly contain any information of value because it is too cheap and easy to get. A book that is more expensive seems to (in the mind of the customer) have a lot more value. In the mind of the customer, *They* (meaning the publisher) *couldn't charge so much if it wasn't valuable.*

This concept works in many fields. Cheap consulting is perceived as less valuable than expensive consulting. More expensive health treatments are perceived as more effective even when research shows them to be less effective than cheaper alternatives. Increasing the price of items may change the perception of value of the products or services.

Cost of the Product or Service

The most influential factor in the price of the item is the cost (though we shouldn't necessarily consider cost a limitation, as we will see when we discuss pricing strategies). Furthermore, the cost of a product or service is often influenced by the volume of item sold.

I'm sure you've heard about clueless entrepreneurs who are losing money on every sale, thinking they will make it up in volume. Underlying this old joke is a misunderstanding about the break-even analysis. We always lose money on every sale (no matter how many items we sell) *until the fixed expenses plus the variable expenses are paid off*. Once the fixed expenses are paid, we make money on every sale. So, in a way, we can make it up in volume—but only under certain circumstances. Over a certain volume, we can sell enough products to make a profit. Under that volume, we cannot make a profit.

But if the variable cost of the item is higher than the selling price, we lose money every time we sell an item. The higher the sales volume, the higher our losses.

Market Demand

Earlier, we discussed that it is difficult to create a new market. In most cases, the demand is what the demand is. There is a certain percentage of people who have a need for, and money to purchase, our products and services. No matter how much product and service we have available, we can only sell what the market is demanding to buy. Advertising and branding can increase demand in the long haul, but the cost to increase the demand may outstrip the margin we receive on the products we sell to fulfill that demand.

Perceived Scarcity

Market demand is not completely inflexible, however. In addition to increasing demand by advertising and promoting the characteristics of a product or service, we can increase demand by making it appear that the product or service is scarce. An inexpensive product or service easily available at all times becomes a commodity, and is doomed to a low margin (or even a loss). A product or service that is perceived as difficult to obtain ends up with increased demand. The scarcity prevents our product or service from being perceived as a commodity, which enables us to raise our prices.

Pricing Strategies

Recognizing the factors that impact costs, we still must establish a pricing strategy. How do we properly price our products and services?

Bob groups the pricing strategies under a general description called discrimination pricing, which means that we should price based upon the intersection of the characteristics of the products/services and the characteristics of our target customer base.

Discrimination pricing can be broken out into several pricing strategies. Some of them can be utilized by large established corporations, but tend to be less effective for entrepreneurs. In this section, I decided to identify them as *Pricing Strategies to Avoid* so that we can clearly see that they are not recommended. The recommended pricing strategies for smaller organizations, startups, and entrepreneurs are presented and discussed individually. They are—What the Market Will Bear, Highest Quality, Brand Status, Restricted Availability, Convenience, Consultive Selling, and Community Support. Our final section will discuss why it is important to include all the costs when calculating our price using each of these pricing strategies.

Pricing Strategies to Avoid

A larger established corporation has resources, cash, and usually a plethora of products and services so that they can employ several pricing strategies. Two of them are usually out of reach to smaller entrepreneurial organizations because of a lack of resources and cash. In most cases, these two pricing strategies should be avoided by small startup organizations. They are lowest price and loss leader.

Lowest Price

Fred Beste tells of the entrepreneurial statement that he's heard way too often, and every time he hears it, he gets nauseated because he knows it means the entrepreneurial endeavor is headed for the big toilet. The entrepreneurial statement (always accompanied by big smiles) is: "We're going to have the best product at the lowest price!"

Hopefully, I don't have to tell you that failure is bound to result from this strategy. It is impossible to have the best product at the lowest price.

We can have an acceptable-but-not-the-best product at the lowest price. We can have the best product, anywhere, at a higher price. But it is essentially impossible to do both at the same time. There is always a trade-off. A technology manager I knew would traditionally stop, look the client directly in the eye, and pointedly say, "Low Price, Fast, or High Quality. Pick one." Similarly, low price or high quality—pick one.

Large multinational businesses (think Walmart) will always have the edge in costs over smaller entrepreneurial or regional companies due to volume. Entrepreneurial endeavors (think Joe's Corner Store) generally cannot sell volume. Since volume is often the basis for low pricing, usually only larger businesses can compete on price. For us to try and compete with them on price when their costs are x and our costs are $2x$ is a recipe for failure. We must find some other differential on which to compete other than price or we are doomed.

Loss Leader

A loss leader is when a company provides a product or service at less than its market cost (sometimes even free) in order to gain market share or to sell other products and services at a higher markup. A convenience store that sells eggs, butter, and milk at a low price (while charging 200 percent markup for candy bars and sodas) is one example. Providing free web services in order to attract an audience for advertisers is another loss leader strategy.

For entrepreneurs, this is a risky strategy and needs to be carefully considered. Loss leaders only work well when the company has enough cash and enough profits from somewhere else to cover the losses. Sometimes those profits come after the market share has been attained when the organization can raise prices. Other times profit from other products and services cover the losses.

One of my clients sells canned training at a loss, but the gross margins obtained on the custom training and consulting services more than cover the losses of the training services. In this situation, the canned training serves as a marketing cost for the more lucrative services. But they would not be able to do this if they were just starting out; if we need to be profitable right away, we can't start with a loss leader.

What the Market Will Bear

"What the market will bear" is a oft-repeated phrase by salespeople seeking to establish the price of something. Basically, this strategy is to identify what the perceived value of the product or service is in the mind of the customer.

The auction is the prime place to see this pricing strategy at work. How much is an item worth? Whatever someone is willing to pay for it. This pricing strategy works well for scarce, highly valuable items (think paintings and sculptures). It also works well for products and services that are sold individually, person to person, such as real estate or life coaching services. Unfortunately, sometimes the market will only bear a price that is well below the cost of the product or service, making this a losing pricing strategy at times.

Additionally, the price of each individual sale is highly dependent upon the skill of the salesperson, which makes it difficult to reproduce or scale. This works best if we, ourselves, serve as our own sales force.

Highest Quality

We can provide, and charge more for, higher quality than otherwise available. Large businesses usually sacrifice quality in order to achieve volume.

Let us consider violins, for example. There is just no way to mass produce high-quality Stradivarius violins. Peccard violins, however, are mass produced by the millions. Stradivarius violins must each be painstakingly handmade, using specialized materials. If Stradivarius tried to sell violins at the same price as a Peccard, they would quickly go out of business because the price wouldn't cover the costs. But a Stradivarius, we believe, is higher quality. So, it can cost a hundred times more than a Peccard.

Very small organizations can often produce high-quality results (albeit at a higher cost). Higher pricing works especially well in industries where knowledge of the domain or talent is a factor. People with higher than typical knowledge and understanding of a particular product or service can provide a higher-quality product or service than available anywhere else.

This pricing strategy works especially well for small shops and artisans (people who sell a superior version of what would typically be a commodity such as bread or bowls). Artisan bread, for example, typically sells for between $8 and $15 a loaf. Regular bread might sell for less than $2 a loaf, making the price differential a 400 to 750 percent markup.

Quality at a higher price can sell, especially now that the Internet makes it possible for us to sell all over the world. The key to success for this pricing strategy is the reputation that must be built, often slowly over time, so that the markets (i.e., the buyers) recognize the higher quality.

Restricted Availability

A related strategy (often used in conjunction with high quality and brand status) is to (perhaps artificially) restrict availability. By restricting availability of a product or services to *just under* market demand, we can create the appearance of scarcity. It is human nature to want what we cannot have, so when customers are told they cannot have something, demand for that thing tends to build, increasing the value of the service or product.

Artisans, by their very nature, can only produce so many products. An artisan bread maker might be able to fit only 30 or 40 loaves into their ovens every day. A flute maker might be able to hand-make only two flutes every year. Doctors and consultants use this method when they make clients and patients wait weeks or months for an appointment. Disney uses this method when all of the copies of children's movies, such as *Snow White* or *Cinderella*, are pulled from the shelves and only released every 10 years or so (Brenda 2013).

Restricting availability causes pent-up demand, which enables a higher price for when the product or service is finally available.

Brand Status

Often, the extra value of a product or service is the perceived status based on marketing and branding rather than any real difference. Recently, a number of well-known music experts took part in a double-blind test by listening to a Stradivarius violin and another, mass produced, modern, less expensive violin. The experts could not tell the difference between them.

Note that this result does not impact the price of the Stradivarius. The value of a Stradivarius is in the brand. A musician's credibility and reputation increase when it is known that the musician plays a Stradivarius.

A Movado or a Rolex watch may not necessarily keep time as well as a Timex. But these watches are not purchased just to tell time (especially in this day of cell phones, when no one needs a watch to know what time it is). Brand-name watches are status symbols. Wearing one publicizes to everyone the success of the business people wearing them without the need to tell them verbally.[1]

When we purchase designer clothes, we are paying for the name, the branding, and the marketing. The clothes themselves are often made of inferior material with inferior stitching methods, but the perceived raised status among our friends and frenemies when we wear the clothes (with the designer name proudly appearing on the outside of the clothes where everyone can see) is enough to get us to plunk down extra dollars over the Kmart or Walmart brands. Therefore, this pricing model must include the costs (apportioned and accrued appropriately) of all of the marketing, branding, and selling instead of solely the cost of the material goods or services.

Convenience

Often, we can sell our products and services on the basis of the convenience of the purchasing process. Are we easier to deal with than the competition? Do we have a human being answer the phone instead of an IVR (Interactive Voice Response system, the most heinous of all the customer non-service products) commonly utilized by large companies? Do we have a retail location close to our customer base?

Consultive Selling

Another pricing strategy is based in more knowledgeable salespeople. If our salespeople are more knowledgeable and responsive than typical salespeople in the field, we can sell at a higher price. Home Depot used this pricing strategy when they started offering competitive salaries to trades people (plumbers, carpenters, drywall installers, painters, etc.) to get them to become salespeople in their retail stores.

One of the most difficult transition periods for entrepreneurs is when we hire salespeople. If our business is service-based, our product choices complex or highly configurable, we are using our expertise in the sales process. Because professional salespeople do not have our expertise, they cannot sell the same way. The extensive index of knowledge in our heads, possibly developed over decades in the industry, cannot be shared with someone in weeks or months of training.

The most successful entrepreneurs understand this limitation of consultive selling, and limit their staff to administrative support positions (generating leads, scheduling meetings, following up with billing, etc). If we try to hire someone who is also already highly knowledgeable in the domain, we may find twofold difficulties. First, those already highly knowledgeable in the industry would charge a lot of money for their services. Second, they may compete with us for clients, and end up quitting, and taking some of our client base with them.

If we build our business on consultive selling (and pricing) strategies, we need to be cognizant of the limitations in transferring to the next generation or selling our business. Typically, this problem is handled as part of the sales agreement by our continuing on for a few years after the business has been sold or transferred. Alternatively, when a business owner who has used consultive selling is ready to sell, they may first modify their business model, and tweak the products and services so that they no longer require consultive selling methods to sell.

Community Support

Another pricing strategy is to connect the product or service with a community-supported interest that benefits by the sale. Customers pay a premium for fair trade coffee because they care about the farmers and producers of that coffee, and don't want to contribute to unfairly exploiting them (which some coffee producers have been accused of in the past.)

Hershey Foods sells candy bars through school groups at a premium price, but the school or club gets to keep a large portion of the margin, so friends and family of the students purchase the candy bars in larger quantities than they would if they were just buying them through a store.

PBS sells music and videos and other products by linking them to a pledge. A DVD of 1960s' rock and roll videos and music might cost $35 each to produce, but if you give $150 to the PBS station fund drive, you get a copy of the DVD as a premium for your contribution.

People don't mind paying a little extra for the products or services if they know the proceeds (or at least some of the proceeds) are going to a community supported nonprofit interest.

Calculating All Costs

It is important to consider all the costs involved in calculating the costs using these pricing strategies. A common mistake among entrepreneurs and small business owners is to calculate the cost of a product or service without considering any indirect costs such as sales, administration, marketing, facilities, and so on. In a large company with high volumes and/or a large number of products and services, the percentage of indirect costs is often negligible when apportioned across hundreds of services or products. That's why some accounting textbooks and classes ignore fixed costs when discussing how to calculate the price of an item. To a small company, however, the price of indirect or fixed costs is a major factor in the cost of our products and services. We must apportion those costs fairly across all products and services in order to calculate the price of each one.

For consultative selling to be part of an effective pricing strategy, for example, we must include the cost of the consult in the selling of the service and/or product. Otherwise, we are just giving away our services for free (never a winning pricing strategy in the long term unless you have other products or services with lucrative margins).

The bottom line is that we need to include the costs of convenience, branding, and knowledge level when we price our products and services. If we offer a product or service more conveniently than our competitors but price it the same, we will go out of business while our competitors survive because they are not paying the extra costs for humans to answer the phones or rent the locations that are more convenient. If we pay a lot of extra money for branding and marketing, but don't include them in pricing the product, we won't meet the break-even point, and we will go out of business.

Common Mistakes in Apportioning Costs

As noted earlier, some entrepreneurs make the mistake of apportioning the fixed costs to one product, and ignoring fixed costs for another product. This makes it appear that one is profitable and the other is not. You can see in the fictional example in Table 8.1 and Table 8.2. (Well, the numbers are all fictional. We are using three book titles in the series for the products as an example.) Let's say that the fixed cost of this publisher is $1,000,000 a year. They sell three book titles. They expect to sell 10,000 copies of the first book, 8,000 copies of the second book, and 23,000 copies of the third book. They are trying to price the books, and start out with $39.95 price to see if they can make a profit at that price.

If they equally apportion the fixed costs to each book, it looks like the first two books are dogs and the third book is the only profitable one. If they apportion all of the fixed costs to the third one, it looks like the first and the second are profitable and the third one is a dog.

Table 8.1. Misapportionment of Fixed Costs—Equal Distribution

	EGT Selling	EGT Advertising	EGT Managing IT
Number of Units Sold	10,000	8,000	23,000
Price per Unit	$ 39.95	$ 39.95	$ 39.95
Sales (# units * Price per unit)	$ 399,500	$ 319,600	$ 918,850
Variable Costs	$ 180,000	$ 96,000	$ 276,000
Gross Profit	$ 219,500	$ 223,600	$ 642,850
Fixed Costs	333,333	333,333	333,333
Net Profit	$ (113,833)	$ (109,733)	$ 309,517

Source: HPL Consortium, Inc., copyright 2014, used with permission.

Table 8.2. Misapportionment of Fixed Costs—Loading on One Product

	EGT Selling	EGT Advertising	EGT Managing IT
Number of Units Sold	10,000	8,000	23,000
Price per Unit	$ 39.95	$ 39.95	$ 39.95
Sales (# units * Price per unit)	$ 399,500	$ 319,600	$ 918,850
Variable Costs	$ 180,000	$ 96,000	$ 276,000
Gross Profit	$ 219,500	$ 223,600	$ 642,850
Fixed Costs	–	–	1,000,000
Net Profit	$ 219,500	$ 223,600	$ (357,150)

Source: HPL Consortium, Inc., copyright 2014, used with permission.

This type of financial analysis mistake is much more common than we realize. Entrepreneurs frequently start a business based upon a single product or service. When they add a second product or service, they only consider the direct costs of the new product or service when calculating the price, so they often underprice. They may be thinking that they have to pay the administrative costs anyway for the first product, so it shouldn't count against the second product. But the second product is using the administrative and organizational resources.

One of my clients, Jan, had a plumbing business. Jan started a second division in one of the empty buildings owned by the business—a gas station. Jan kept thinking the gas station was profitable and the plumbing business was losing money because administrative costs of running the gas station weren't calculated as part of the cost. Jan reasoned that since the same people and same office as the plumbing business were running the gas station, there were no added costs.

If Jan had correctly apportioned the fixed costs, it would have been clear that the gas station was a money pit that was draining needed resources from the only profitable division—plumbing. As plumbing sales went down and gas station sales went up, the business was losing more and more money every month because the gross margin on plumbing was high and the gross margin on gas was low. What Jan needed to do was properly apportion the indirect costs.

Of course, the only way to tell at what price point we can achieve a volume that is profitable for each product or service is to calculate the break-even point. We can use the Goal Seek function of Excel to calculated exactly what price we would need to get the desired profit (as explained in detail in Appendix E).

Properly Apportioning Costs

Which brings us back to the question—how do we apportion fixed costs? The best thing to do would be to figure out exactly what portion of our fixed costs each product or service uses, but that entails making everyone keep time sheets on how much time they indirectly spend on each product (which adds even more to the administrative costs because keeping track of time takes time away from production). We would also have to segregate equipment and facility space, marketing resources, and so on. For most business operations, tracking actual costs by product or service is unfeasible (another reason why it is often ignored).

There are a couple of ways to apportion the cost based upon the specific business other than the misleading ways shown in Table 8.1 or calculating actual time and resources. We can apportion them by volume or by sales.

Apportioning based on volume is easy to calculate, and works well when the gross margin on all the units is equivalent. We can see in Table 8.3, where the variable costs do not work when the gross margins are different. The first product has a cost of $18 per unit and the second and third units have a variable cost of $12 per unit. Basing the apportionment on volume would make the first product seem unprofitable even at higher volumes than the second book.

A better way would be to apportion fixed costs based upon gross profit dollars, which is a function of both volume and gross margin. Table 8.3 illustrates that under this scenario, each of the products appears profitable, proportionate to each other because each bears a proportionate amount of the fixed costs.

There are two difficulties with these methods. Little of this information (volume, gross profit, fixed costs) is known when calculating the optimum pricing. This means we need to do this calculation twice. The first time, we estimate the profitable pricing and the volume needed to obtain the desired profit. To do that, we play with the numbers either by entering in different numbers to see the results, or by using the Goal Seek function to calculate the price based upon a set volume. We can also calculate the volume based upon a set price. This becomes our pricing strategy.

Table 8.3. Apportioning Fixed Costs Based on Volume

	EGT Selling	EGT Advertising	EGT Managing IT
Number of Units Sold	10,000	8,000	23,000
Price per Unit	$ 39.95	$ 39.95	$ 39.95
Sales (# units * Price per unit)	$ 399,500	$ 319,600	$ 918,850
Variable Costs	$ 180,000	$96,000	$ 276,000
Gross Profit	$ 219,500	$ 223,600	$ 642,850
Fixed Costs	243,902	195,122	560,976
Net Profit	$ (24,402)	$ 28,478	$ 81,874

Source: HPL Consortium, Inc., copyright 2014, used with permission.

Table 8.4. Apportionment Based on Gross Profit

	EGT Selling	EGT Advertising	EGT Managing IT
Number of Units Sold	10,000	8,000	23,000
Price per Unit	$ 39.95	$ 39.95	$ 39.95
Sales (# units * Price per unit)	$ 399,500	$ 319,600	$ 918,850
Variable Costs	$ 180,000	$ 96,000	$ 276,000
Gross Profit	$ 219,500	$ 223,600	$ 642,850
Fixed Costs	202,127	205,903	591,970
Net Profit	$ 17,373	$ 17,697	$ 50,880

Source: HPL Consortium, Inc., copyright 2014, used with permission.

Then, at the end of the month, quarter, or year, we must do the calculation again based upon the actuals instead of the estimates to see how close we got to guessing the volumes and costs. If we do this every month, quarter, and year, over time, we will get better and better at doing the estimate so that eventually, our pricing strategy will always be right on the money instead of wildly inaccurate. If we do not compare the actuals to the estimates (and you might be surprised at how often business owners skip this essential step), then instead of getting better and better at pricing strategy, we get worse and worse. If not corrected occasionally, our poor pricing strategy will put us out of business.

We shouldn't worry too much about getting it right the first time. The estimates for a new product or service always start out wildly inaccurate. The most common mistake is overestimating the volume, followed closely by underestimating the fixed costs. But if we haven't fixed the estimated break-even point within a short time frame, we are setting ourselves up for trouble. It is during the follow up, when we compare our estimates to the actuals, that our pricing strategy can be proven effective.

Apportioning costs correctly leads to proper pricing. Once we've established our pricing strategy, we are ready for the next phase. Depending upon our business, that might be writing proposals.

WRITING PROPOSALS

Proposals are not about us, our business, or our products and services. The proposal should be about the reader, the customer, the client. Dennis articulated the First Law of Persuasion Dynamics to explain—*writers persuade only to the degree that we talk about the reader's concerns.*

A company may have the greatest service in the world, but if it is not a service people need, then they will not even listen to the pitch (nor should they).[2] Our proposals should deal solely and specifically with the client's needs and concerns. Otherwise, they won't achieve our goal, which is to sell.

Proposals That Sell

Some industries, such as consulting, thrive on proposals. Any industry where products, services, and pricing are individualized or customized generally requires a quote or proposal stage in the sales process. But even in these proposal-heavy industries, we may be better off modifying how we use proposals.

COMPUTER EDUCATIONAL
SERVICES & ETM ASSOCIATES, INC.: CASE 4

When I started my first business, I developed a sales proposal template. It was beautiful. Pictures of our training rooms. Descriptions of all the services we offered. Testimonials from satisfied clients. The backgrounds of all the top team members, the people who might be working on a contract from any one of the clients. Highly professional font. Good level of whitespace. We automated the whole system, inserting the client name throughout the document, providing paragraphs of choices, depending upon what type of client we might be talking with. Every time I met with a prospective client, I would find out what they needed, and then, I would spend hours customizing the proposal to what the client needed. I would carefully fill in the sections set up for the customized portion of the sales proposal.

Many clients commented on how professional and nice-looking the proposal was. Clients loved the in-depth analysis of their needs and the comprehensive options I provided to solve those needs. We got many compliments.

What we didn't get was sales.

I couldn't figure out why until many years later, in my fourth business venture, when I started taking sales coaching from Dave Bosler.[1] After taking one look at a sample proposal, Dave described to me what happened after I had delivered them to a client (before I had a chance to tell him). After I would present a proposal, the prospective client would compliment me on the proposal, and tell me they would be making the decision shortly. Then, they would read my proposal and utilize all of my carefully done analysis. The prospective clients would again get back to me full of compliments about how wonderful my proposal was and how much the committee or the boss (which until this point I hadn't even known were in the decision-making process) appreciated it and loved it, and that they would get back to me soon.

That would be the last I would hear from them.

I, of course, would spend time trying to follow up. Initial replies to my queries would be *too busy just now—we'll get to it shortly*, until eventually all my calls, e-mails, even visits would go unanswered.

Dave described this exchange and called it *Lie, Steal, Lie, Hide*. Prospects would lie about the decision-making process, steal my intellectual property (my analysis of the problem), lie about their intent to hire me, then hide when I tried to follow up. Until Dave pointed it out, I hadn't recognized the pattern. It was my own fault; I needed to find a better way to do proposals.

Dave told me to stop working on proposals entirely. Give them up. Never write another one again. As a consultant, to be told to give up writing proposals left me aghast and seriously doubting the credibility of my newfound sales coach. No proposals? How would I get business? All the consultants I knew wrote proposals. But, by that time, I was getting pretty desperate for clients, so I decided to give Dave's plan a try.

Instead of writing proposals, Dave told me to simply ask the client what they wanted to see in the proposal. And then to write that down, word for word in a letter. I was not allowed to use buzzword terminology. I was not allowed to include any boilerplate information, or my resume or anything at all about me or my business. Instead, I was to send them the information they wanted to see, assign a price, and send it back to them with a blank line at the bottom for them to sign, agreeing to allow me to start the work. I went from 30-page proposals to single-page agreements.

I also went from desperate for clients to flooded with work. Within one month of working with Dave, after giving up proposals, I had doubled my business. Within two months, I had tripled it. Within three months, I had quadrupled my business.

---

[1] Dave Bosler is still coaching business owners at the time of publication, and can be contacted by phone at (610) 207–2265, or by e-mail at davidbosler@gmail.com.

Ten Commandments for Writing a Killer Proposal

Dennis advocates an approach similar to Dave's when writing proposals. You will see what I mean when you read Dennis's first of 10 commandments for writing a killer proposal:

One. No boilerplate. Not even one paragraph.
Two. Begin with the assurance of compliance.
Three. Describe in your own words, not the language of the RFP, the exact outcome that the prospect is seeking in vocabulary the prospect understands.
Four. Deal with the money up front.
Five. Avoid writing about the company for 10 pages longer than you can stand it.
Six. Follow all rules for 21st-century grammar and punctuation.
Seven. Let one writer create the entire first draft, and let it be original to this project.
Eight. Avoid all clichés.
Nine. Create a Work Breakdown Structure or a Gantt Chart for your proposal project.
Ten. Do not delegate a proposal to junior people.

You can see from the beginning that this list of commandments is similar to the concept of asking the client what they want in the proposal and just putting what they want in it. Without any boilerplate text, the proposal becomes a document that simply describes what we heard the client say, and what our company can do for them (using the language they gave us). The second commandment, assurance of compliance, should be used in the case of responding to an RFP (request for proposal), and refers to a table listing the proposal requirements in one column and the response (including, perhaps, the page or section) to the requirements. It would provide the committees reviewing the proposal, at a glance, what they are looking for so the proposal can be quickly handed off to the real decision maker.

In his fifth commandment, Dennis cautions us to write as long as possible (for at least 10 pages longer than we can stand it) about the potential client and avoid writing about our own company. In practice, I've found that we can avoid writing about our company at all, especially if we have a web page or a LinkedIn profile that the prospect can review if they wish to look into our background or the company's history. Those external sources of information are infinitely more powerful than any standard text we might want to include in a proposal. Only information about our company that is directly relevant to our prospect's decision making should be included in the proposal.

The Art of Writing a Proposal

The art of writing a proposal is the ability to provide a document that:

- is all about the prospect
- communicates that we understand their situation completely
- communicates that our company has the solution to the problem
- outlines the cost to the prospect of failing to solve the problem
- shares how much it will cost the prospect to solve the problem
- discusses the value calculation (the difference between the cost of not solving it, and the cost of solving it)
- does not reveal any techniques or solutions that could be used to solicit a cheaper supplier

Of course, we also use all the techniques for good writing discussed in the chapter on writing our business plan, including clear and concise language, avoiding clichés, using professional fonts, spacing, and color.

SUMMARY OF PRICING AND PROPOSING

It is essential to properly calculate the break-even point for our products and services in order to establish the proper pricing strategy. Once we've established our pricing, we can meet the clients' needs by focusing our proposals on them and only them.

- ☑ Proper pricing is essential for business health.
- ☑ Our pricing strategy is influenced by price elasticity, product cost, perceived scarcity, and market demand.
- ☑ Entrepreneurs of startups might want to avoid two of the pricing strategies—lowest price and lost leader.
- ☑ Pricing strategies we might want to try include; what the market will bear, highest quality, brand status, restricted availability, convenience, consultive selling, and community support
- ☑ We need to include all the costs involved in our pricing strategy when calculating pricing.
- ☑ Pricing needs to include a fairly apportioned amount for indirect costs.
- ☑ Goal Seek is an Excel feature useful in calculating pricing.
- ☑ Proposals should be free of boilerplate or standard text.
- ☑ Proposals should be all about the customer, not about our company.

9

Selling

When I originally reviewed the proposal for the book *The Entrepreneur's Guide to Selling* from Jonathan London, I was immediately struck by the fact that Jonathan's book outlined many of the same concepts and techniques that Dave Bosler had taught me. Further investigation revealed that many sales methods have common elements. Terminology and specific techniques differed, but the keys to learning how to sell have a common base among all methods.

Sales training guru David Sandler notes that there's been nothing new in sales methods since World War II (Sandler 1995), and he is right. Despite all the new technology, new channels, and new methods to attract new customers, the actual final sales process has not changed at all.

LEARNING HOW TO SELL REQUIRES A COACH

When I first started in business, I believed that selling (like leadership) was one of those skills that people were born with, and I was not born that lucky. Then, I learned to sell from Dave Bosler, and I realized that selling (like leadership) can be taught.

If you are one of those people born with the natural talent of sales, congratulations! You have no idea what the rest of us go through.

Selling and leadership can be taught, but they can't be learned from a book. To learn to sell, one must be coached. In addition to reading the books in this series, I encourage you to find a live coach who can teach you, little by little, experience by experience, how to lead your team and sell your products, in your industry, in your marketplace. We can share specifics on what to do in these books, but only through practice under the guidance of a live coach can people move from the sidelines to the game. As the title of David Sandler's book says, "You Can't Learn to Ride a Bike at a Seminar."

COMMONALITY AMONG SELLING PROCESSES

Paraphrased here is a compilation description of Sandler's, Bosler's, London's (and hundreds of other sales method gurus) sales process:

1. We must uncover our prospect's *pain.*
2. We must discover the decision-making process our prospect uses when deciding to buy or not buy a product or service.
3. We must deal with the money issues.
4. We must present scenarios that enable our prospects to envision the cost of not getting rid of the pain.
5. We must present a solution that will get rid of the prospect's pain that is less than the cost of not getting rid of the pain.
6. We must post-sell our prospect so that they don't change their minds later.

ETM ASSOCIATES, INC.: CASE 5

I found myself, in 2001, trying to sell my technology consulting services in a recession-based world filled with unemployed technology consultants who were much better than me at pure technology. I knew I was in trouble after working hard, doing my best, authoring, and presenting dozens of proposals for three solid months, and only getting a run rate of $2,000 a month in sales. I knew what my fixed costs were, and they were more than $2,000 a month. I became a bit desperate, so I asked a fellow consultant for help. Tom Casey was a fellow consultant who I had originally gotten to know after he had made a great presentation at one of my many networking groups (Unit of One). (Incidentally, Tom later talked me into joining the Institute of Management Consultants—one of the best things I ever did—and if you are a consultant, I encourage you to join.) I asked Tom what I might be doing wrong. The first sentence out of his mouth was, "How do you find pain?" I responded, "What do you mean by pain?" He knew immediately that I was clueless about sales. I didn't even know how to look for pain, which is the key to selling! He told me to take a beginning course on sales. I followed his advice, and took a workshop through the local Chamber of Commerce from a sales coach named Dave Bosler (about whom you've already heard in Chapter 8 on Pricing and Proposals).

Finding Pain

One might think that pain is just another word for need, but pain is more than just need. Once we identify their pain, and if our products or services can soothe or heal their pain in any way, we have reached the sweet spot of sales. We have put ourselves in a place where we have the highest likelihood of success—a sale.

It is important to recognize that the cost of pain is not always financial. The key to understanding pain? Pain is often emotional. Pain is an aching wound that begs someone, anyone, to help it heal at any cost. Prospects are embarrassed by their pain, or in denial about their pain. They will not, often cannot, acknowledge their pain to anyone, much less a salesperson. They hide their pain, being unable to consciously attach any importance to it.

Emotional pain is a much stronger motivation for purchases than financial pain, and more likely to end up in a sale. The combination of both financial and emotional pain is the most powerful of all.

Consider the amount of money we spend on our pets in this country. The American Pet Product Association estimates that we spend over $55 million on our pets. There is no financial gain in owning a pet, but the emotional benefits are quite powerful. Another powerful pain that often prompts a purchase is avoiding the perception of being ignored by our peers and bosses. Many products and services are purchased to gain recognition, which may (or may not) lead to financial benefit. Designer products and media services take advantage of this all-too-human instinct to stand out above the crowd and be admired by others.

Sweet Spot

The first question to ask ourselves is whether or not our products and services are really, truly, a good fit for the customer. Will the product or service sooth their pain? If the answer is no, then we need to move on.

One of the most important lessons I learned about sales was that the purpose of a sales dialog was not to make a sale. The purpose of a sales dialog is to eliminate, as quickly as possible, those people for whom our products and services are not a good fit. The name for this process is called prospecting. We are looking for those few tiny nuggets of gold (people with the pain that is soothed by our products) among the mountains of rock (people who don't have pain, or whose pain would not be soothed by our products or services). The sweet spot is the combination of a person with pain that is soothed by our products and services. Our next step is to ensure that the prospect recognizes their own pain (which, as noted earlier, is not always easy to do) so that we can help them.

Being Trustworthy

As with marketing, selling is all about relationships. Relationships are all about trust and likeability. Salespeople have learned to develop the skill of being able to get along with everyone, of appreciating everyone.

This state of affairs is not our natural instinct. Human beings have an initial filter. If we suspect someone doesn't like us, doesn't appreciate us, doesn't share our values, we won't be able to like them (without concerted effort). We like people who, first and foremost, like us and are like us.

That means that we, as salespeople, have to like everyone, and to be like everyone. We cannot have politics or convictions so strong they would interfere with our ability to respond positively to a potential client. Conservative? Liberal? Gun toting fanatic? Wimpy peacenik? Doesn't matter. Our first impression must be one of likeability and appreciation.

When I first heard the Dale Carnegie quote (Levine et al. 1993) about never meeting a man he didn't like, I thought it was bunk. At the time, I was full of judgments about people. This person was good, that person was evil, or at least not so good (or so I thought). Like many people, I valued people who valued the same things that I valued and felt that people who didn't meet my criteria didn't measure up. It was their responsibility to measure up to my standards, not my responsibility to lower my standards to accept them. My own judgmental nature was one of the reasons I was such a poor salesperson—until I learned the error of my ways.

It took me a while to understand that the problem was not them, the problem was me. I'd never even tried to put myself in their shoes, or understand their thinking. I never considered the possibility that my so-called high principles were damaging, or that my intolerance was insufferable. I did well with a few people, and I thought the problem was everyone else.

I was flat out wrong.

What I learned was that we have to respect and like everyone. Everyone. We can ignore those few behaviors or characteristics of people that we might find objectionable. Instead, we focus on the behaviors and characteristics we like and admire (even if we have to go searching for them). I now live the Dale Carnegie statement—I never meet anyone that I don't like.

The key is learning to listen.[1] By listening to people, we can figure out what we like about those people. We must be willing to devote the time necessary to get to know people at a deep level. We need to get beyond "what do you want" or even "what do you need." We move to that space where our prospects have learned to trust us. Our prospects know that we have the prospect's own best interests at heart.

We don't get there by lying, or bluffing, or showing off. We get there by actually being trustworthy, by actually having our prospects' best interests at heart.

There is more to it than that, of course. But being trustworthy is the foundation for everything else. If our prospects don't like us, if they don't trust us, they will not purchase anything from us.

Holistic Process of Sales

Jonathan views sales as a holistic process, from end to end. He delineated how each part of the sales process positively or negatively affects each phase. He identifies the following items as critical:

- Starting a sales opportunity in our "Sweet Spot" so we are ahead of the competition from the beginning
- Consciously creating an environment where people feel more comfortable with us so they tell us more and listen more to what we say
- Having a full sales funnel, which impacts our ability to sell and negotiate more effectively by giving us confidence
- Showing benefits from three perspectives—technical, business/financial, and individual/company
- Brainstorming solutions so we can differentiate our offer as much as possible
- Prospecting in the 21st century using Internet technologies to reach more people who need our products and services
- Being the best salesperson (as opposed to just relying on having the best product to sell)
- Knowing how best to present over the phone, over the web, or in person
- Honing our presentations and demonstrations to increase our percent of wins
- Eliminating objections to accelerate sales cycles and make our negotiations easier
- Handling the most common negotiation issues or tactics
- Avoiding the emotional roller coaster of selling by learning to deal effectively with stress and rejection

The Art of Selling

Selling is not a science, though there is a lot of underlying technique that is based upon psychology, neurology, neurolinguistic programming, and personality assessments. To identify whether or not we are in a good position to practice the art of selling to any particular prospect, we might want to answer the following questions:

- How good a fit is our product or service to the prospect's pain?
- How well do we get along with prospects?
- What further information do we need to know?
- How much time have we spent with the prospect?
- Is the prospect really interested?
- Is the prospect the right person to talk with (i.e., the decision maker)?
- How well do we know our own products and services?
- How well are our products and services differentiated from those of our competitors?
- How full is our sales funnel?

By answering these questions honestly, we can pinpoint exactly where we can most improve our sales process. The most common mistake is talking with someone who is not the decision maker (and wasting all of our time), or not spending enough time with the decision maker. Of course, getting to the decision maker is difficult; there are obstacles in the way, the biggest is the lack of time of the decision makers themselves. We tend to spend all our time with people whose company we enjoy who aren't in a position to purchase something from us. It is easy to convince ourselves that we are prospecting and networking when we are actually wasting time because facing the possibility of rejection from the decision makers is a hard thing to do.

But it is to our benefit if we can learn to recognize, early on, when the person we are talking with is not in a position to make a decision so that we can move on to the next person quickly. This skill is essential; it means the difference between wasting time and real prospecting.

Personality Characteristics: DiSC

One tool that sales trainers often utilize is the DiSC profile (a personality assessment offered by Inscape Publishing, briefly mentioned in the chapter on hiring people). DiSC has been around since the early 1960s. More than 37 million people worldwide use the profile to get insight into their behavior, as well as the behavior of others. Unlike the Myer's Briggs personality profile (which is commonly used in team building and group dynamics activities), DiSC isn't based upon innate tendencies, but rather, on emotional and behavioral responses to certain situations. The assessment is based on Dr. William Marston's studies of the emotions of normal people done in the 1920s. Marston's studies showed that human behavior is observable, situationally based, flexible, and dynamic. DiSC categorizes human behavior into four primary areas or behavior styles. Though we may behave differently in different situations, we tend to behave the same in similar situations, such as in a selling or buying process. Each style has its own preferences, as seen in Table 9.1 (Center for Internal Change Inc. 2013).

As salespeople, we need to be aware that desire and fear are important factors that drive people to take action. Selling is helping people get what they want. We also help them avoid what they don't want.

The most effective way to know which DiSC style our prospect might be is to pick up on their pace (fast or slow), tone (friendly or serious), how much data they want (a lot or little), and then mirror that subtly by tapping into our own behavior style that matches the prospect's. (Can you see why this needs to be coached?) We basically must learn to be a chameleon, and change our own style to match that of our prospect. Table 9.2 lays this out.

Table 9.1. DiSC Characteristics

DiSC Style	Pace	Tone of Voice	Desire	Fear
Dominance	Fast	Dominant, assertive, confident, impatient	Control, Power, and Results	Being out of control, taken advantage of, and failure
Influence	Fast	Expressive, outgoing, wordy	Influence, results, and being liked or popular	Not being liked
Steadiness	Slower	Calm, easy, comfortable, supportive	Stability, cooperation, maintenance of status quo	Change, conflict
Conscientiousness	Slower	Analytical, removed, cynical	Perfection, quality, and accuracy	Being criticized for poor quality

Source: Jonathan London, *The Entrepreneur's Guide to Selling.* Santa Barbara, CA: Praeger, 2009.

Table 9.2. Matching Our DiSC Style with Prospects' Styles

DiSC Style*	Pace	Tone of Voice	Amount of Information
Dominance	Fast	Dominant, assertive, confident, impatient	Less—bullet points—direct and to the point —focus on control and results
Influence	Fast	Expressive, outgoing, wordy	More than the D but not so much as the S or C—be more positive and effusive—paint a big picture
Steadiness	Slower	Calm, easy, comfortable, supportive	Lots of details, with a focus on how things are done, processes, stability
Conscienti-ousness	Slower	Analytical, removed, cynical	The most detailed, with a focus on perfection, quality and accuracy; the more-independent and unbiased the information, the better

Source: Jonathan London, *The Entrepreneur's Guide to Selling.* Santa Barbara, CA: Praeger, 2009.

Using the DiSC Traits to Gain Credibility

As salespeople, we should be aware that these behavioral traits are one of the factors that drive people to trust us and take action. We can help people get what they want, and avoid what they don't want, but only if we see ourselves through their lens.

People will buy from people they like and trust. There are many things we can do throughout a sales process to enable a prospect to choose us as someone with whom they are comfortable—find common ground, honestly present ourselves as competent, demonstrate our knowledge and experience, utilize the language of the client, empathize with them, actively listen to them, follow up with them.

The first step is to find some common business or personal experiences, background, or interests. We use informal conversation to explore our likes/dislikes, where we grew up, where we shop, hobbies, sports—anything that might form common ground between us.

The next step is to come across to them as competent. Without being pushy, again—as part of the informal conversation—we demonstrate preparation, knowledge, and experience. We share examples of times we followed up, and portray ourselves as reliable.

We also (again, informally, in conversation) demonstrate knowledge about our own products, as well as about the industry or environment the prospective customers are in. We need to be able to use the language of their business or the environment, and demonstrate knowledge of the acronyms familiar to them.

But what if we don't know their industry (or them) very well? Above all, we must be honest about what we do and do not know. We don't try to fake it, because nothing loses credibility faster than pretending to know something we don't or using an acronym incorrectly. If our clients and customers don't trust us, it is time to move on. If the prospect is not a good fit for our products and services, or if we don't know enough about their business, we should say "no" to the process and move on.

As noted earlier, one of my less successful clients was in the plumbing business. I thought that my general knowledge of business would be enough to help the client, but the client could not get past the fact that I didn't have any experience in the plumbing industry. Everything I suggested in terms of improvement was dismissed. The client simply did not believe that someone without plumbing experience could provide advice.

We want to mimic the language style of the person with whom we are speaking. We empathize them with them, putting ourselves in their shoes. We listen beyond what they are saying and feeling, to what they are not telling us. We don't just act concerned, we must truly *be* concerned. We want to help them, not just sell them something. Prospects can tell the difference. People can feel what we are feeling about them. And will respond accordingly.

You've heard the joke; "Sincerity is the key. Once you learn to fake that, you're golden!" Sincerity is, indeed, the key—but only if we learn to generate sincerity deeply within ourselves for another person. We can't fake it.

Perhaps the most important skill is to be a good listener. We need to learn to listen in many different ways. We can listen appreciatively in a relaxed manner, seeking enjoyment, entertainment, or inspiration. We can listen empathetically, without judging. We can listen comprehensively, trying to make sense of what we hear in order to organize and make sense of information by understanding relationships among ideas. We can listen discerningly, making sure we understand the main message, and determine important details. We can evaluate as we listen in order to make a decision based on information provided.

Of all the ways that we can listen, listening empathetically is the most powerful. Consider a time in your own life when you truly felt heard, where the person you were talking to had no objective or motive except to be there for you. Think about how it felt. If we can enable our prospects to feel the same way, this would help us gain their trust so that we can help them.

There are several techniques that can help us become empathetic listeners. We should remove anything that might distract us when we speak to someone. Ensure no cell phone or text will interrupt us, close the door, and be sure to focus entirely on our prospect. We listen not only for the words, but for the underlying issues (desires, fears, and concerns). The more people feel that we *get* what they are saying, the more they will trust us and feel safe with us.

Remember that this is an emotional, not a cognitive process. We must get used to letting go of our own desires and fears while we are hearing the desires and fears of the prospect. We can open up the process by making suggestions or summarizing what we have heard to create some momentum for them to talk. Some example phrases might be:

- "I hear you are saying _____ and I can also imagine that _____ is happening as well."
- "I imagine that is scary."
- "Sounds upsetting."
- "Are you saying that what you are currently trying to do is not working?"
- "Can you tell me more about what you've tried?"

We should not ever be in a rush to talk. The more we hear, the more completely we can respond. I found out that some people are only able to open up after many such long conversations.

One of the hardest things for me to learn was to sit back and take a couple of full, deep breaths before responding or saying anything after someone has spoken. Often, before I could take that full breath, I discovered that they weren't quite finished. If I had started speaking when I thought they were finished, they would have felt like I was interrupting them. Getting to this stage, to the point where we are in a position to listen empathetically and deeply to our prospects, when they feel fully listened to—that is often the point when they move from being prospects to being clients or customers.

Finally, the most important step is afterwards—follow through. Follow through should be apparent from our first interaction. We should send a Thank You note and confirm our next steps. If we promised to send information to people, we need to get the information to them in the timeframe we committed, or even earlier. We need to set the right expectations so people know when things will happen. Even the smallest promise, once broken, can derail a prospective sale. Under promise and over-deliver rather than the opposite; our prospects will see our reliability as a refreshing differentiator.

SUMMARY OF SELLING

Selling is one of the most important skills we can learn, made easier with the help of a coach.

- ☑ Sales is a holistic process that begins by establishing our sweet spot, the point at which our products and services soothes or heals the pains of our customers.
- ☑ Learning to sell is a hands-on process that usually requires a coach.
- ☑ Selling requires us to understand personality characteristics, and the ability to modify our own presentation to match the characteristics of our prospect.
- ☑ Listening is an important aspect of selling.
- ☑ The process of selling involves a multistep method:
- ☑ We must uncover our prospect's pain.
- ☑ We must discover the decision-making process our prospect uses when deciding to buy or not buy a product or service.
- ☑ We must deal with the money issues.
- ☑ We must present scenarios that enable our prospects to envision the cost of not getting rid of the pain.
- ☑ We must present a solution that will get rid of the prospect's pain that is less than the cost of not getting rid of the pain.
- ☑ We must post-sell our prospect so that they don't change their minds later.

10

Financials: A Picture of the Business

When I first took over as editor in this series, I started immediately looking for someone who could explain the financials to entrepreneurs. In addition to working with my business owner clients, I often judge business plan competitions due to teaching entrepreneurship at Kutztown University. I am constantly seeing entrepreneurs struggle to understand their own financial statements. Many business owners are unwilling to ask their accountants what this number or that number means, or where the numbers came from. Few understood the difference between capital accounts and income accounts, or liability accounts and expense accounts.

I was lucky. In part, I learned how to understand financials from a variety of experiences. In addition to the local SBDC, and SCORE, I also gathered a lot from my classes at Lehigh University while working on my doctorate. Mostly, however, my financial knowledge came from my own willingness to appear dumb. I would grill my accountants endlessly to be sure I understood the source of every single number on my reports and tax forms. If I couldn't understand their explanations, I found a new accountant who could explain it in enough different ways that it finally made sense to me. I also served on many different boards of directors and did the same thing. When I eventually became treasurer for several nonprofit organizations, I figured out ways to share financial data with board members so that they, too, understood every number (which wasn't easy; nonprofit organizations generally attract people for their altruism, not their financial knowledge).

Some people think that being good at math is a requirement to understand financials, which adds to the fear factor in learning about them. Some might think that because I enjoy financial analysis and understand financial statements, I would be good at math. But nothing could be further from the truth.

Luckily, financial statements don't require math skills.

People who can do math in their heads tend to look down upon people (like me) who don't have the ability to remember or come up with "the numbers" quickly. Never was this more apparent to me than when I became vice president in the Finance department at a Fortune 500 financial firm. I was surrounded by people who could do advanced math in their heads.[1] I was in awe of their ability because they seemed never to drop a decimal point or misplace a comma, and could quote the fundamental numbers of the organization extensively without notes. When I was seeking venture capital, I found that potential investors also expected me to be able to come up with the numbers off the top of my head. I was never able to do that, and what little math I could do when I was younger completely disappeared after my 2002 auto accident that left me with some specific memory issues and a complete inability to do even simple math in my head. And yet—my abilities in understanding financial statements remained. I share this story so that we recognize that we have nothing to fear. Even if we aren't the greatest at math, we can learn to understand our financials. Understanding financials requires an understanding of business, not math.

---

[1] Being surrounding by financial people and missing technology people was one of the factors (plus the added salary) that induced me to take a position at a competing Fortune 500 financial firm, which turned out to be a mistake—as you may have remembered reading about in the chapter on leadership.

I tried to find an author to write the book on financial statements early on, but could not. Almost a half-dozen years later, I finally was referred to David Worrell through a friend in the Institute of Management Consultants. David understood what entrepreneurs needed to know about financial statements, and was interested in writing about it. David Worrell speaks of finance as the language of business, and does a wonderful job of explaining what entrepreneurs need to know. Additionally, Don Yount, Chief Finance Officer (CFO) of technology firm Corente, Inc. and former CFO of Mid-Atlantic Venture Fund, helped out, especially with the concept of the inside and outside pictures of the business. Of course, I will also intersperse my point of view on many financial statement issues and techniques that I found helpful in managing my own businesses over the years.

DIFFERENT PICTURES

As David noted, businesses speak in numbers. Even an art gallery or a cupcake shop tells its story in numbers—how many cupcakes are made, how many paintings are sold, how much profit is returned to the owner, and so on. The life story of a business is best understood when it is quantified.

There are at least three pictures of a business. The financial picture is the language the outside world speaks (bankers, venture capitalists, stockholders, and investors). The managerial picture is the internal view, needed by the advising board, the managers, and the employees of the business. We may also need to track things a third way in order to calculate taxable income. This may, or may not, coincide with the other two pictures of the business.

Many entrepreneurs, especially technology entrepreneurs (who tend to be engineers and computer scientists), know that both views exist. Often, however, they don't know how they relate. Understanding the relationship will make it easier for us to understand which picture should be at the forefront.

To understand the difference, it is helpful to know the rules the accountants are using for the financial picture. Commonly, they utilize rules codified by *GAAP*, or Generally Accepted Accounting Principles.

Mind the GAAP?

GAAP was developed for accountants to be able to easily audit and track numbers, as well as determine net income for purposes of comparison between companies. GAAP presents our financial numbers in a way that is externally comparable. But GAAP is not very good at enabling us to manage or determine the value of our businesses. Therefore, in addition to tracking things based upon GAAP, we need to figure out how to track things according to our own inside rules for managing the business.

I first noticed this gap regarding GAAP (pun intended) with my first business, Computer Educational Services (CES). As you've read, CES was a technology training and consulting firm. In order to be able to teach many different software programs, I became adept at quickly learning new programs and writing instructional manuals (usually between 30 and 100 pages). Using a template my brother and I developed, I could produce a professional-looking high-quality instructional guide on any new software within two weeks. My manuals impressed several other local training firms, and before you knew it, we were selling our manuals to them in order to supplement our income.

Dealing with inventory was the first GAAP issue. I learned that when I purchased other's manuals and put them on my shelf to resell in my training, I could add the cost of the books (generally $15 to $30) to my inventory, bumping up the value of tangible assets (but lowering my gross margin). But if I wrote them myself and printed them as I needed them, the value could not be put on my balance sheet as an asset according to my accountant. The tools that I used to write the manuals (word processor, the software, etc.), the paper, covers, and binders were all expenses, not assets. The time that I spent to write them was not valued. The only way to add them as a tangible asset was to print them out and put them on a shelf. Then, I could capitalize the tools and the time.

In reality, printing the manuals would have been a mistake. Manuals on a shelf about software were worthless. By the time someone needed to learn that particular software program, the software publisher would have already upgraded to another version. That would force me to throw away the old books and purchase new books. However, if I wrote the books myself and only printed them when I needed them, when the software publisher came out with a new version, all I had to do was update the electronic version of the manuals—something that only took a few hours. To my internal view of the business, the electronic versions of the instructional manuals were extremely valuable—much more valuable than the actual books. Paper versions of the manuals were wasted money and space. The external view based on GAAP, however, valued the paper manuals in inventory and assessed no value to the electronic ones.

I knew better, however. I carefully assessed a reasonable dollar value to every hour I spent writing manuals. I then placed that value every quarter in the intangible asset account under each title's name so that when it was time to sell my business, that asset did not get forgotten in the valuation. In the sales agreement, I was able to sell a license to the acquiring company for the intellectual property contained in those electronic files.

I could give you hundreds of similar examples where traditional accounting overvalues or undervalues an asset. It is up to us to know what is valuable in our business and what is not. For example, if we feel that a database of past customers would be valuable to some future buyer of our business, then we should assess a value for each customer, and each year, add that value to the intangible asset account. If we feel our brand has value, we can assess that value and record it.

What this calculation does is pre-value the intangibles that would not normally be valued (according to GAAP) until after we sell the business (at which point, they would appear on the balance sheet of the acquiring business). The difference between the book value of the tangible assets of the acquired company and the value paid for the business is usually entered as goodwill, but it can also be entered as intellectual property or branding value. We can think of this intangible asset value as "the amount we would sell our business for today if someone were to make an offer." It is not the GAAP book value reported to the IRS because the book value generally reflects tangible, not intangible, assets.

Furthermore, traditional accounting does not provide guidelines on determining the difference between fixed costs and variable costs—an important value that entrepreneurs need to know. As I mentioned in Chapter 2, the break-even analysis is not just a banal calculation; it is a method that allows us to better manage our businesses. It is up to us to develop and manage some of our own financial reports so that we can track the break-even point on all of our products and services. We must break up the numbers in a way that is useful to us in managing our business.

Accountants will often resist this activity because breaking up the numbers makes their job more difficult. Breaking up the numbers this way is also a pain for the bookkeepers and clerks. But in the end, it is essential that we take control of the financial statements so that we get reports on a daily, weekly, monthly, quarterly, and annual basis that are actually useful to us.

Simplifying Categories

A standard set of expense categories (such as rent, insurance, advertising, supplies, etc.) is usually included in financial systems and tax reporting forms. It is customary for accountants to use this standard set of categories, but they don't often help us in our specific business.

Personally, I find it most useful to track expenses by the following categories:

- Direct (variable) costs: People
- Direct (variable) costs: Promotion
- Direct (variable) costs: Office
- Direct (variable) costs: Administration
- Indirect (fixed) costs: People
- Indirect (fixed) costs: Promotion
- Indirect (fixed) costs: Office
- Indirect (fixed) costs: Administration

Just eight categories, instead of the typical 20 or 30. Putting everything in just one of these eight categories enables me to see when my overarching costs for any one category are out of bounds. We still track those standard categories (insurance, advertising, rent, etc.) for the accountant and the

IRS, but they all roll up to one of these four categories in either the direct or indirect costs. This enables me to see quick simple overview reports, seeing if the majority of cost was people, or promotion, or office, or administration. It groups expenses in a much more meaningful way for me. For example; if I want to know how much we spent on promotion, I want to see one number, not separate numbers for brochures, advertisements, travel, or software, all of which might be part of our promotional campaigns.

This simplified list also lets me easily do a break-even analysis for any product or service at any time. For example, advertising might be a promotion cost for a particular product or event (which would make it direct), or a promotion cost for a generic branding advertisement (which would make it indirect). If we only track the category as advertising, we would lose the distinction.[1]

As business owners, it makes sense for us to go through an exercise to come up with categories that will make sense to us instead of leaving it up to bookkeepers and accountants. We can ask ourselves the following questions:

- What are the overarching measurements that determine the success of my business?
- What are the precursors of those measurements?
- What categories will make sense to me when reviewing the financials?
- How much detail do I want to see on a monthly basis?
- What can be rolled up together and still help me manage the business?

It usually takes a few years of trying different things before we begin to get monthly reports that really help us to make the right decisions about our business.

Manage by the Numbers

Becoming familiar with finance is the key to unlocking the secrets of our business success. The best part about using finance to understand our business is that the results are dynamic—the picture can change as a result of our actions. Watching the financial numbers change over time gives us the feedback we need to take actions that will improve the financial health of our business. Every decision we make and every action we take impacts the numbers going forward.

Finance works best when it is comparative. A single number or ratio by itself can be important, but the whole story comes from looking at the same number over time—past, present and future. We should review our numbers frequently.

Passion or Business

Why do some entrepreneurs avoid looking at their own numbers? We entrepreneurs usually start businesses in fields in which we are passionate. We sometimes aren't that concerned about making money. We just want to help our clients and customers. We want to make a living, playing at our hobby, without worrying too much about getting rich. As long as there is enough cash in the bank (or an alternative form of income), we might be inclined to ignore important things such as balance sheets and income statements.

We *should* care passionately about our businesses. (And there are some entrepreneurs who go too far in the opposite direction; they care only about making money and have no passion for the business or their customers.) But we *should also* make sure that we have more income than expense. We can't make decisions based solely on customer needs and not at all on whether or not we can afford it. We must turn away clients or customers who can't pay for the products or services. Otherwise, we end up giving away our business, bit by bit, until it can run no longer. Running the business into the ground doesn't help anyone, least of all our customers.

The best entrepreneurs are passionate about their business, about the industry the business is in, about the topic and values upon which the business is based. But we also pay close attention to ensuring that there is enough income to pay for all the expenses and to ensure the financial future of the business is stable. We review financial statements frequently, plan strategically, and budget for the future.

THE BASICS: FINANCIAL REPORTS

Every business has three basic financial reports that integrate into the complete financial picture of the business—income statement, balance sheet, and cash flow. To those basics, I will add two more—the trial balance and the break-even analysis.

Income Statement

Companies track their income (sales) and expense (spending) in an income statement, or sometimes, a profit and loss statement. We will use the common abbreviation, P&L.

The P&L is the single most important measure of a company's health and sustainability. Only a P&L can tell us whether our overall operations are resulting in profits, which will help our company continue. Of course, the P&L might tell us that the results are losses, which will spell doom on a long-term basis.

There are four sections to a P&L.

- Income
- Cost of Sales
- Expenses
- Other Income and Expense

Income is also known as revenue or sales. Cost of sales is also known as direct costs or cost of goods. Gross profit is income minus cost of sales, or the amount of our sales that is not used up by the variable or direct costs of the sales. When it is expressed as a percentage, it is call the gross margin. The gross profit amount must be large enough to cover all the fixed, or indirect, expenses. Gross profit minus expenses is our operating profit, also known sometimes as EBITDA (Earnings Before Interest, Taxes, Depreciation, and Amortization). Operating profit minus interest, taxes, depreciation, and amortization is our net profit. The net profit is also known as the Bottom Line, and it determines whether or not the business is profitable.

These terms are all applicable to every business, no matter which industry they are in. But beyond that, the details for each particular industry and each particular business will differ.

Take something simple such as sales (also known as revenue or income). Not every dollar that comes into a business is a sale, so there must be rules around which dollars coming in would go into this category and which would go into another category. There are rules of thumb to help a business owner decide:

- Control: Did the business control the terms of the income?
- Customers: Did the income come from people we want to describe as customers?
- Transaction: Did the company sell a product or service in exchange for the revenue?
- Timing: Did the sale happen during the time period measured by the P&L?

If the answer for all these questions is *yes*, then the dollars would go into the income statement as income.

Balance Sheet

Just as the P&L tells the story of how a business makes money, the balance sheet tells the story of how the company manages its money. The balance sheet reflects the book value and the net worth of the business.

Has the company racked up a lot of debt? Has it taken money from—or paid money to—investors? Does the company have any money in the bank? Those are questions answered only by the balance sheet.

In short, a balance sheet answers the question "How much do we have?" while the P&L answers the question "How did we get it?" Or, said another way, the balance sheet says where we are while the P&L shows how we got here.

This definition highlights one important difference between a P&L and a balance sheet—the P&L describes events that happened over a period of time, but a balance sheet describes only what exists at a particular instant. Because of this, the balance sheet is often called a snapshot of the company's financial health—it depicts conditions at a single moment, and it does not show how things have changed over time.

Historically, a balance sheet was created by drawing a line down the center of a piece of paper. On one side was a list of what a company owned, called assets. On the other side was the list of what the company owed, either to lenders (liabilities) or owners (equity).

A company always starts with nothing—the balance sheet is the original financial statement and can exist even before any income or expense has happened. At the beginning, of course, a company has no money of its own—no intrinsic value simply because it exists—so a business must get its economic value from either owners, lenders, or investors. The balance sheet records these amounts; every business naturally creates a balance sheet at the instant it forms. Whether we write it down or not, the balance sheet exists and the amounts are always in natural balance.

In short, the amount of money a company has (or spends) must equal, or balance with, the amount of money it has received—not just from profits, but from borrowing and investment. By looking at the graphic illustration in Figure 10.1, we can imagine the income going into and the expenses coming out of the balanced formula: asset = liabilities + equity. If at any point the assets don't equal the liabilities plus equity, the business is out of balance, which means that somewhere, there is a mistake because, by definition, the amount of equity is what's left over after the liabilities have been subtracted from the assets. In order to keep this formula in balance, accountants use double entry accounting.

Assets are composed of the cash in the bank accounts, the amount our customers owe us, our value of our product inventory, the value of our furniture/equipment/land/buildings (also known as tangible or fixed assets, not to be confused with fixed expenses), and the value of intangible assets such as intellectual property, branding, and goodwill.

Liabilities are composed of loans, lines of credit, credit card balances, the amount we owe our suppliers, or any other amount that we are expected to pay in the future.

Figure 10.1. Graphic illustration of Balance Sheet and Income Statement

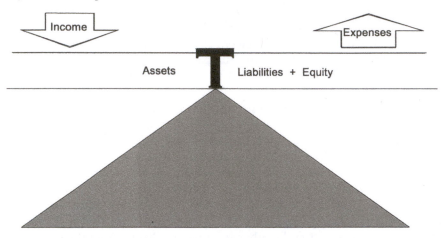

Source: HPL Consortium, Inc., copyright 2014, used with permission.

Equity is the difference between the assets and liabilities. The equity section usually has an account called retained earnings, which records the value of profits left in the business from a previous period, profits from the current period (net income or current retained earnings), the amount that owners and investors have already put into the business, and any amounts paid to the shareholders/owners (distributions or owner's draw) against the amount put in.

Statement of Cash Flow

As described in Chapter 2, cash is more important than your mother. A cash flow statement shows where the money went during a period of time. Remember how we said the balance sheet is a snapshot of your finances? One way to imagine the cash flow statement is as a comparison between two balance sheets (and thus, a description of how money flowed between the balance sheet accounts during the period between the two snapshots).

A business may be profitable, but if the cash isn't managed right, it will go bankrupt despite the profits. Additionally, a business may have enough cash, but is still not profitable (because there is some alternative form of cash that is fueling the business, such as credit or owner's equity). Again, that situation can only be maintained for so long—at some point, the business will go bankrupt if it continues to spend more money than it makes.

At the simplest level, the cash flow statement is like a bank account statement; it does not pass judgment on whether or not the dollars are assets, liabilities, income, or expenses; it just records what goes in and what goes out. For that reason, many entrepreneurs prefer to review the cash flow statement because it is more understandable than the split revenue/expense of the income statement and the assets/liabilities/equity of the balance sheet.

Trial Balance

David didn't talk much about the trial balance, but I think it is very important. A trial balance is a listing of all the accounts in your general ledger and their balances on a specific date (usually, the last day of an accounting period or year). Most accountants view the trial balance as something they look at to make sure they didn't make any mistakes in their general ledger. They don't typically share it with the business owner.

However, over the years (especially when trying to explain finances to nonprofit organization boards of directors), I have found the trial balance report to be the most believable and understandable financial report. For a typical small business owner, it is highly useful. It is the only financial report that shows both the income/expense accounts and the asset/liability/equity accounts on the *same* report. For that reason, I usually advise business owners to ask their accountant for a trial balance to review regularly because, from a management perspective, it is often the one report that can be reviewed as a complete picture of the business, including both income/expense and balance sheet accounts.

Making Sense of Accountant-Speak: Translating the Financials

Accountant-speak has developed over the years to accommodate all of the special situations, exceptions, different industries, and comparisons from company to company. What has been explained in this short summary of the basics is just the tiny tip of the iceberg when it comes to reviewing financials—for large and/or public companies. You'll note, for example, that we didn't go over the Other Income & Expense line of the income statement, or explain where income goes that does not fit into the description of income criteria, such as income we don't control (winning the lottery, for example, or a refund on an earlier purchase) or income outside of the P&L period described. We didn't talk about asset depreciation or calculating taxes. We didn't mention the difference between extraordinary income and operational income, nor when expenses are actually income items instead of expenses (or vice versa). It is all these exceptions and situations and conditions and calculations for which we need accountants; it doesn't make sense for us to need to learn everything accountants know in order to enhance our businesses. Indeed, that time is much better spent on our business.

But we must understand what the accountants are talking about. We must understand accountant-speak. We have to translate accountant speak into something useful for us to manage. To consider why there is a difference, let us review the simple monthly transaction regarding office space.

If we rent, we pay a monthly amount that is an expense.

If we own the building, but have a mortgage on it, the monthly amount that we pay is split between the amount of principal payment on a liability (the mortgage), which is offsetting the asset (the building) and the amount of the interest, which appears as an expense (and often set apart from normal operating expense because interest is one of those categories accountants like to track separately).

If we are typical business owners, we don't care whether the dollars that go out for office space is categorized as expense or asset/liability. But since one will appear on the income report and the other will appear on the balance sheet, it makes a big difference to an accountant. One will change our profit number. The other will change our asset/liability/equity numbers.

As good entrepreneurs, we instinctively understand that the amount we bring in for sales has to be more than the amount we have to pay for office space. But there is a difference between needing enough sales to cover the rent costs in a single period and needing only enough to cover the costs of just the interest in a single period (because the asset/liability transaction doesn't affect profits). That could mean the difference between a profitable month and an unprofitable one.

There are dozens of decisions like that—decisions which will impact our profitability or our equity for a particular period. I've known many business owners who completely ignore depreciation, for example, because it does not involve cash and the amount depends upon a judgment call about the proposed life of an asset (which, strangely enough, sometimes has little to do with the usable life of an asset). Assets are usually depreciated over 5 years, 10 years, 15 years, or 30 years (in the case of a building, large equipment, or a large computer system).

Booking too much depreciation hurts profitability as effectively as spending too much on box tickets to the top sports teams. Booking too little depreciation can make an organization appear profitable when it is not.[2] Often, we book depreciation according to the rules of what is deductible according to the IRS. For example, there is a special depreciation (called Section 179)[3] that allows business owners to depreciate a large amount the first year an asset has been in service. Depreciation, therefore, might not be reported consistently for all items. Why should our profitability be determined by a specialized tax deduction rule? It shouldn't. We should not let this depreciation impact the way we manage our business. If we don't know if this special depreciation is included in the financial or managerial reports we are viewing, however, we might be misled about the profitability of the business.

As business owners, we are more concerned with the overall start-to-finish view of our business. We are not as concerned (or should not be as concerned) with whether or not we made a profit in this one particular quarter; instead we would want to know if we have been trending toward more profit each month or less profit each month (and why).

We also should be much more concerned with direct versus indirect costs than accountants typically are. It is a lot of transactional work to post a percentage of salary that has been focused on a particular product or service, but if we don't do so, we overstate our gross margins and understate our cost of goods. Furthermore, only *we* can tell the difference between a direct and indirect cost for our products and services. So, if our accountant has set up the accounts in the financial system and we didn't tell them to create an account for direct and indirect costs, chances are the fixed and variable costs have not been separated.

The Managerial Picture: Fixed and Variable Costs

In order to create our own managerial picture of the business, we would create our definitions of revenue and variable costs based on our business models. We would tie them to specific products or services. Consider, for example, a bill of materials, which is the list of all of the components that make up our final product or service. In general, the items in the bill of materials are all variable expenses. Next, we would identify any other costs that exist. These would be costs that don't relate to each individual product or service.

Some businesses, such as health providers, insurance companies, technology companies, or large consulting firms, don't have any variable costs; all costs are fixed. Other businesses, such as wholesalers, boutique consultants, or drop-ship Internet storefronts, don't have any significant fixed costs. They don't have to pay out anything if they don't sell anything. Most businesses are somewhere in between.

The break-even point has a great deal of impact on the cash flow of a company. That's why tracking it is so important to us. One way to keep a good day-to-day handle on the break-even point is to utilize the break-even analysis as we develop our dashboard (discussed in the next section). What you put on the dashboard winds up being the assumptions you make when you prepare your projection model for the break-even point.

Using Break-Even Point for Decision Making

Financial people can see the results of number changes in their heads (just like they can do math in their heads). If you are like me, not only can't you do math in your head, but you can't envision the results of a number change on a spreadsheet of numbers. People like us, entrepreneurs who aren't necessarily mathematicians, are more likely to be able to see the numbers if we use graphic illustrations of the numbers. Because financial people don't need this step, they tend to think it is unnecessary. If we are smart, we get the financials from our accountants every quarter and use Excel or some other graphing program to just to look at the numbers and graph them.

One of the reasons the break-even analysis is so useful to entrepreneurs is because it can be evaluated graphically. We don't consider a single break-even point; we rather consider the break-even chart, that is, the amount of break-even at different price points or different cost points.

Below is a break-even analysis decision-making illustration example for Sandy, who owns a tai chi studio. Sandy's business model is to sell monthly subscriptions to the tai chi and fitness classes at the studio. Students may take as many classes during the month as they wish. The fixed costs for providing and advertising three classes each week is $689 per month. Sandy is not sure what the monthly pricing should be next year. The studio currently charges $49 per student. Sandy is also considering purchasing a water service at $150 per month to save the hassle of buying water at the store and lugging it in each week, which takes approximately five hours each month.

The variable costs are $40 per student. That pays for the guest instructors and the credit card processing charges for the monthly subscription. The current table for the break-even analysis can be seen in Table 10.1.

The decision-making choices can be seen in Figure 10.2. Sandy has not been making any money, and the answer is glaringly obvious when we look at the chart that shows the break-even point—at a $49 fee, the break-even point is 80 clients. Sandy has 27 clients. That's not even close to being enough. The studio cannot make any money at all with a $49 price, and is losing over $400 a month.

Table 10.1. Current Break-Even Analysis Table Example

Monthly Break Even

Number of Clients	10	20	30	40	50	60	70	80
Fixed Expenses	$689	$689	$689	$689	$689	$689	$689	$689
Variable Expenses	$400	$800	$1,200	$1,600	$2,000	$2,400	$2,800	$3,200
Income	$490	$980	$1,470	$1,960	$2,450	$2,940	$3,430	$3,920
Net Profit	-$599	-$509	-$419	-$329	-$239	-$149	-$59	$31
Price Per Client	49	49	49	49	49	49	49	49

Source: HPL Consortium, Inc., copyright 2014, used with permission.

Figure 10.2. Break-Even Analysis for $49 Price

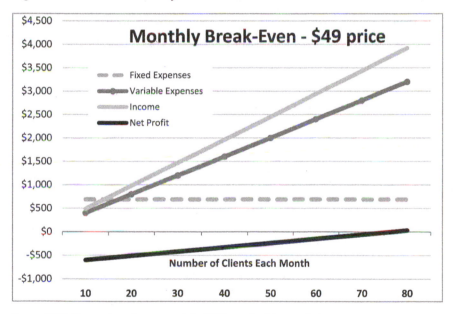

Source: HPL Consortium, Inc., copyright 2014, used with permission.

After playing with the numbers, Sandy sees that if the price were $70 a month, the break-even point is reached with less than 27 clients, and the studio would be able to survive (Figure 10.3).

The problem is that the going rate for competition in the area is $50, so it might be difficult to get clients to pay such a large premium over the

Figure 10.3. Break-Even Analysis for $70 Price

Source: HPL Consortium, Inc., copyright 2014, used with permission.

going rate. Sandy has a loyal following, however, and many more certifications than some of those competitors, so feels it might be possible to get $60 a month instead of $49. Sandy began to play with the numbers. She set the price to $60 and looked at the break-even analysis graph, as shown in Figure 10.4.

That would mean that the studio would have to attract at least seven more clients a month to survive—something that Sandy feels is possible. But Sandy would really like to get that water service. Sandy wanted to see what would happen if she ordered the water service for the students at the $60 price.

After changing the fixed costs by adding the $150 (Figure 10.5), the break-even analysis shows that if the studio can get 40 clients instead of 35, it can afford to hire the water service. Sandy decides to wait until 40 clients sign up before ordering the water service. In the meantime, five hours a month lugging water doesn't sound so bad.

Using any financial report, and then re-casting it based upon a number of variables is known as a what-if analysis. If we are attempting to find a particular number (such as the exact break-even point), we can use a Goal Seek process to do the analysis. (Details on how to do a Goal Seek analysis can be found in Appendix E.)

Figure 10.4. Break-Even Analysis for $60 Price

Figure 10.5. Break-Even Analysis for $60 Price with Water Service

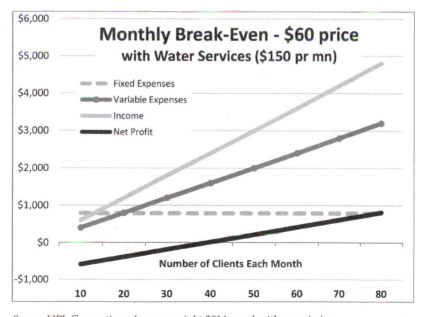

MANAGERIAL AND FINANCIAL PICTURES

Financial statements always involve some judgment. Flexibility allows business owners to review different aspects of the business, or review the business financials for different purposes. Some are straightforward, such as purchasing a building (an asset) instead of paying rent (an expense). Some decisions are less clear-cut, such as classifying rebates as income rather than a reduction of expenses.

When the rules allow flexibility, our decisions should be shaped by clear management objectives—we want to measure and manage one aspect of the business, so we record transactions a certain way.

What if, as business owners, we simply want to make the financial statements look more favorable? One business owner may wish to show more profit in order to position the company for sale, while another business owner hopes to minimize profit for tax reasons. It may seem like walking a thin line, but there are plenty of situations where modification of the financial reporting produces more meaningful financial statements. This modification and recasting is both legal and ethical.

Two Sets of Books

Businesses should have at least two sets of books. One set of books is the inside management picture in order to enable day-to-day operational decisions. Another set of books is to enable reporting for the external financial picture (usually following GAAP rules). We may need a third set to accommodate specific taxation requirements, or a fourth to meet the needs of the managers.

Sometimes, when speaking to entrepreneurs, I get an open-mouthed reaction to the concept of multiple books, as if doing so is a sign of nefarious or criminal activity. Not only is there nothing wrong with having more than one set of books, it is the right way to manage our finances. Multiple sets of books would only be unethical, immoral, or illegal if: 1) we hide one set of books, 2) one set contains fraudulent transactions, 3) the two sets of books cannot be reconciled to each other, or 4) the two provide vastly different results.

Of course, in this day and age, we don't have physical books for bookkeeping anymore; we simply produce different sets of reports from the same data from our financial system. Furthermore, in addition to managerial and financial reports, there will be cash and accrual reports.

Accrual versus Cash

One of the most important issues that may be reflected differently in managerial versus financial reporting is accrual versus cash accounting, and the timing of posting of income and expenses.

Most people are very familiar with cash accounting. Income is the checks we've received and an expense is the checks we've written that someone else has cashed. Straightforward and easy.

For most businesses, however, cash accounting would be a misleading way to track financials. Checks often come in weeks or months after products and services have been delivered. Checks for products and services often go out weeks or months after we've received them. As a result, our businesses usually use accrual accounting.

In accrual accounting, booking a sale means increasing accounts receivable (an asset), which increases net income. When we receive checks for the invoices, we increase cash and decrease accounts receivable. When we receive bills from vendors, we increase accounts payable (a liability) and decrease net income. Paying the bill with a check means decreasing accounts payable and decreasing the cash account.

Accrual accounting has some flexibility regarding exactly when we book the income and expenses. One of the decisions we must make, therefore, is establishing the rules for transactions, which may be different for the managerial and financial pictures.

Capital versus Expense

The most common way to enhance or delay a company's profits is to shift expenses off the P&L and onto the balance sheet. When a business makes a large purchase, the purchase could be capitalized, meaning we create an asset rather than an expense. As we have seen, an asset is depreciated, so the expense that shows up on the P&L is quite small compared to the initial purchase price (although, of course, depreciation lasts many periods, whereas a purchase expense occurs once). Capitalizing, therefore, increases short-term profits while sacrificing long-term profits. Expensing decreases short-term profits while enhancing long-term profits.

There are general rules about what should, and should not, be capitalized. Some costs, such as leasehold improvements (building new walls in a rented office, for example), are correctly classified as an asset. Other times, the rules are open to more interpretation. It wasn't too long ago that desktop computers were always classified as assets and were often given depreciation timeframes of 30 years because that was the typical depreciation timeframe of mainframe computers when they first came out in the 1970s and 1980s. But as desktop computer costs went from thousands to hundreds, and the typical life cycle went from decades to years (and now, perhaps, to months), desktop computers are now often expensed and sometimes aren't even considered assets.

The decision to capitalize expenses works both ways. We also discussed in the Information Technology chapter that ERP systems are usually booked as an asset, along with the cost to train the staff and customize the code. But we might want to expense the value of the customization and training, even if the invoice from the vendor says the training is free when we buy the ERP system.

Shifting items to the balance sheet boosts the assets we have listed on the balance sheet. Conversely, choosing to record the purchase as an expense rather than an asset puts the entire expense into one period, which decreases the taxable income in that period, but would increase taxable income in future periods.

Capitalizing or expensing an item becomes a strategic decision that impacts profits, taxes, and other areas of business. It should not be a decision left to the sole discretion of the accountant; it should be a strategic management decision in consultation with financial advisors.

Note that capitalizing costs doesn't increase profits or reduce losses. It just defers the expense until the future, and some times, like the case of depreciation, spreads it over time. Depreciation, in particular, is an important concept in the managerial to financial translation, since capital is a fixed cost that, by definition, should be spread over time, and especially in the case of manufacturing, spread over the units or products made.

Time-Shifting Transactions

Accounting requires a single moment in time when all the transactions are wrapped up or done. Business, however, can't be so neatly containerized. Sales and spending continue past the end of a month or year, so there is some leeway on whether or not the income and expenses are booked in one time period or another. There are some good reasons to do this, including simply correcting quirks in the calendar. A power bill, for example, is a monthly expense. If we do not receive the February power bill until March 1, it would be misleading to skip the expense in February. Adjusting the date on the bill is a reasonable and legitimate use of this technique.

Time shifting can be an important way to smooth out revenue and expenses on periodic reports. It can be difficult to manage a business when several large invoices land arbitrarily in one month, so assigning part or all of the expense to another month may help make sense of what is actually going on in the business.

In some cases, time shifting is mandatory. Businesses with multimonth delivery cycles and big invoice values are expected to spread income out as it is earned, rather than showing it all in the month when an invoice was created. Spreading revenue across multiple periods is often not only a good idea but also a legal requirement. While it is not a legal requirement to spread out the expenses associated with that revenue, it would be the smart thing to do. Otherwise, the financial statements might show tremendous profits one month and huge losses another month. Our goal is to align the timing of the income with the timing of the expenses.

Inventory is another decision-making issue. When a company buys or creates inventory that has a rapidly changing price (gasoline, for example), we can create or destroy profits simply by deciding how to recognize the cost of the inventory we are holding. Should we value it at the price we paid for the oldest part of it we still have on hand? Or the price we paid most recently for the newest pieces? Or at the price we will pay to replace it next week?

There are generally accepted rules for guiding this decision, but there is a lot of leeway in the guidelines that require decision-making on our part. The important key is to remain consistent. Changing the method at any point can have a substantial impact on profitability, since it will shift the cost of goods and/or change the value at which the inventory is recorded.

As discussed in an earlier section, the other way to change the balance sheet of an organization is to value (or adjust the value of) its intangible assets. Since the value of an intangible asset is, by necessity, subjective, it can be adjusted to reflect real market values at the whim of the management (that is, us).

Don't Cross the Ethical Line

As we've seen, there are plenty of legitimate reasons for changing the way we record things on our books. With all that flexibility, it should not be shocking that some people choose to cross the line—bending the rules so far as to misrepresent the facts or hide important items. The headlines are full of such transgressions—from the Enron debacle of the 1990s to the Wall Street meltdown of 2008. There seems to be no end to how creative managers can get when generating financial statements.

As long as reports are designed to inform us and help us make better decisions and accurately reflect reality, they are ethical. Deviations from GAAP may need to be footnoted, but there is nothing wrong with it. The key is full disclosure of everything.

Full disclosure eliminates the "you didn't tell us that" complaint, which may be very important from a retroactive view. It is also a good idea to get into the habit of deferring good news, but immediately reporting the bad news—as soon as possible. When possible, defer revenue, but book expenses immediately. Write down assets and write up liabilities sooner rather than later.

When modeling, the financials should have accounting integrity. The numbers must paint the picture of reality.

Financial statements that are knowingly false, that twist reality beyond recognition, or that are based on wants instead of facts, will not provide useful management information. Misleading financial statements make it very hard to raise money credibly, and even harder to manage cash effectively. No good can come of creative accounting that is deceptive accounting.

Financial Reporting and Taxes

One of the most common issues I find as a strategic management consultant helping business owners make decisions is the difficulty faced when business owners who have run a successful business for years (perhaps even decades) decide to try and sell their business. The problem occurs if those business owners expensed (rather than capitalized) as much as possible in order to minimize the amount of taxes they paid. This is true whether they are a corporation (which pays taxes separately), an S corp (which is registered as a corporation, but pays taxes through the owners tax forms as if it was a sole proprietorship), a partnership or an LLC (Limited Liability Corporation, which is a fancy name for a partnership, which pays taxes through the owner's tax forms), or a sole proprietorship. No matter what form of business we have, there is an instinct to minimize the amount of taxes we have to pay to the government.

But there may be a reason to pay more in taxes rather than less. If the business is going to be valued for sale or any other reason, and we want the business to have more value (so that we can sell it for a higher price, for example), then suppressing those profits year after year will go against our goal. We can't change the amount of profits after the fact through capitalization because we reported the profits when we paid taxes on them. We also can't get loans from a bank or attract investors if our business has not been shown to be profitable in the past. Banks, investors, and potential buyers always request several years of tax forms, and utilize that data when evaluating and assessing the value of a business.

Kim was one of my business owner clients who was looking to expand and sell. When I did the strategic assessment, I found that the business had been just barely profitable for the past 15 years. When I reported that back in my assessment, Kim became agitated, and noted that it wasn't true. Kim insisted (angrily) that the business had actually been profitable, but that the accountant had made it *look* less profitable to minimize taxes. Unfortunately, there was nothing that I could do; since we didn't have accurate information for the historicals of the business, there was no way to use the supposed-higher-profitability upon which to get a loan or base a sale of the business. In order to get the valuations Kim was looking for, we would need another three years of history where taxes were paid on actual profits. The moral of the story is—we are better off accurately report profits, and paying taxes on them. Deception will hurt us in the long run.

DASHBOARDS, MODELS, FORECASTS, AND BUDGETS

The business data cycle process forms a cyclical loop monthly, quarterly, and/or annually.

1. Financial statements show results from operations and help us understand weaknesses and opportunities.
2. Dashboards unlock the interrelation of financial statements and show how operating results are related to certain other inputs or parameters.
3. Models use those relationships to build "what if" and "what could be" scenarios.
4. Forecasts take the model results and add a dose of future thinking; what we think will happen.
5. Budgets use the forecast goals to justify and assign financial resources to the business operations.
6. The business uses budgeted resources to operate, which creates actual results that are presented in the financial statements.
   . . . and the cycle continues

When this cycle is operating correctly, and when the entrepreneur is diligent, this six-step process becomes a continuous feedback flywheel loop, helping the business grow stronger and stronger with each cycle. The data shows us opportunities and we set strategies to capture them. The data shows us threats and we set strategies to avoid them. Each strategy brings new results and new data . . . which can reveal new threats or opportunities. All the while, the owner and managers are learning how the business works and how the market reacts. Think of the four tools as looking at the same situation from four different viewpoints:

1. Model: What could happen
2. Forecast: What we believe will happen—within the model
3. Budget: What must happen to reach the forecast
4. Dashboard: What actually happened

Models describe how we make and spend money. Models start with the big picture—external market conditions and available resources—and attempt to distill the size and scope of a business that could be built within those parameters. Forecasts start with a known size and scope of business and project how the business might change over time. Forecasts are predictions of future results that are rooted in past experience. Budgets take the predictions of a forecast and describe in as much detail as possible exactly what income and expenses are likely to result. Dashboards are the daily management tool that summarize the most important metrics.

Like the dashboard in a car, a business dashboard is a tool that tells us how things are going. If we are worried about the engine overheating, we have a temperature gauge. If we want to know whether we are likely to get a speeding ticket, we glance at the speedometer. All the car's vital systems can be displayed on the dashboard—oil, water, gasoline, rpm, distance, and even the direction of travel. A well-constructed business dashboard can, likewise, tell us a great deal about the function and health of our business.

Entrepreneurs who are concerned with the future will want to use these tools (or pieces of them) at different times and for different reasons. One day, we may settle for a quick forecast based on current conditions; another day, we may need a model to look at an entirely new line of business.

Budget versus Plan

Don Yount feels strongly about using the term "budget." He shared with me his thinking on the subject in a conversation in July of 2013:

> I never use the term budget. Budgets are static and too reminiscent of governmental accounting. Instead, I like the term "plan" since they can be managed with flexibility and an aim toward "preservation." In keeping with a quote from a 19th century Prussian General, Field Marshal von Moltke, in which he says that no battle plan ever survived the first twenty minutes of battle, the only thing I know for sure about a financial projection or plan is that it's wrong the minute you print it. So, I'd advise entrepreneurs to create flexible plans that can be altered to "preserve" the bottom line.
>
> The bottom line is not net income, by the way, it is cash flow. Advertising, for example, should be purchased monthly or quarterly, and not up front for a whole year. Then, if sales slump, advertising can be trimmed, rationalized and re-directed to the most efficient outlets in an effort to "preserve the plan." At Mid-Atlantic, [a venture capital fund] we did lots of Plan Preservation for portfolio companies over the years. I'd close with that piece of advice—work your plan, and use it to preserve cash.

The next section will discuss these tools, and how to use them to preserve cash, in the order of the importance to the entrepreneur.

Dashboards, Balanced Scorecards, Executive Information Systems

Dashboards are the essential daily management tool of the smart entrepreneur. Another term used over the past few decades for dashboard is balanced scorecard, and before that, executive information systems.

Accountants don't typically care about high-level summaries or integration with nonfinancials numbers because they are focused on recording and not managing. Employees often don't care because they focus on their piece of the puzzle. Only the dashboard contains the underlying whole, the daily numbers that enable us to predict (and prevent) problems down the road.

A dashboard is nothing more than a chart of the most important numbers, reviewed daily or weekly, with both financial and nonfinancial drivers for the business. The point of a great dashboard is not to introduce complexity or confusion, but rather, to show the key metrics in a business and how those metrics change over time.

I'm not talking about dashboards driven by expensive software. My personal opinion is that such software is mostly a waste of resources. It takes five minutes per day to have someone enter the bottom number from several different financial reports and tracking logs into an Excel spreadsheet. I've been involved in dozens of dashboard projects (and often I've been paid quite a bit to automate those five minutes). In the end, I've determined that this is one process that doesn't make any sense to automate. Entrepreneurs should do it themselves if they have no one else, but once the key metrics have been determined, recording them into the dashboard can easily be done by any clerk or administrative person.

Use Colors

A balanced scorecard/dashboard often uses color to indicate good/bad. This makes it easy to see what's going on in a glance—a concept known as "managing by exception." Typically, red means a number is going in the wrong direction, yellow means it should be watched because it might be going in the wrong direction, green means the number is okay—nothing to worry about. In addition to the summary values given in P&L statements, balance sheets, and cash flow statements, a dashboard will include non-dollar values, such as number of new clients, number of return clients, average number of days outstanding for receivables, and so on.

David Worrell uses the acronym TIGER to delineate the characteristics of a great dashboard:

- Time—results are shown over several periods
- Impact—the metrics displayed can be controlled through management decisions

- Goals—results are shown relative to a business goal
- Ease—the metrics must be easy to measure and to understand
- Relationships—interrelated metrics are shown in a way that their relationship becomes obvious

Examples of some dashboard metrics might be:

- Sales
- Accounts receivable
- Accounts payable
- Days sales outstanding
- Number of units sold
- Number of errors, or error rate
- Number of new customers signed up
- Website visitors
- Total overhead expenses
- Net profit

A dashboard is an essential tool that good leaders use to manage their business. If possible, the dashboard should be published, frequently, so that everyone can see how the entire company is doing. Bonuses and incentives should be based upon the most important of the numbers.

Dashboard Example

One financial firm I worked for accrued up to $750,000 every quarter to be distributed to all the nonmanagement employees (averaging about $300 a person each quarter) based upon a list of key metrics that were previously identified by those employees. They called it a customer satisfaction test, but it was nothing more than a dashboard. The key metrics included number of customers, total number of loans, and so on. The metrics were updated and posted on the walls of every building every day, and on the computer screens of every employee every day (shown in Figure 10.6 and Figure 10.7)

When the metrics were in the red, everyone pulled together (working nights and weekends) in order to get them green again because a missed metric meant no bonus—and that hit the pocketbooks of every employee throughout the company. When a particular division was having a hard time with something, employees from other divisions would offer to help. The system encouraged the entire company to work together to ensure that bonuses were not missed. Everyone knew how every other division was doing, and we approached it as a shared goal, not a competition.

Figure 10.6. Dashboard Example—Standards

CUSTOMER SATISFACTION TEST

SATISFACTION STANDARDS

Ready to Serve: Percentage of staff people who are here to serve the Customer.

System Availability: Percentage of time that staff systems are available and responding within standard.

Two-Ring Pickup: Percentage of direct-extension calls that are answered within two rings.

Speed of Answer: Percentage of Customer calls that are answered within standard.

Product Replacement: Percentage of product reissues that are processed and mailed within standard.

New Account Setup: Percentage of new accounts that are opened within standard.

Account Adjustments: Percentage of address changes, non-monetary adjustments, and monetary adjustments processed within standard.

No-Error Processing: Percentage of divisional processes completed accurately.

Credit Line Increases: Percentage of line increase requests received by telephone that are processed within standard.

Customer Correspondence: Percentage of Customer correspondence acknowledged and/or processed within standard.

Statement Generation: Percentage of Customer statements processed accurately and mailed within standard.

Payment Processing: Percentage of Customer payments processed accurately and posted within standard.

GLOBAL SATISFACTION STANDARDS

INDEX	STD%	TDY%
Ready to Serve	99.5	100
System Availability	100	100
Two-Ring Pickup	100	100
Speed of Answer	100	100
Product Replacement	100	100
New Account Setup	100	100
Account Adjustments	100	100
No-Error Processing	100	100
Credit Line Increases	100	100
Customer Correspondence	100	100
Statement Generation	100	100
Payment Processing	100	100

CUSTOMER SATISFACTION TEST

MONDAY, AUGUST 25, 2027

100%

YTD Index: 99.2%
Standard: 98.5%

TODAY'S DIVISIONAL INDEXES

Consumer Deposits	100%
Consumer Finance	100%
Credit Sector	100%
International	100%
HHNA Callmark	100%
Insurance Services	100%
Marketing	100%
Regional Management	100%

What Gets Measured Gets Attended To, What Gets Attended To Gets Done.

Figure 10.7. Dashboard Example—Bonus Incentive

CUSTOMER SATISFACTION TEST

BUSINESS INDICATORS

Total Customers: Number of loan Customers.

Total New Accounts: Number of new accounts opened.

Total Managed Loans: Combined balances of all loan accounts.

Delinquency: Consolidated percentage of delinquency on all loan products.

Cardholder Volume: Total dollar volume of purchases and cash advances charged by Customers

Payments: Total dollar amount of payments made to loan accounts.

Customer Transactions: Total number of purchases and cash advances charged by Customers

Merchant Services: Merchant and professional services dollar sales volume.

Total Deposits: Combined balances of all retail deposits.

Customer Phone Contacts: Total number of Customer calls answered.

BUSINESS INDICATORS

INDEX	TDY	YTD
Total Customers		18,863 M
Total New Accounts	36 M	2,696 M
Total Managed Loans		$28,952,100 M
Delinquency	3.94%	3.94%
Cardholder Volume	$130,900 M	$16,897,500 M
Payments	$94,800 M	$15,166,900 M
Customer Transactions	820 M	94,550 M
Merchant Services	$3,169 M	$301,189 M
Total Deposits		$6,172,376 M
Customer Phone Contacts	211 M	20,386 M

M = 1,000

SATISFACTION EARNINGS

Earned Yesterday
$29,092

Earned Quarter To Date
$494,564

Earned Year To Date
$3,417,491

Total Program Earnings
Since May 1986
$29,142,255

Choosing the Metrics

The right dashboard metrics are those that will discover weakness in vital systems, evaluate activity, or predict disaster. In other words, a dashboard should answer the following questions:

1. What's always important?
2. What's effective now?
3. What's ahead?

What is important in a business may not be obvious at first, even to the entrepreneur. It's easy to say sales—and every owner's dashboard should track sales—but let's go deeper. What is the real engine of sales? An online retailer's sales engine is far different from the sales engine at a lumber mill or real estate office. Different business models have different key ingredients.

The online retailer can only sell when people come to the website, so the key metrics might be traffic, number of ads running, or click-through rate. The lumber mill can sell as much wood as they can cut, so the key to sales might be the tons of wood processed or the board-feet produced. The real estate brokerage makes money when sales close, but that is driven by number of homes under contract, or total value of pending transactions. The tai chi studio gets members from their quarterly events, so the number of people who attend those events is a major driver.

By identifying the underlying drivers of sales, we can measure and monitor those operational items that we can actually impact or control through careful management. Plotting sales is important, but not all that helpful by itself. A business that drives sales should observe and record the factors that result in sales as well as the sales themselves.

When we correctly identify both the key drivers of sales and measure sales, we get a nice bonus—the ratio of the two. For example, a real estate broker might track the number of houses under contract, and commissions earned. By calculating and tracking the ratio of these two numbers (dollars earned/houses contracted), we can get a feel for how fast houses are closing, how efficient agents are at finding buyers, and how much houses are selling for. Tracking each of those specific numbers every month would be arduous. By tracking just the ratio of houses to dollars, the experienced broker can spot trends or anomalies, which can direct further investigation.

The whole purpose of plotting the most important metrics (sales and sales drivers, for example) is to gain deeper insight into the external market and a clearer understanding of the inner workings of our own business. Trends, opportunities, and dangers are hidden by a typical financial statement, but become crystal clear when we plot a few metrics on a dashboard. By identifying key drivers, the results, and the ratio between them, we will have our thumb on the pulse of the business.

The Magic of Dashboards

There is something magical about a well-constructed business dashboard. The act of creating a dashboard forces us to find, examine, measure, calculate, and record those things that are most important to our business success. If we update the dashboard often enough, then that process alone should be enough to shape the decisions we make in the day-to-day business operations. The dashboard not only makes our priorities obvious, but also provides a feedback loop so we can see the results of the decisions we've made.

There is one more step that can make the magic of a dashboard even more powerful—printing it out. Ignore the temptation to keep a dashboard file on a PC or website (unless you make it the screensaver that appears on everyone's PC). Instead, print it out. Carry it. Tape it to the wall. Update it with magic marker. Share it with others. Make it obvious!

Just as a car dashboard is always right in front of us, our business dashboard should be within our field of view as much as possible. The process of creating a dashboard and keeping it in front of us commits us to work on the priorities we've measured. It is amazing what our focused attention can accomplish—and the dashboard is the lens that can focus us on those things that matter most.

Models

A small business model should capture the market conditions and resources that are most important to the scope and scale of the business (now or in the future). It might be as simple as four variables in a spreadsheet (Excel, Google Sheets, Open Office Calc, Apple Numbers, or any other spreadsheet). For example, if the business is a neighborhood grocery store, the number of houses in the neighborhood might be an input variable. If the business is a tai chi studio focusing on seniors' health, the number of people over the age of 50 within driving distance might be an input variable. If the tai chi studio also has classes focusing on the martial aspect of tai chi, then the number of young adults would also be an input. Through experience, for example, we might know that $2,000 of local newspaper advertising will generally attract about five new senior students out of a population of 15,000 and three new young adult students out of a population of 6,000. We would build formulas that represent those relationships in our spreadsheet—and that would be the model.

Models can get complex, or can be simple. They are simply a way of mathematically representing our experience regarding what works, what doesn't, how many people we need, and so on.

Some example variables we might consider for our model are:

- Current number of customers or employees
- Capital available for expansion
- Size of region served (square miles or states)
- Number of square feet in our store
- Hours available for operation
- Likely downtime or inefficiencies
- Gross margin or markup
- Advertising opportunities or budget
- Maximum number of sales per hour or day
- Population in the area we serve
- Number of competitors
- Cost of raw materials
- Number of distributors serving our industry
- Total web searches on a key term
- Price of web hosting, bandwidth, gasoline, or any other input
- Number of certain events per year (trade shows, hurricanes, satellite launches, etc.)

In general, anything that drives demand, supply, or price of our product or service should be considered as an input. We are looking for variables that impact our ability to produce, sell, or profit from the goods and services we sell. Consider all possible customers, competitors, and costs when collecting possible inputs. Then, keep those that are most directly related to the success of the business and can be most easily verified.

The downside to using a business model is that we have to build it from scratch. No one model can predict the business results for every business. In fact, although there are generic models that apply to particular industries, each business should create a model that specifically and uniquely captures its own operating inputs and variables.

A model might rely on exactly the same inputs as a dashboard. In fact, the relationships and ratios we discover while making a dashboard (which plots events as they happen) might become the inputs and calculations for a powerful and accurate model. If we have an operating business, and can build a dashboard that measures meaningful and predictive ratios, then that work will flow naturally into a model that can be used to predict the future and to play "what if" with the business inputs we select.

Forecast

While a model tells us what may be possible, a forecast defines what we want to accomplish.

Since the scope and scale of a business depends entirely on how much we sell, every forecast starts with an estimate of what sales will be. Within the parameters set by the model (and perhaps, using the mathematical relationships established by the model), we must look into the future and set a reasonable and attainable goal for sales. From that sales goal, every other aspect of the business can be forecast—prior to sales, we need advertising and awareness; after sales, we need production and product support; those functions must be backed up by administration and overhead.

The forecast begins to fall in place when we answer five questions:

1. How much will we sell?
2. What is needed to attract those sales?
3. What is needed to complete those sales?
4. What else will customers need?
5. How big must the other parts of the company be in order to support all of that activity?

A rolling forecast is quite useful for small businesses. Rolling forecasts have two important attributes: (1) They predict results over a specific, constant period of time, (2) We update them frequently. In practice, a 12- or 15-week rolling forecast, updated weekly, is a powerful tool. Twelve weeks—about three months—is enough time to start and complete significant projects, and see their impact on business.

Budgets

With a complete forecast in hand, a manager should be able to estimate—calculate, really—the amount of money that will be made and spent in every part of the business.

If our company is large enough to have departments, then each department can be responsible for its own budget. Frankly, any employee who has spending authority should also have the responsibility of keeping a budget. This is an excellent way to reinforce the need for frugality and reduces the budgeting burden on the business owner at the same time. We shouldn't forget, however, to roll-up the departmental budgets into one consolidated company budget.

It is typical (especially in government agencies and large companies) to begin with last year's budget of P&L as the basis of the budget for the following year. Since the P&L already lists every income and expense account, it is easier to estimate every detail when each line item starts with last year's number.

However, it is often better for us to do zero-based budgeting, as we did when we were first starting out. Zero-based budgets assume that each period begins with no pre-set level of spending and any unnecessary expense is cut. It can be a powerful tool for controlling costs and making staff members think critically about purchases. Zero-based budgets work well for both small and large expenses. In fact, the concept can be applied to all three kinds of expenses in a business—cost of goods, ordinary expenses, and capital expenses.

SUMMARY OF FINANCIALS

When we know how financial statements work, we will be rewarded with a new and more complete understanding of our business and where it is going. When we learn the language of finance and data, we can grow a company that is more profitable, more sustainable, and more fun.

- ☑ Finance is the language of business.
- ☑ GAAP (Generally Accepted Accounting Principles) are guidelines for accountants and tax professionals to follow so that financial reporting is comparable between companies and across timeframes.
- ☑ GAAP does not provide guidance on how we should manage our business effectively.
- ☑ Simplified categories, separated into direct and indirect expenses, may be more useful to us than the typical breakouts reported by accountants.
- ☑ Income statements or P&L gives the profit or loss of a business within a specified timeframe.
- ☑ Balance sheets gives us a snapshot view of the net worth or book value of the business at a particular moment in time.
- ☑ Cash flow statements illustrate how much cash is flowing into or out of the business over a specified timeframe.
- ☑ Break-even analysis can help us make better decisions.
- ☑ Recording financials requires strategic decisions regarding capital versus expense, how much to depreciate and when, as well as when to book income and expenses.
- ☑ Dashboards can help us manage our business by measuring the key drivers of our business frequently.
- ☑ Budgets, forecasts, and models can be helpful in strategically planning for improving our business.

11

Sources of Capital

I know many people who are very knowledgeable about sources of capital. In addition to David Nour, who wrote *The Entrepreneur's Guide to Raising Capital*, I received a lot of help in this chapter from two other people:

- Bob Thomson from Ben Franklin Technology Partners of Northeastern Pennsylvania, a government-backed venture funding group
- Jane Morris, founder of Liora Partners and heavily involved in the private equity industry for over 30 years in a variety of roles

While their help was invaluable, few have the wide scope of experience and can communicate the details of raising capital as well as David Nour. From bootstrapping to huge mega deals, David knows the playing field for entrepreneurial investments of all types and sizes. I will relay just the highlights from his book regarding how to find and choose the sources of capital. For more specific details on the terms and conditions of highly complex venture capital deals, however, you should read David's book.

At the end of this chapter, I will also convey some stories from my decision making regarding varied financing methods I used for my own companies.

OUTSIDE FINANCING

How do entrepreneurs navigate the capital-raising labyrinth? David's book deals with the most common, yet often perplexing, questions:

- How do I realize the promised benefits of raising outside capital?
- How do I avoid the risks associated with various sources of capital?
- How do I plan for the right type, amount, and source of capital as the business evolves in its natural lifecycle?

- How do I avoid diluting my ownership with current and prospective investors?
- How do I maintain my credibility with current and prospective investors?
- How do I choose wisely from the plethora of financial and strategic investors, consultants, merchant bankers, and middlemen?
- How do I avoid wasting precious capital that won't help me move the business forward?
- How do I get the most out of every dollar of outside capital I raise?

If we can get through the maze set up by those who might fund our dream, if we can understand the broad sources of available capital from different sources, if we can survive the beauty contests set up by those who judge the quality of the deal—all while making a stand for the business we have built—the capital we receive can become the fuel for making our larger vision a reality.

Options for Funding

There are several options for funding our business, summarized along with advantages and disadvantages in Table 11.1 Financing Options. Many factors influence the choice of internal or external funding. For example, a typical lifestyle business (in which the owner and/or the owner's family can make a good living) is not going to be attractive to an external investor, so it often can only get internal funding for any expansion or development efforts. The timing of the funding in the life of the business (early stage, also known as seed funding stage, or a mature, profitable, already-existing business) is also a factor.

All financing options are not equal. Before getting into the specifics of how to get capital, we must delve into the decision to seek capital at all and review the risks. Bootstrapping is relying solely upon internal funding—a decision which should be carefully considered. When Ernie Post (Executive Director of the Kutztown University Small Business Development Center) and I did research on entrepreneurs, we determined that a decision not to start or expand a business was just as much a success as a decision to start a business (Rhoads and Post 2013). In Chapter 12, I outline my own past funding decisions and discuss why, in my most recent funding decision, I decided to bootstrap.

If we choose to go for external capital, we need to choose the right investors and the right kind of capital at the right time. The source of the funding and the amount of the funding can be critical to the success of our plans.

Table 11.1. Financing Options

Option	Description	Typical Timing	Advantages	Disadvantages
Bootstrap	Funding expansion from savings, existing profits, or previous retained earnings.	Small or lifestyle businesses, anytime	No external pressure or risk. No debt or future payback required. Allows owner to retain total control over company.	Slow growth, possibility of missed opportunities. Limitations on size. Relies solely on skills and network of owner to expand.
Friends and Family	Asking personal friends and family members to provide funding, either by lending or giving money. May or may not involve formal agreements and ownership shares.	early stage	Relatively quick and easy to obtain, based upon personal relationships.	Very risky to personal relationships. Investors are not professional and may not be prepared to lose their money. Investors may try to control or interfere with operations.
Business Plan Competitions, Innovation Contests, and Business Incubators	Competing against others for a financial prize that can be used to fund expansions or startups.	early stage	Democratic (usually) and often network connections are valuable in later funding stages. Allows owner to retain total control over company.	Low probability of funding. Time consuming and takes focus away from primary business.

(Continued)

Table 11.1. (*Continued*)

Option	Description	Typical Timing	Advantages	Disadvantages
Grants and Incentives	Applying to a government agency, agency, or corporation for funding. For example, the National Institute of Health provides SBIR grant funding for innovative business ideas.	early stage	Funding does not usually need to be repaid. Network connections are valuable in later funding stages. Allows owner to retain total control over company.	Low probability of funding. Time consuming and takes focus away from primary business.
Credit Card or other unsecured debt	Using a credit card or borrowing money from a nontraditional source of money.	early stage	Unregulated and easy to obtain. Allows owner to retain more control over company.	Costly and Risky. Debt must be repaid at high interest rates, regardless of business success. Never recommended.
Crowdfunding	Requesting donations on a website designed to share your project with others who can pledge money in varying amounts. Usually involves creating a video about the project and creating incentives to reward contributors.	early stage	Relatively easy to request, funding does not need to be paid back. Incentives can be managed to increase funding levels dynamically. Allows owner to retain total control over company.	Low probability of funding, and requires strong online presence. Time consuming to manage. Must be planned carefully.

Angel Investment	Finding an experienced person who enjoys investing money in new projects or startups.	early stage	Funding that does not need to be repaid. Network connections are valuable in later funding stages.	Angel may become overly controlling, and may interfere in future plans.
Bank Debt (including SBA loans and/or lines of credit)	Applying for a loan or a line of credit from a bank. May be guaranteed by SBA, which makes it more likely for a local bank to make funding available.	mature	Secure, and allows owner to retain more control over company. If owner or business has tangible assets, relatively easy to obtain.	Funding must be repaid, regardless of business success. Requires pledging significant assets for security.
Venture Debt	Obtaining funding from a venture capitalist, but structuring the funding as a debenture upon which interest is paid. Usually set up to be convertible to stock at a future date.	early stage to mature	Funding usually does not need to be repaid if business is not successful. Relatively easy to structure. Network connections and knowledge of startup processes are valuable in later funding stages. Allows owner to retain more control over company.	May be more difficult to find. Requires interest payments, regardless of business success, and may lead to less control of company in later stages than bank debt.

(Continued)

Table 11.1. (*Continued*)

Option	Description	Typical Timing	Advantages	Disadvantages
Private Equity Venture Capital	Obtaining funding from a venture capitalist who takes a percentage of ownership in the company.	mature	Funding usually does not need to be repaid if business is not successful. Network connections and knowledge of startup processes are valuable, raising the chance of business success.	Requires giving up a percentage (sometimes, a majority) of control. In order to be successful, must be "well introduced" (i.e., already have some connections in the venture industry). Business management team must be relatively stable with proven product or service and high-potential return on investment.
Strategic Investment	Obtaining funding through a corporation, usually one in an industry that would benefit from the new project or startup.	mature	Funding usually does not need to be repaid if business is not successful. Network connections and knowledge of industry are valuable. Potential for buyout if successful.	Requires giving up a percentage (sometimes, a majority) of control. In order to be successful, must fit in very well with funding industry. Business must be fast growing and have a high chance of liquidity event to be attractive.

Institutionalt Venture Capital	The "big guns." Professionally managed firms for high-growth short-term funding from expansion to maturity for proven products and services.	mature	Funding usually does not need to be repaid if business is not successful. Network connections and knowledge of startup processes are valuable, ensuring business success.	Requires giving up a percentage (sometimes, a majority) of control. In order to be successful, must be "well introduced" (i.e., already have some connections in the venture industry). Business must be fast growing and have a high chance of liquidity event in next five years to be attractive.

Source: Based on information from David Nour, *The Entrepreneur's Guide to Raising Capital*. Santa Barbara, CA: Praeger, 2009.

Understanding the Risks

There is always a risk when raising capital. While all the different sources of capital have some risk and are explained in more detail in David's book, there are some funding sources which will be discussed here—crowdfunding, easy venture capital, friends and family.

Crowdfunding: A New Option

One item David did not discuss was crowdfunding because when he wrote his book, crowdfunding did not exist. Crowdfunding is an offshoot of crowdsourcing, which is obtaining needed products and services from a large population of people, most often conducted through online channels. Rather than goods or services, crowdfunding focuses on obtaining funding for a project. Crowdfunding has been around for a few years, but was mostly used to support artists, film makers, and musicians. Someone with a worthy project asks people to contribute money without any kind of formal agreement regarding what they can expect in return—a donation-based model. Typically, people would create a short online video that describes some intellectual property (movie, book, CD, artwork) that they would like to work on, and others viewing the descriptive video would contribute whatever they felt they could afford. Generally, the performer or artist would promise to send the completed item to the contributors, sometimes describing additional incentives for larger contributions.

There are several websites that provide a platform for people to request funding for projects, including Kickstarter.com, Indiegogo.com, Crowdfunder.com, and Rockethub.com. Most are set up so that if the goal amount is not raised, no money changes hands. If the goal amount is pledged, however, then the amount is deducted from the credit cards of the pledgers and transferred, minus a small fee, to the requester.

In 2010, for example, I contributed to a project started by a friend, Qiang, through Kickstarter, the most well-known of the crowdfunding websites. Qiang wanted to take a trip to China and play an instrument at a concert. The premium was a copy of one of Qiang's music CDs, which I received within a short time of the expected date.

In 2011, another friend, Aeron, wanted to make a short film. Aeron advertised the project through Kickstarter. There were nine levels of funding, each with a different level of incentive associated with it. In all, Aeron asked for $9,500 and raised $10,600. So that you can see a typical donation profile, the numbers and levels for Aeron's project were:

10 people pledged $5
20 people pledged $15
21 people pledged $30
28 people pledged $50
27 people pledged $100
5 people pledged $250
3 people pledged $500
1 people pledged $1,000

At the level I contributed, I was to have received a special thanks in the film and on the website, a digital and DVD copy of the movie, signed by the director, PLUS an original movie poster and a signed copy of the adapted screenplay by the cast, crew, and writer/director. The expected date for completion was October 2012. Knowing my friend, my expectations were very low regarding actually receiving the incentives by October 2012. Perhaps I may, someday, receive them—or not. As of May, 2014, there has been no movie made yet.

In both of these cases, I was simply donating to the project. It wasn't a charitable deduction. The transaction was not a sale. The premiums might be considered Thank You gifts. Generally, people donate to help friends achieve their dreams, or simply because they like the idea.

Not everyone gets funded; the majority who create their video and describe their projects do not get any funding. But some hit the jackpot. Robyn Jasko, test marketing a line of hot sauces, ran a campaign from March 27, 2013 to May 11, 2013, and requested only $850. She raised $53,419. She had learned from previous failed campaigns how to attract funding. "There are so many scenarios where a successful Kickstarter ends up costing the project creator more money than they raised to fulfill the rewards," she warned. She knew that prior to launching the fundraising portion of the project, the requester needs a robust social media presence, a large following of potential backers, and a strong online community presence in order to attract funding. The beauty of the system, however, is that incentives can be increased dynamically as the amount raised becomes larger, which was how she was able to raise 6,284 percent of her goal (Scheid 2013).

Crowdfunding is fast becoming a viable alternative for startup costs or market testing grounds for small businesses. In 2012, President Barack Obama signed into law legislation that would allow people to invest and become stockholders through crowdfunding sites, though as of this writing, the rules are not yet established by the SEC (Luzar 2013). Still in donation-only mode, several high-profile startups have relied upon funding from crowdfunding websites. Pebble Technology Corporation, for example, raised more than $10 million on Kickstarter, and was able to develop a smartwatch ahead of Apple and Samsung. Ouya raised over $8 million to develop a game console. HiddenRadio raised almost a million to develop a tiny speaker, and Supermechanical raised half a million to develop a tiny sensor device that is programmable over the web (Des-Marais 2013).

Though there are still a lot of questions that need to be answered about the legality and risk of crowdfunding, it is definitely a viable possibility for funding projects of all types.

Should We Take Advantage of Easy Capital?

The process for finding capital is volatile and dependent upon the current conditions. At times, venture capital is difficult to find, no matter how stable and laudable the business and team. At other times, venture capital seems easy to obtain, even for what might be considered questionable ventures.

Easy capital is funding that comes to us from angels, venture funding, or strategic funding without our needing to spend large amounts of time going after it. During the late 1990s (just before the dot-com crash) and during the years 2004–2008 (after the recovery from the Internet bubble bursting, but before the devastating recession), capital was relatively easily available. Many entrepreneurs who were originally planning to run a small lifestyle business changed their plans after reading about successes of others in the big leagues. There is a mode of thinking that says when there's capital to be gotten, we should go out and get it.

Larry Bock serves as chairman of the Lux Ventures advisory board, a collection of industry experts advising the firm's investment team. He advises, "When the cookies are being handed out, you take as many cookies as you possibly can." He adds, "The kinds of companies that I get involved in . . . are broad-based platform technology companies. I'm always one who thinks you should raise as much money as you can."

I remember speaking with a good friend of mine, Jerry, in the year 2000 (at the peak of the Internet Technology bubble, when any dot com could attract hundreds of thousands of venture capital just by having a few web designers on board and a half-decent pitch). Jerry and the team had been given three times the investment they had originally sought. They believed success was assured. They had a great business model, well-connected investors, and were about to hit the big time, moving from hundreds of thousands to millions of dollars invested. They were looking at the optimistic future and were not thinking about the downside—until a few months later, when the bubble burst and the dot com market crashed.

Jerry's situation demonstrates the risks of taking more capital than we feel comfortable with. Everyone on Jerry's team lost their entire investment, including their houses, which they had used as collateral. The investors lost all their money, too. As we saw in October 2008, market crashes and capital valuation downgrades can happen at any time, for many reasons beyond our control. While it is possible to win big, it is also possible to lose everything.

Should we accept easy capital? It depends. My experience is that easy capital fails the entrepreneur more often than it succeeds, but there are always exceptions. As of this writing, the venture capital industry is heating up again, and the cookies are being handed out, so some may want to take advantage of the opportunity before it is lost through another economic downturn.

Friends and Family Funding: Tread Carefully

Many experts recommend that entrepreneurs raise seed money from friends and family. Friends and family funding is often the cheapest money we can obtain. But getting financing from friends and family is fraught with peril. When we take money that puts people at significant financial risk—because the early stages of a business are simply not predictable—we have to be careful.

"Never accept money from anyone you might have to sit next to at Thanksgiving dinner," warns Tim Knox, serial entrepreneur and author of *Everything I Know about Business I Learned from My Mama.* Even if friends and family are begging us to take their money, we should think long and hard before accepting. When we ask friends and family for a loan or investment, we are appealing to them emotionally, not necessarily to their rational sense of investing. Capital raised through friends and family can be emotionally draining as we become more and more consumed with not disappointing them.

Furthermore, family and friends can lose out even if the business becomes a success. Later funding rounds can dilute the holdings of early investors until they get very little in the end. On the other hand, terms that are too restrictive in early rounds might dissuade potential venture capital funders from investing in later rounds. In either case, family and friends rounds can complicate the financing options. But the biggest risk is not financial, but personal relationships.

One of my ventures (CommerceLinks.net) lost big time when the market crashed in 2001. We had just finished a friends and family round of financing, and were working on a deal with some venture capitalists to provide the next round of funding to enable us to finish the development of the technology. We had applied for a provisional patent, but needed funding to finish it. We never did.

Luckily, I am fortunate to have very forgiving family members. Of course, I only accepted money from those who were not putting their own futures at risk. Nonetheless, I felt the weight of that debt for many years, even after it had been fully discharged, legally. I continued to strive to find a way to pay my family investors back, even though it took more than a decade. I gave them money out of my own pocket, even when I couldn't really afford it. And I would do it again. To me, it is a matter of integrity.

I was fortunate, but I've talked with many entrepreneurs who weren't. They had raised funding through friends-and-family rounds and then lost it. The losses led to damaged, even destroyed, relationships. Given business failure statistics, unless we are careful, we may find ourselves sitting at Thanksgiving dinner next to someone who is not happy about losing money in our venture.

If we do decide to take friends and family capital, it is critical that we set up a repayment schedule in writing and stick to it, so that family gatherings don't become a battleground. It is also critical that we are completely honest and upfront about the chances of losing the money.

Other Considerations Regarding External Funding

There are risks to external funding that aren't related to the specific types of funding.

Remember the Failures

When reading about rising stars and overwhelming successful entrepreneurs, we might want to remember that media loves the winners, and rarely talks about the losers. I share my stories—even the failures—because often, entrepreneurs are not willing to talk about when they lost money. Who wants to admit failure?

I don't know any successful entrepreneurs and business owners who haven't failed—multiple times. Motivational guru Tony Robbins reminds us that all of our past failures and frustrations are actually laying the foundation for the understandings that have created the new level of living that we can enjoy. Nanci Raphael reminds us to celebrate the gift of failure. Learning from our failures is the key to success.

Ready for External Funding?

In order to determine whether or not we are ready, willing, and able to receive external capital, whether from a bank, an angel investor, or a venture capital source, we can ask ourselves the following questions:

- Can I succinctly articulate and credibly convince others of the realistic potential of my business?
- Am I willing to think big, start small, and scale fast?
- Have I developed a strategic plan to attract venture or bank funding?
- Do I have what it takes to impress investors?
- Do I have the opportunity to be well-introduced?
- Do I have a proven track record of delivering on my milestones in the past?
- Am I willing to toil day and night to achieve the plan that I have envisioned, no matter how long it takes?
- Am I confident in my ability to physically and mentally deal with the challenges coming my way?
- Have I developed the necessary leadership skills to inspire others to accomplish these goals because they want to, and not just because I'm paying them?
- Does my team have the bench strength necessary to achieve our stated financial goals?

If we can answer most of these questions positively, then attracting outside capital may be the right thing for us and our business at the present time.

Note that we should only go for external funding if our business is doing well. If we are desperate for money, if our business is in trouble, we cannot/should not go after external funding. We either put the business in order so that it is profitable and then go after funding, or close it down, find a job, and start saving for our next venture. When we have a vision, a good history, a great team, and the wherewithal to expand beyond our own assets—that is the time to look for external funding.

CHOOSING THE BEST EXTERNAL
FUNDING OPTION

Once we've made the decision to go for external funding rather than bootstrap our business, we need to seek out a good match for our business. Different sorts of businesses with different goals require different funding options.

Considerations in Our Choice of External Funding

Venture funding options range from early stage seed funding (friends and family, angels, business incubators, government grants) to mature venture funding (strategic financial partners, private equity funds, venture capital funds, corporate capital funds, and institutional investors). The advantages and disadvantages are discussed in Table 11.1, *Financing Options*.

If we already have significant assets and a profitable business, then we can go to a bank for financing in order to invest in expansion efforts. Of course, borrowing against those assets puts them at risk. But if we are sure that the expansion will pay off, borrowing from a bank is a great way to convert our balance sheet strength into future profits without giving up any control. However, the numbers have to clearly show how the bank will get paid back. Banks are not looking to invest. We need to pay them back whether our business succeeds or fails.

If we are looking for funding that wouldn't have to be paid back if our business fails, then we might want to seek angel or venture capital. Some entrepreneurs recommend venture capital because if the business goes south, they don't have to pay it back. Additionally, with venture capital usually comes a whole host of help and support coming from the network of the investors since they have a vested interest in our success.

Venture capital has a cost, however. Investors may expect us to leverage everything we own, so that we have skin in the game. Attracting venture capital requires developing an advisory team (usually a formalized Board of Directors), which integrates management, lenders, investors, and advisors into a working support group. We must manage the expectations of the investors and carefully balance the relationship between strategic planning and the investment time horizons.

Furthermore, with venture capital, the investment time horizons (the time between investment and liquidity event) become important. Venture capitalists are concerned about the liquidity event because it is how they will achieve a return on their investment. The investment time horizon is controlled by the economy and the marketplace, and may not fit neatly into what we, as owners, would like. Periods of exceptionally low interest rates and bond yields such as we have seen in the last few years have a profound impact on valuations and the downstream effects of investor expectations. For example, a 15 percent annual return on investment, when bond yields are at 4 percent, might lead our investors to want us to cash out. Fifteen percent is a valuation that would give them a return while leaving us, as founders, with insufficient cash flow on which to live or fund another company.

Venture debt is similar to venture capital, and may be an option in the mix. The addition of some debt allows the entrepreneur to keep more of the equity in the company. Debt funding can also come from a bank. Many banks have stricter criteria for lending money than other sources of investment, so they aren't always an option. Not all banks are the same, however. Banks such as Silicon Valley and Square One are more receptive to new ventures.

Getting a government grant may be a good way to get seed capital, especially for businesses in biotechnology or other highly technical industries. Several companies have greatly profited from Small Business Innovation Research (SBIR) or Small Business Technology Transfer (STTR) funding. ViaSat, a California digital communications company specializing in satellite and wireless networking technologies, was founded in 1986 and received its first SBIR contract to develop a Communication Environment Simulator in 1987. Since then, they've grown to more than 2,100 employees and $688 million in sales. ViewPlus was founded by John Gardner, a physics professor who unexpectedly went blind from minor eye surgery. John initially funded the company with family and friends' money, but after a few years, he applied for and received a SBIR award, which was renewed 14 more times to perfect or develop new uses for ViewPlus products. ViewPlus is now a $5 million dollar firm with 40 employees.

My experiences getting government grants have been frustrating and fraught with difficulty. The applications require an inordinate amount of resources, are very time consuming, and there is no guarantee of success in obtaining the grant. Even when I got them, they turned out to be much less lucrative than I thought.

I learned my lesson the hard way. After wasting too many hours on applications and being disappointed in the rewards, in 2009, I decided government grants were a poor investment of my time.

But I'm a glutton for punishment and couldn't shake the notion that, perhaps, next time would be different. In 2011, I tried again. A grant to study *telehealth*[1] became available through my university. Since

I monitor progress of such technology to assess how close we are getting to my vision of videoconferencing ubiquity, and could use the information in the expansion of my business, I thought I should give grants another chance. The application took three months of my time. I got the grant, but the rules for reimbursable expenses were so restrictive I ended up funding most of the work myself. And the changes and requested revisions took six months longer than I had originally planned. As I write this, I am still waiting for approval from the government agency to publish the results. Another six months wasted.

This time, I've vowed on my father's grave, never, ever, ever to apply for another government grant.[2] The only saving grace was that I actually did learn a lot and had a lot of fun doing the research and writing the report. As I explain in Chapter 11, working on the telehealth research impacted my decision to bootstrap the expansion because of how much I enjoyed it.

---

[1] Telehealth is utilizing information technology tools to provide health care remotely.

[2] Of course, I also swore up and down in 1995 that I would never learn to play that stupid game where people chased a little white ball all over acres of grass (golf), but by 2001 I was hitting birdies, chipping and putting with the best of them. Until my back injuries put the cabosh on the activity, I was an avid golfer, usually out there every weekend. Additionally, I'll be happy to work on grants for which other people successfully apply as long as my own time investment is minimal.

Business incubators are often wonderful and a godsend, but they might also be expensive and not as helpful as we think they might be, especially in actually providing capital. The Kutztown University Small Business Development Center has a great business incubator with inexpensive office space, top-notch consulting help included in the price, and a full array of technology and marketing support tools. There have been many successful businesses coming out of that incubator.

But I've also seen business incubators where the rents were higher than market prices, the supportive consultants charged extra for every hour of their help, and the graduation rates (the businesses that leave the incubator and go on to successful independent locations) were abysmal.

Smaller amounts of funding are often available through business plan competitions, or innovative incentive programs available through universities or research organizations. Given the right product at the right time, these small incentive funding opportunities may be a good option.

Angels, usually cashed-out entrepreneurs looking to help the next generation, can be helpful and a good initial funding round. However, sometimes angels can also be a little too hands-on. They may end up inter-fering in the smooth running of the business. If the strategic plan is bold enough to attract institutional venture funding, it may be best to skip the early stage angel funding unless the perfect angel can be found. A success-ful angel/entrepreneur partnership is as much about personal chemistry as a marriage, and can be just as devastating if the partnership ends in a divorce.

Learning about External Funding Options

All capital investors are looking for an eventual exit (also known as a liquidation event) that is profitable to them. No matter how nice they are, no matter how much they come across as supportive and caring, they are not looking to make us, or our friends and family, wealthy. They will only do so if they can get a large return on their own investment first. Some-times, they will sacrifice the prosperity and well-being of the owners, the owner's friends and family, as well as the founders and management team in order to achieve their goals. The term vulture capitalist is not a term of endearment; it is a very real outcome if we aren't able to produce the returns we promised when they gave us the financing. It is up to us to ensure that we enter into an agreement we can live with, no matter which way it goes, up or down. That's why doing our homework and ensuring the quality of the character of the people with whom we are considering partnering is essential.

We also don't want to waste our time with people who aren't actually good candidates for investing in us. Sean Mallon recommends asking the following questions to qualify potential investors:

- Has this investor made any investments within the last year?
- If so, in what sector(s) did they invest?
- How big are the checks that they have written?
- Who have they co-invested with?

Talking with other business owners who have investigated and/or ob-tained external financing is essential—and not just one or two. Now is the time to get out and speak with dozens of different entrepreneurs and find out all about their experiences.

It used to be that the only way to do that was networking face to face among friends or at venture funding conferences. But the World Wide Web has changed that. Now, the best resource for entrepreneurs is www.thefunded.com, an independent online community where entre-preneurs contribute great insights regarding their investor experiences at varying stages of their company's growth. The site is free for CEOs searching for funding. For everyone else, a registration fee from $200 to $500 is required and venture capitalists are not allowed on at all. The entrepreneurial members rate hundreds of venture capitalists, venture funds, and openly talk turkey about sources of funding.

We also must take care at this stage. Once we have made it known that we are interested in expanding and obtaining external financing, a bevy of consultants, supporters, recruiters, and opportunists will beat a path to our door. There is a full merry-go-round of "experts" who will undertake to introduce us to the right people, write our business plan for us, and find the best people for our new management team. Many will make appealing promises. Not counting the fact that many of these tasks we need to do ourselves and should not outsource, there is a lot of difficulty in separating the trustworthy individuals (far and few between) from the rest. Background checks are essential. Talking to previous clients is important. Before taking on any consultant, be absolutely sure they can deliver actual help instead of just empty assurances.

A sure sign that we have moved outside of trustworthy realms is when someone offers to find us funding for a fee. The industry does not work that way. You cannot pay someone to get access. Another sign is if they say they can't disclose any previous clients due to confidentiality. It might be true, but it might also be an excuse because previous clients aren't happy, or there are no previous clients. While no consultant can divulge proprietary information or confidential operational secrets of their clients, the names and contact information of their clients is only kept secret in the rarest of cases.

> Years ago, one of my entrepreneurial clients, Emerson, was sure that a consultant found on Monster.com was going to lead straight to the promised land of strategic partnership funding from a company we had targeted. Emerson booked a flight for both of us to meet in Chicago with the consultant and the supposed funding source. As I suspected from the beginning, the consultant was simply a has-been who had talked a good game. To justify the $5,000 fee, the consultant had arranged the meeting with a close friend who had an impressive-sounding title in company we were targeting. The close friend actually had no decision-making power at all, and seemed clueless as to why we were there. Our time and resources were completely wasted.

As described in Chapter 4, there is no substitute for the time-consuming task of finding a personal connection to the decision maker who might provide venture funding.

Attractive to Investors?

We may decide on a particular funding source, but that doesn't mean that we are able to get the funding source. The other side of the coin is whether or not our business will be attractive to investors. Sometimes, entrepreneurs feel that their business is valuable, and a good investment, because they make a good living at it. The thinking goes, *It makes money for me, why wouldn't someone else want it?*

External investors, however, are not looking for businesses at which they can make a good living. They want the business to be large enough to go public or be sold to another company. External investors are usually looking for a large return on their investment.

David Nour published an excellent test to help an entrepreneur recognize if their own business is going to be attractive to different kinds of external capital (angels, venture, strategic, or institutional). Take the test by giving each feature a score of 1–4 on each point on the table in Table 11.2.

Table 11.2. Attractive to Angels and Venture Capital?

	Venture Capital Attractiveness Quiz	
Feature of Business	**Criteria**	**Score**
Unique concept/market-dominating potential	(1 = not really; 4 = strong)	
Unique market approach/value-add	(1 = not really; 4 = strong)	
Cash to market	(1 = <$10 million; 4 = $100 million)	
Channels	(1 = build your own; 4 = leverage others)	
Support cost after the sale	(1 = high; 4 = low)	
Gross margins	(1 = <10 percent; 4 = >50 percent)	
Profitable growth	(1 = >$10 million but <$15 million 4 = >$100 million business)	
Strategic value to others	(1 = not really; 4 = very high)	
Global appeal	(1 = not really; 4 = strong)	
IPO potential	(1 = not really; 4 = within 5 years)	
	Total	____

Source: David Nour, *The Entrepreneur's Guide to Raising Capital.* Santa Barbara, CA: Praeger, 2009.

Add up the score. If the score is less than 10, perhaps external funding is not a viable alternative. The business might be better off by bootstrapping. If the score is more than 10 but less than 15, perhaps angel and early-stage venture capital would be an alternative to bank financing. If the score is between 16 and 30, the company might be a good target for limited venture capital, perhaps some strategic investors, or some smaller private equity firms. Companies with scores of greater than 30 would be appealing to larger private equity and high-profile venture capital firms and bigger, perhaps even international, strategic investors.

Only businesses with a score of up around 40 would be a good fit for large institutional capital sources. Institutional capital investors are looking for a scalable, profitable, business with strategic value to others.

SUMMARY OF SOURCES OF CAPITAL

☑ There are many issues involved in the decision to seek external funding.
☑ Before we seek funding, we should understand the risks.
☑ Friends and family may be a good source of initial capital, but we should be careful about accepting money from them.
☑ Banks generally require a borrower to have collateral to back any business loans.
☑ Investors are looking for businesses with a unique advantage, market dominating potential, low cash to market, an already established sales channel, low support costs, high gross margins, profitable growth, strategic value, global appeal, and IPO (initial public offering) potential.
☑ The best way to learn about external funding options is to talk to other entrepreneurs who have been funded in the past.

12

Funding Decisions and Giving Back

No one can tell us if and when we should borrow money, look for investors, or go for the big bucks. It is truly a personal decision that only makes sense in light of our own lives and situations.

PREVIOUS FUNDING DECISIONS

I've been involved in four startups. It may be instructional to share the decisions that I made over the years, and how I feel about them years after the fact.

First Business: Computer Educational Services

I shared stories in several chapters about Computer Educational Services (CES), my first business, a technology consulting and training firm. When I borrowed $175,000 for CES, it was the right decision at the time, despite the fact that months later, the recession hit and I almost lost my business. The combination of an unexpected hike in interest rates and reduced sales was a big blow to the budget. CES survived, but the difficulties I had influenced my decision to start looking for someone to partner with. If I hadn't borrowed that money and expanded at the time I did, I would not have been able to fortuitously sell the business three years later because I wouldn't have been looking for a partner.

I started CES in 1986 and sold it in 1993, when it had a tangible book value of $36,000 and annual sales of about twice that (with a peak of around $100,000 several years earlier). The deal I negotiated totaled over $600,000 when you count all the sources of income. In addition to some cash up front, there were bonus payments based upon performance, lease payments for intellectual property, guaranteed salaries, and stock in the buying company. Then, when the acquiring business was acquired by a public company seven years later, my brother and I sold our stock at values exceeding $300,000. (Not bad for a clueless school teacher-turned-entrepreneur.)

Millstar and CommerceLink.net

I joined my second startup after being (fortuitously) laid off from my position as vice president in a Fortune 500 financial firm. I was brought in by the investors at the height of the Internet bubble as chief technology officer to support the expansion of a technology firm into an e-commerce software development powerhouse, funded with a few million in venture capital. I didn't last long, but my short-term hiring and firing was a good thing for me. In those few months, I learned more about the world of web development than I could have anywhere else.

The third startup was a true entrepreneurial venture, and the one that lost so much money in the dot com crash. We tried to develop Live Video Customer Service, but we were more than a decade too soon. The underlying technology foundation simply wasn't there in 2001. Nonetheless, I wouldn't be where I am today if I hadn't worked on that patent or went out seeking millions in venture financing. It's a good thing we didn't get those millions, or we would have closed our doors millions in debt instead of only $95,000 in debt (most of which I've paid off since). It was a great learning experience, and I wouldn't trade it for the world.

HPL CONSORTIUM, INC.

My fourth business, Enterprise, Technology, Management Associates, Inc. (ETM) was started in 2001. It was a boutique[1] consulting firm, and I counted among my team the many friends I had worked with virtually over the years. It was also an opportunity to return to my hometown in Berks County, Pennsylvania. My adorable and long-suffering husband had dutifully followed me through all my travails and jobs in other states, but we were both homesick and longed to return to our roots. Furthermore, we both had ailing parents to take care of, and the hours of traveling back and forth to Maryland were getting old.

ETM has been financially successful despite my years of disability due to a devastating car accident on November 5, 2002. Luckily, I had chosen the right team who just kept the darn thing going even when I couldn't get out of bed for months at a time. (Most especially critical was the choice of Gene Brown as my office manager. Sadly, as I was recovering, his health began to fail. Gene passed away before he could see the company flourish again.)

Recently, I made a change to my business linked to my own ongoing recovery from my injuries. As a result, I was faced with a strategic funding decision regarding my business.

Change in Focus

Three years ago, after 10 years of running ETM, I decided to change the focus and potential of my business. After finally getting back on my feet healthwise, I wanted to focus my efforts on development tools and processes that would help organizations and individuals connect so that more people would flourish despite business and personal crises (such as the one I went through).

Few people understood the importance of connecting with others, and the central role that healthy living plays in health and prosperity, as I did. Going through the period of loss, chronic injuries, and depression that resulted from my accident was not fun, but it was highly instructive. Two years after my accident, I had dropped to the bottom of the barrel. My husband and I had spent all of our savings and were borrowing money for groceries. We began to contemplate selling the house to survive and the future looked bleak. I still couldn't work and was in constant pain.

It was only a few years later, however, that I had zoomed to the top of the world. I now have an unbelievably great life. I have more money than I need, and the freedom to spend my time as I wish. ETM Associates was no longer important to me. It was time to give back. It was time to share my story and see if others could benefit from my experiences.

Since the help and support of others, as well as my newfound dedication to integrative health practices were responsible for my recovery, I wanted to find a way to use my technology and entrepreneurial skills to enhance the possibility that others would gain the same support and help that I did.

The HPL Consortium Plan

After two and a half years of planning, I was ready to launch the new strategy. I changed the name of my business from ETM Associates, Inc. to HPL Consortium, Inc. for Health, Prosperity, and Leadership. I spread out and started to prepare a team for launch.

The new business plan described a business with a unique concept, market-dominating potential, low cash requirements to market, an already established sales channel, minimal after-sale support costs, high gross margins, and a profitable global appeal that would be of high strategic value to others. We were hitting all cylinders of Dave's Venture Capital Attractiveness Quiz.

Our business plan was a masterpiece (if I do say so myself). Our mission statement was compelling (Figure 12.1). The initial pro forma results (Figure 12.2) and the long-term pro forma results (Figure 12.3) demonstrated all of the aspects that would be attractive to a bank, angel, or venture capitalist. The financials forecasted a skyrocket trajectory of growth.

In March 2013, I was just about to join a business incubator. I had prepared my loan application for an SBA guaranteed loan. I had drafted the employee contracts for the initial team I had chosen to put into place (all of whom had worked on my team for years as 1099 employees). I had also chosen the underlying technology platform upon which we were going to build our technology tools, and chosen the developers who were going to build the infrastructure. That infrastructure was going to accomplish our mission and help thousands (initially) and millions (eventually) of others connect with each other. We were going to help those who were on their own path to health and prosperity through leadership.

Figure 12.1. Mission: Statement for HPL Consortium, Inc. Expansion

Our Goal: To Enable Health and Prosperity Through Leadership.
Our Mission: To profitably support the community by developing proprietary processes, technologies and educational opportunities that lead to connections providing the exact right knowledge at the exact right time for the exact right value.
Our Tag Line: Hyper Linking people who need help with the people who can help them toward Health, Prosperity, and Leadership—anytime, anywhere.

Source: HPL Consortium, Inc., copyright 2014, used with permission.

Figure 12.2. Five-Year Financials for HPL Consortium, Inc. Expansion

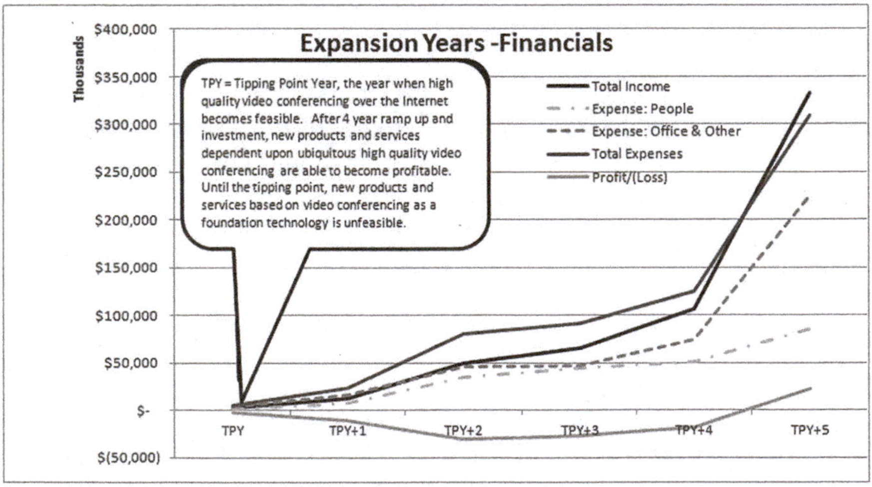

Source: HPL Consortium, Inc., copyright 2014, used with permission.

Figure 12.3. Fifteen-Year Financial Pro Forma for HPL Consortium, Inc.

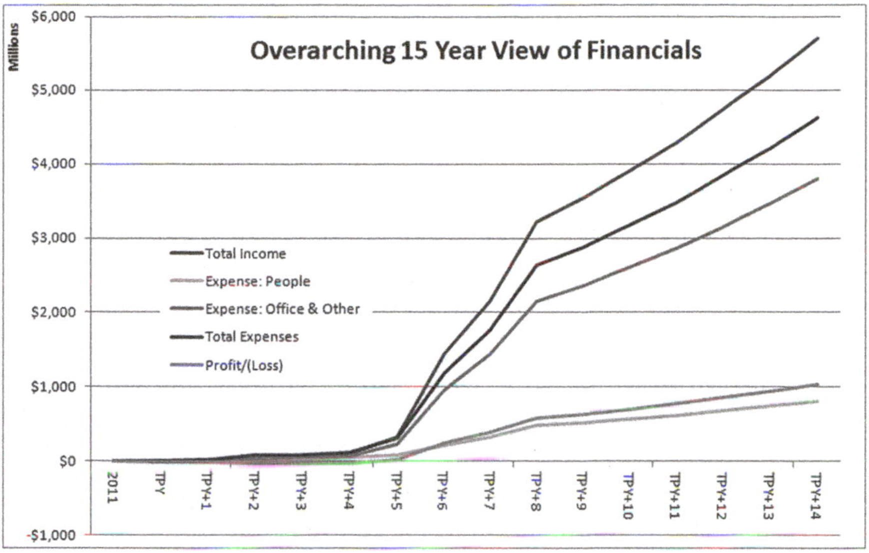

Source: HPL Consortium, Inc., copyright 2014, used with permission.

Poised for launch, with all the players in place, I was on the precipice of the go-no go decision in March 2013 as I worked on the business plan, the business model canvas, and the Pitch-Then-Plan presentation with Scott Schaeffer from the business incubator. Did I want to seek external funding, or not?

About-Face Decision for Funding

So, what happened?

Well, as I considered my own plans for seeking external capital, I did an about-face. I have decided to avoid borrowing any money, or getting involved in the incubator, or attempting to get any external investments from anyone. I've decided that I don't want to go blasting at rocket speeds toward my goal using other people's money. I've decided to continue to plod along, at a snail's pace, going in the direction of my goal without employees or financial obligations.

The goal and the mission of HPL Consortium, Inc. have not changed. What has changed is the focus and speed with which we are going to accomplish our goal.

But why the change?

Whenever life-changing decisions occur, it is always perilous to go back and try to put one's finger on exactly why the decision was made.

More often than not, the reasons people communicate do not match the real, underlying, actual reason. That's because the gut reaction might sound—well—unreasonable. *You gave up all of your plans and undid three years of work for THAT?* would be a typical reaction. It is with this caveat that I attempt to share with you the situation that led to my drastic change in March 2013.

- The number of people who responded to one of the initially planned events to discuss our expansion plans did not equal the number necessary to launch.
- Every time I tried to explain the plan to someone, they misunderstood what we were trying to accomplish and how we planned to achieve the goal. Despite three years of trying, I couldn't adequately convey the vision in my head because it was long term, without immediate returns.
- The financial analysis revealed a requirement for many times the amount of investment and a much more ambitious sales forecast to meet investors' expectations than I had originally expected.
- A trusted advisor gave me only a weakly positive response to my plans rather than the strong endorsement I had hoped for.
- Despite my excellent credit rating (one bank told me I had a perfect score!), I discovered that it was unlikely that I could get a loan without putting my house up as collateral, which I wasn't willing to do.
- After further investigation, the platform upon which we had expected to build our application turned out to be buggy and flawed. We would have to start over.
- The telehealth report for which I received a grant took six months longer than I expected to complete. My launch timeframe was critical since I was trying to fit it into my sabbatical from teaching.
- I realized that my sabbatical, upon which I had counted to get the bulk of the launch execution work done, was going to be over before I could complete the initial expansion work.
- Some potential investors with whom I spoke nixed my plan to work on the business while still teaching full time at the university. They expected me to quit teaching.
- Some personal health setbacks renewed my fears that I could not sustain the typical physical pace of an entrepreneur's schedule.
- The opportunity to work on this book, the final book in *The Entrepreneur's Guide To* series, arose.
- I attended a luncheon where Kathleen Passanisi,[2] an author and humorist, spoke.

While this last item was the actual decision point, the previous items were all influential in that final moment—the moment when I decided that I was going to completely reverse course. There I was, just listening to Kathleen tell hilariously funny stories about getting her business and career off the ground. Then, she led an exercise. She had us all write down our to-do lists (and, of course, I just pulled mine out since I am a fervent to-do-lister and always have mine handy). Then, she told us to reflect on the items on our list. Kathleen asked: *Which of those items makes your heart sing?*

As I looked at the list of all the actions on which I was about to embark within the next four weeks (move into the incubator office, hire a bunch of new employees, negotiate with strategic partners, borrow money, pitch to investors, implement the technology platform I had spent three years designing), I realized that not a single one made my heart sing. My reaction to that list was one of dread.

There was nothing wrong with the plan. I knew that if I embarked on that plan, I was going to make a ton of money and be very successful. I'm sure that some other intelligent person is going to exploit the coming videoconferencing revolution and make a boatload of money instead of me. I know because I've been watching and waiting for 12 years for the tipping point of videoconferencing technology to be financially feasible for the masses. I know because I've been watching and waiting for 12 years for IPv6 to be adopted, for mobile devices to be sold video-ready, for touch screen interfaces to become prolific.

But I also knew the truth. I realized, in my gut, that I would not be happy if I embarked on that plan, no matter how much money I made.

I thought about my just-completed project, the grant-supported telehealth report. I relished the thought of doing more research and writing on the topic. I thought about another potential project that had come along—the book you are reading now. The idea of writing this final book for *The Entrepreneur's Guide To* series filled me with delight. Doing conferences again, going out, and speaking about my experiences and my research—these activities elated me to no end. Having the time to write columns, blogging, and doing short videos containing the lessons that I had learned—these activities thrilled me. These notions made my heart sing.

Managing people? Nope. Pleasing investors? Nada. Without realizing it, I had changed. When I was younger, running my own business was a joy, a calling, the playground in which I was happiest. But I was older now. Starting a new business venture no longer sounded to me like the fun challenge it had been when I was 25. Back then, I was full of an unquenchable fire to be on the front lines, to achieve. Now—not so much.

I faced facts. What made my heart sing at this stage was writing, researching, teaching, and speaking. I wanted to inspire others rather than continue to add to my already-long list of accomplishments. I don't need any more money. I certainly don't need any more stress.

I realized that I would get much more joy by sharing my experiences, my plans, my thoughts. I could launch a thousand other ships, and continue to watch the different components as they inevitably come together to form that web of connections that I envision. Perhaps one of them would morph into the cruise liner that would change the world in the way that I knew was inevitable.[3] Perhaps they would invite me in to help them make their dreams a reality.

In the meantime, I could work on the technology tools myself with my own rudimentary skills that would help people to connect rather than hire a team of programmers to do it for me. I realized that I could work toward the mission of health, prosperity, and leadership for all without putting my own fragile health at risk. I realized that I could maintain the freedom I like and still focus on my nonprofit interests such as HPL 501c3 Institute, Entrepreneurship Club, National Qigong Association, Taijiquan Enthusiasts Organization, and dozens of others. I realized that I could continue without giving up my much-loved teaching position at the university.

Decide for Yourself

There comes a time in every business owner's life when they must decide what they will do afterwards. Some are forced into a change through unexpected impending bankruptcy or loss of business. Others welcome a change by selling the business or retiring from the business. Some hand the business over to employees or family members. Others shut the business down. Sometimes, the end involves a liquidation event that provides one-time or ongoing financial bounty. Other times, the business shuts down with continuing debts and financial obligations.

No matter which of these choices, opportunities, or situations faces us as we go through our lives, we can look upon them as delightful pinnacles to dot our careers. Obviously, the negative ones take a bit longer to feel comfortable about. Whenever something unexpected happens, especially if it costs us money or impacts our reputation, emotional adjustments need to occur.

We can help ourselves greatly, however, by envisioning all the different possibilities, and preparing for them. We can create our goals and lists, sit down, and think about them, to see which ones make our hearts sing. We can identify what our real underlying purpose in life is so that we can sleep well at night, get up refreshed in the morning, and feel good all day long.

We do have responsibilities to others, but they cannot eclipse our responsibility to ourselves. It is only by knowing ourselves, understanding our own internal motivations, that we can identify the best course of action for ourselves.

Having said that, one thing that I've decided is that the emotional charge that one gets from giving back to others is hard to beat. There is, however, more than one way to give back. One of my main motivations over the past three years of planning for growth was to be able to provide jobs for the many people I know who are talented, but who, because of the economy, are unemployed or underemployed. I've had to give up on that part of the dream, but I can continue to help as I can through working on the technology infrastructure that will help them connect with others more easily. They are all on my list to get a complimentary subscription to the platform when I'm further along.

So, for all of us entrepreneurs, I share these questions that we can ask ourselves to achieve our dreams so that we can get into a position where we can spend the bulk of our time giving back:

- What kind of funding, internal or external, debt or venture, will best meet my needs at this point in my life?
- How can I improve my skills in finance, sales, marketing, information technology, and leadership in order to achieve more for my business?
- What planning do I need to do now in order to get where I want to go five years from now?
- What makes my heart sing?

I hope that sharing the lessons from all the books in the series, as well as many other sources of wisdom which I have come across over the years, has been helpful to you. I hope that sharing my personal story has enhanced those directives for you, and provided some context for the difficult-to-learn topics. No matter what business you are in, what path you choose to walk, I wish you luck in your journeys.

Appendix A
About the Authors in the Series

THE ENTREPRENEUR'S GUIDE TO
MANAGING GROWTH AND HANDLING CRISES

Theo J. van Dijk MSc (Eng), MBA, has over 20 years experience in guiding small and medium sized enterprises (SME) through the crisis of leadership/direction in the United States, the United Kingdom, Australia, Ireland, South Africa, The Netherlands, and South Eastern Europe.

Theo completed an MSc (Eng) degree in 1975 and an MBA in 1983 from the University of the Witwatersrand, Johannesburg, South Africa. Since 1983, Theo has been actively associated with the transition of growing entrepreneurial businesses into professional SMEs.

Currently, Theo is assisting an Ireland-based entrepreneur, active in the building supply industry in Ireland and England, to develop his business in a controlled and effective manner.

THE ENTREPRENEUR'S GUIDE TO
WRITING BUSINESS PLANS AND PROPOSALS

K. Dennis Chambers is a former officer in the U.S. Navy and a veteran of two tours in Vietnam. He holds a BA in English literature from the University of Memphis and an MA in English literature from Boston University. He is an adjunct instructor in literature and writing at several local colleges.

He is the founder of Chambers Communications, a Massachusetts-based advertising and marketing agency that brings top freelance talent together on a project-by-project basis to provide clients with inexpensive yet powerful marketing tools. Chambers is the author of three books: *Writing to Get Action*, Velocity Publishers; *The Entrepreneur's Guide to Writing Business Plans and Proposals*; and *Corporations That Changed the World— Toyota*, both by Praeger Publishing.

THE ENTREPRENEUR'S GUIDE TO
HIRING AND BUILDING THE TEAM

Ken Tanner began his career scrubbing dishes in a Pizza Hut and eventually became the youngest manager in that chain's history. What followed was a 20-year career in the hospitality industry. He served as regional vice president, director of training, and COO of companies such as Taco Bell, Long John Silver's, and Advantage.

Ken founded an HR consulting firm to help companies build teamwork and retain employees as well. His achievements featured dramatic customer service turnarounds, record-low employee turnover, and the development of dozens of leaders in the industry. He is especially proud of the number of women he helped advance into executive positions. Ken is also the author of six books, including *The Boomers' Career Survival Guide*; *Recruiting Excellence*; and *Common Sense*.

THE ENTREPRENEUR'S GUIDE TO
MANAGING INFORMATION TECHNOLOGY

CJ Rhoads is the founder and CEO of HPL Consortium, Inc. developing technology tools to help people connect toward health, prosperity, and leadership. She speaks and writes about entrepreneurship, business strategy, leadership development, information technology, and the economics of healthcare and integrative health practices. She's also a professor in the College of Business at Kutztown University, an avid researcher, an incurable community advocate, and a serial entrepreneur. In 2009, she was honored as one of Pennsylvania's Best 50 Women in Business; in 2011, she received the Athena Leadership award; in 2013 was named one of 25 most Influential Women in Lehigh Valley Business, and in 2014 was awarded the Top Faculty Researcher of the Year by Kutztown University.

THE ENTREPRENEUR'S GUIDE
TO SUCCESSFUL LEADERSHIP

Dan Goldberg, MBA, is an internationally recognized business developer, master marketer, speaker, trainer, and coach. He was the founder and former owner of the highly successful international optical company "For Eyes," whose cutting-edge approach to the sale of eyewear and related services irrevocably changed the entire industry and had a major impact on how all service businesses are marketed.

After selling "For Eyes," Dan created an international management, marketing, public relations, and advertising firm. He received the Citizen Diplomacy Award for American Business by the International Visitors

Council of Philadelphia (IVC) for his work in teaching Russian business executives strategic planning.

Dan is an adjunct professor at the Fox School of Business, Temple University, the Smeal College of Business, Penn State University, and Kutztown University's College of Business. He has been featured in major newspapers and magazines, as well as on radio and television stations, throughout the United States.

Don Martin is a regionally recognized trainer, mentor, business developer, public speaker, and master salesman. He was the founder and former owner of Learning Resources Technical Training Consultants, Inc. and Partners In Change Inc. —both highly successful companies in training and organizational development. He served as program manager of Learning Resources for the Kutztown Small Business Development Center for many years, helping to make them a leader in the field of online learning using programs that encompass the full range of needs for entrepreneurs.

Don has taught at the high school and college level and created one of the first alternative high schools in the United States, working with troubled high school students. He is a graduate of West Chester University with a Bachelor's degree in the Social Sciences and holds a Master's Degree of Education from Pennsylvania State University.

THE ENTREPRENEUR'S GUIDE TO MARKETING

Robert F. Everett, PhD, has taught marketing at Kutztown University in Pennsylvania as well as at the Johns Hopkins University and the University of Maryland, College Park. Besides working as an independent business consultant, Bob has been regional director for the American Management Association, vice president at software developer The Orcutt Group, director of Business Development for the high-tech consultancy Selbre Associates, and a principal in an advertising agency.

THE ENTREPRENEUR'S GUIDE TO RAISING CAPITAL

David Nour is founder and managing partner of Relationship Economics, Inc. He is a social networking strategist and one of the foremost thought leaders on the quantifiable value of business relationships. David has been named in *Georgia Trend*'s 40 Under 40, *Atlanta Business Chronicle*'s Up and Coming, and Who's Who in Atlanta Technology Awards. He has been featured in a variety of publications, including *The Wall Street Journal*, The *New York Times*, The *Atlanta Journal and Constitution*, The *Atlanta Business Chronicle, Georgia Trend,* Smart Money.com, and *Success Magazines.*

David earned an Executive MBA from the Goizueta Business School at Emory University where he's often a guest lecturer and a BA degree in Management from Georgia State University.

THE ENTREPRENEUR'S GUIDE TO SELLING

Jonathan London, president and founder of the Improved Performance Group (IPG), has extensive experience (working with over 18,000 people) in training, coaching, and development in the areas of sales, leadership, and customer service. Based upon his 31 years of sales and management experience and an accomplished track record in both domestic and global sales, Jonathan's contemporary approach to time-tested practices has well-served the interests of IPG's clients.

While working for corporations such as The Olivetti Corporation, NBI, ROLM, Wyse/Amdek, Business Land, and Picture Tel, Jonathan was the No. 1 salesperson and manager in all of his sales or management positions, company or industrywide. He received a Bachelor's degree in History from American University in Washington, D.C. and is a member of ASTD.

THE ENTREPRENEUR'S GUIDE TO ADVERTISING

James R. Ogden has been consulting with various businesses for over 30 years as CEO of The Doctors Ogden Group, LLC (TDOG, LLC) consulting. In addition to his duties at TDOG, Doc serves as a professor of Marketing at Kutztown University of Pennsylvania (Kutztown, PA).

Doc Ogden sits on numerous boards and boards of directors and was recently elected chair of the Group 8 Think Tank for Business and Education. Dr. Ogden holds a PhD from the University of Northern Colorado, a Master of Science from Colorado State University, and a Bachelor's degree from Eastern Michigan University. He has also been active in postgraduate training and education.

Scott Rarick is currently the director of Media and Account Services at The Stevenson Group, a strategic advertising firm, with its greatest strengths in brand development and management, as well as strategic and creative execution. Since graduating in 1997 from Kutztown University, with degrees in Marketing and Management, Scott has worked at multiple advertising agencies within the Philadelphia Direct Marketing Association. Scott has serviced both business-to-business and consumer clients, which have ranged from global industrial manufacturers to regional financial institutions.

Scott completed the Institute of Advanced Advertising Studies program through the American Association of Advertising Agencies in

Philadelphia. Scott has been a member of the American Marketing Association, American Advertising Federation, and Sales and Marketing Executives International.

THE ENTREPRENEUR'S GUIDE TO
MASTERING THE INNER WORLD OF BUSINESS

Nanci Raphael, founder of Leadership and Executive Development (www.keyleaders.com), coaches executives, entrepreneurs, professionals, and their teams to accelerate the production of significantly advanced and sustainable results. These business leaders increase performance, sharpen the ability to execute and follow through, develop stronger problem solving and decision-making skillsets that lead to quicker, more innovative solutions, gain greater clarity and confidence, fortify team commitment, engagement and accountability, and strengthen business development—leading to an achievement of higher level results.

Nanci is hired by Fortune 500s as well as entrepreneurial enterprises, to help leaders overcome challenges that block success. Combining her coaching expertise with her experience as a successful entrepreneur and CEO, her passion is to help people reach their fullest potential.

The *Philadelphia Business Journal* named Nanci's organization for two consecutive years as a top management consulting firm and a top woman-owned business. She is also a speaker and contributing writer to many business publications

THE ENTREPRENEUR'S GUIDE
TO MARKET RESEARCH

Anne M. Wenzel is principal with Econosystems, an economics and market research firm located in Menlo Park, California. Prior to founding Econosystems in 1999, Wenzel was economist for the Chemical Economics Handbook program in the Chemical Marketing Research Center at SRI International, Menlo Park, California.

Ms. Wenzel is past president of the Silicon Valley Roundtable and San Francisco chapters of the National Association for Business Economics, and currently serves as a member of the Silicon Valley Roundtable Board of Advisors. She is also past vice-chair for the NABE Financial Roundtable. Wenzel is a lecturer in the economics department at San Francisco State University, and teaches Managerial Economics at Menlo College in Atherton, California. She received her Master's degree in Economics from San Francisco State University, and is a Certified Business Adviser for the Silicon Valley Small Business Development Center.

THE ENTREPRENEUR'S GUIDE TO
UNDERSTANDING FINANCIAL STATEMENTS

David Worrell is an accomplished entrepreneur, executive, and author, specializing in helping businesses grow rapidly to the next level by employing powerful financial and business development strategies.

Worrell is a graduate of The Ohio State University, the Sandler Sales Institute, and the Kauffman Foundation's Fast Trac Entrepreneur Training program. Four times, he has been recognized as a Fast 50 award recipient for building fast growing new companies of his own and now consults with business owners as an on-demand CFO. His current venture, Rock Solid Finance, has helped hundreds of entrepreneurs get the most from their business.

David taught international business planning within the top 10 ranked MBA program at the Fisher Graduate School of International Business, in Monterey, California, and during 2002–2009, was a regular contributor to *Entrepreneur Magazine* on all aspects of business finance, acquisitions, and exit strategies.

Appendix B
Leadership Research

Over the past decade, I've spent quite a bit of time reading the research on leadership in my personal quest to become a better leader. This section starts with a very brief narrative summary on the history of leadership, along with many of the major points. Following that is a comprehensive table on all the major researchers and gurus who have published well-known works on the topic of leadership.

EARLY LEADERSHIP RESEARCH

Initial research on leadership focused on styles of leadership. Lewin, Lippit, and White (1939) appeared early on in the leadership research literature. They identified three styles of leadership based upon the characteristics of the leader–follower relationship. We had the authoritarian, democratic, or laissez-fair leader. The research showed that the most productive teams were run by democratic or participative leaders, though autocratic was the most common type found of people in leadership positions.

Many other researchers built upon this basic foundation and developed more complex and comprehensive theories and studies. Likert (1967) identified four styles, and Shartle (1956) developed the Leader Behavior Description Questionnaire—funded by the government and used mainly to assess the leadership capabilities of the military, which morphed over the years into the MLQ, the Multifactor Leadership Questionnaire. This framework spawned four decades of research dominated by Bernard Bass (1960, 1993, 2003), Ralph Stogdill (1948, 1963, 1972, 1974), and Bruce Avolio (1999, 2001, 2009), who focused again on the specific personality traits of people to determine their ability to lead. This spurred even more leadership studies with people such as William Gardner (1998), Fred Walumbwa (2008, 2008), and Warren Bennis (1990) focusing on Transactional Leadership, Authentic leadership, Transformational Leadership and Charismatic Leadership, Visionary Leadership, and any other type of leadership you might want to name.

One of the problems with paper and pencil assessment is their histori-cal basis; many came out of the leadership research validated only with men, the thinking at the time being that only men could ever be consid-ered as possible leaders. In the 1980s, the focus in the research world of leadership switched to the situation rather than the characteristics of the person in the leadership role. Fiedler (1976) came up with what he called the Contingency Theory. Fiedler believed that group effectiveness was a result of how well the matching of the leader's style was to the situation. Hoy (1987), Miskel, and Hencley (1973) followed up with what they called Situational Leadership. They identified the distinctive charac-teristics of the setting that determined the leader's success. Hersey and Blanchard (1969, 1982) got into the act by identifying levels of maturity of the types of interaction between the leaders and the group: Telling, Sell-ing, Participating, and Delegating.

In 1971, House developed the Path-Goal Theory, which identified which leadership behaviors worked with which situation. This soon led to Vroom's Expectancy Theory of Leadership (Vroom and Yetton 1973; Vroom and Jago 1988; Vroom and Sternberg 2002). This theory basically says that good leaders motivate people. Vroom suggested a formula: Motivation = Valance × Expectancy (Instrumentality). Valance is a per-son's instinct for either extrinsic or intrinsic rewards. Expectancy is the person's belief in his or her own abilities, and instrumentality is the pre-vious experience of the person with either getting or not getting prom-ised rewards.

In the 1980s, Barnes and Kriger (1986) went a step further. They sug-gested that previous theories of leadership were insufficient because they dealt more with the single leader followed by many. According to them, leadership could only be addressed in a pluralistic sense—including the organizational characteristics and factors rather than the abilities of any single individual within the situation.

Bass—the father of the field, if there can be a father of the field—wrote in a recent article, "The challenge still remains how we can best measure such exemplary leadership styles beyond simply using survey tools, as well as to develop them over time in organization" (2003, p. 461).

Because of the paucity of academic empirical research that leads to practical advice, filling the gap are a bevy of leadership gurus, starting with the developer of modern management, Peter Drucker (1987, 2001), but also including Tom Peters (1986), Jim Collins (2001b), Ken Blanchard (1970), Marcus Buckingham (2005), Warren Bennis (1990), Steve Covey (1992), and hundreds of others.

Just about the same time all these gurus started becoming well known, there was a split in the field. In 2003, the *Harvard Business Review* pub-lished "Leadership Insights" edited by Henry Mintzberg (2004) that deftly outlines the changing thinking on leadership during the past 30 years, starting with Abraham Zaleznik's article, "Managers and Leaders: Are They Different," originally published in 1977 which, according to Mintzberg, caused an uproar in business schools all over the country (Zaleznik 2004). The debate was that management skills were generally incompatible with leadership skills. The debate lasted for decades. For most part, today, it is generally accepted that leadership and management are by no means the same thing, and that training for one generally precludes training for the other. Conger (2003) reviewed 15 years' research on leadership, and attributed the added attention to the global business environment, competitive pressures, and the challenges of unmotivated employees. These issues led to the flood of research in the last two years on leadership rather than management.

Differentiating management from leadership in the 1980s meant going back to all the research and gurus of yesteryear and recasting whether or not they were basically talking about management, or talking about leadership. Tom Peters, though known as a management consultant, was of the group that was really more leadership oriented—as were Markus Buckingham, Steve Covey, and Jim Collins. On the other hand, Edward Deming, Peter Drucker, Michael Hammer, and Michael Porter were more management-oriented.

Entered into this fray was the concept of emotional intelligence, first proposed in a doctoral thesis by Wayne Payne (1985). Emotional Intelligence was made more well known by Daniel Goleman (1998); and it proved to be a critical aspect in the difference between management and leadership. Goleman presented data that a leader's ability to resonate emotionally with others is a better predictor of effective executive leadership than general intelligence. Rudderman at the Center for Creative Leadership (CCL) did further research that empirically confirmed the relationship between emotional intelligence and leadership effectiveness (Hernez-Broome and Hughes 2004). Emotional intelligence also proved to be not only measurable, but learnable.

One enterprising researcher decided to categorize the leaders of major corporations at the time by whether or not they were Level 5 leaders (à la Jim Collins), rated highly emotional intelligent (à la Goleman), and/or fit the criteria for narcissistic productive leadership (à la Maccoby). I found it fascinating—especially given that two of the people, identified as top leaders by 1999's *Lessons from the Top: The Search for America's Best Business Leaders*, have since been completely discredited—ending up in jail even.

Since then, I have found another leadership assessment tool that I think is superior to the existing assessments, but it has not yet been validated. It was developed by Mark and Andrea Burgio-Murphy (2006).

What made this particular assessment so good was the subtlety and the length. The "right" answer wasn't immediately transparent, and the assessment was only 10 questions long. (I encourage you to go to: http://www.leadershipiq.com/tests/leadership-test/ and take the assessment.)

The entire list of major leadership notables is listed in Table B.1.

Table B.1. Summary of Seventy-five Years of Leadership Research

Name	Type (Guru or Researcher)	Type/Style/Definition/ Theory
Lewin, Lippit, and White (1939)	Researchers	Three leadership styles: authoritarian, democratic, or laissez-faire
Stogdill (1948, 1963, 1972, 1974), Fleishman (1956, 1957, 1998), Halpin and Winer (1957)	Researchers	Ohio Group: Consideration and Initiation of Structure
Carroll L. Shartle (1956)	Researcher	Leader Behavior Description Questionnaire (LBDQ)
Likert (1967)	Researcher	Four Styles: Participative, Exploitive authoritative, Consultative, Benevolent authoritative
Bass (1960, 1993, 2003), Avolio (1999, 2000, 2001, 2004, 2005, 2007, 2009, 2009, 2009, 1999), Jung (1999), Gardner (1998, 2005), Hunt (1967, 1993), Yukl (1971, 1982, 2008, 2009), Burns (1978), Musser (1987)	Researchers	MLQ, Transformational and Transactional Leadership Charismatic Leadership
Bennis (1990), Smith (2008), Craig (2009), Walumbwa (2007, 2008, 2009)	Gurus	Authentic Leadership

(Continued)

Table B.1. (*Continued*)

Name	Type (Guru or Researcher)	Type/Style/Definition/ Theory
Drucker (1987, 2001)	Guru	Management By Objective
Fiedler (1967, 1976)	Researcher	Contingency Theory, and Least Preferred Coworker
Hersey and Blanchard (1970, 1969, 1972, 1981, 1982), Hoy and Miskel (1987), Hencley (1973)	Researchers	Situational Leadership
Vroom and Yetton (1973), Vroom and Jago (1988), Vroom and Sternberg (2002)	Gurus	Expectancy Theory of Leadership
House (1971)	Guru	Path-Goal Theory of Leadership
Barnes and Kriger (1986)	Guru	Organizational Leadership
Deming (Aguayo 1990)	Researcher	Total Quality Management
Tennant (2001)	Researcher/ Guru	Six Sigma
McLaughlin (2001), Manasse (1986)	Gurus	Visionary Leadership
Maccoby (1981, 2000, 2001a, b, 2002)	Guru	Narcissistic Leaders
Peters and Austin (1986)	Guru	Leadership Excellence
Payne (1985), Goleman (1998), Ruderman (2001), Hannum, Leslie, and Steed (2001), Mayer and Salovey (1993)	Gurus	Emotional Intelligence
Porter (1985, 1991)	Guru	Competitive Strategy
Buckingham (1999, 2005)	Guru	If it ain't broke, break it.
Covey (1992, 2005)	Guru	Principle-Centered leadership

(*Continued*)

Table B.1. (*Continued*)

Name	Type (Guru or Researcher)	Type/Style/Definition/ Theory
Hammer (1996)	Guru	Process Re-engineering
Baldwin (2007, 2008)	Researcher	Leadership Simulation Learning
Barrett and Beeson (2002)	Guru	Leadership Derailers
Murphy (2006)	Guru	Leadership IQ
Collins (1992, 1994, 2001a, 2001b, 2005, 2009, 2011), Harrison and Clough (2006)	Researcher/ Guru	Level 5 Leadership

REFERENCES

Aguayo, Rafael. 1990. *Dr. Deming: The American Who Taught the Japanese about Quality*. Vol. 1. Secaucus, NJ: Carol Publishing Group.

Avolio, Bruce J. 2000. "E-Leadership: Implications for Theory, Research, and Practice." *Leadership Quarterly* 11 (4): 615.

Avolio, Bruce J. 2001. "Winning with a Full Range of Leadership." *Military Review* 81 (2): 54.

Avolio, Bruce J. 2007. "Promoting More Integrative Strategies for Leadership Theory-Building." *American Psychologist* 62 (1): 25–33.

Avolio, Bruce J., and Bernard M. Bass. 1999. "Re-examining the Components of Transformational and Transactional Leadership Using the Multifactor Leadership Questionnaire." *Journal of Occupational & Organizational Psychology* 72 (4): 441–62.

Avolio, Bruce J., and William L. Gardner. 2005. "Authentic Leadership Development: Getting to the Root of Positive Forms of Leadership." *Leadership Quarterly* 16 (3): 315–38.

Avolio, Bruce J., Jane M. Howell, and John J. Sosik. 1999. "A Funny Thing Happened on the Way to the Bottom Line: Humor as a Moderator of Leadership Style Effects." *Academy of Management Journal* 42 (2): 219–27.

Avolio, Bruce J., Rebecca J. Reichard, Sean T. Hannah, Fred O. Walumbwa, and Adrian Chan. 2009. "A Meta-analytic Review of Leadership Impact Research: Experimental and Quasi-experimental Studies." *Leadership Quarterly* 20 (5): 764–84.

Avolio, Bruce J., Maria Rotundo, and Fred O. Walumbwa. 2009. "Early Life Experiences as Determinants of Leadership Role Occupancy: The Importance of Parental Influence and Rule Breaking Behavior." *Leadership Quarterly* 20 (3): 329–42.

Avolio, Bruce J., Fred O. Walumbwa, and Todd J. Weber. 2009. "Leadership: Current Theories, Research, and Future Directions." *Annual Review of Psychology* 60 (1): 421–49.

Avolio, Bruce J., Weichun Zhu, William Koh, and Puja Bhatia. 2004. "Transformational Leadership and Organizational Commitment: Mediating Role of Psychological Empowerment and Moderating Role of Structural Distance." *Journal of Organizational Behavior* 25 (8): 951–68.

Baldwin, Timothy. 2008. *Developing Managers Who Build High Performance Cultures: Why It This So Darn Hard?* Academy of Management Conference, Keynote Speaker, August 11, 2008. Anaheim, CA.

Baldwin, T. T., W. H. Bommer, and Robert S. Rubin. 2007. *Developing Management Skills: What Great Managers Know and Do.* New York: McGraw-Hill.

Barnes, L. B., and M. P. Kriger. 1986. "The Hidden Side of Organizational Leadership." *Sloan Management Review* 28 (1): 15–25.

Barrett, A., and J. Beeson. 2002. *Developing Business Leaders for 2010.* New York: The Conference Board.

Bass, Bernard M. 1960. *Leadership, Psychology, and Organizational Behavior.* New York: Harper & Brothers.

Bass, Bernard M., and Bruce J. Avolio. 1993. "Transformational Leadership and Organizational Culture." *Public Administration Quarterly* 17 (1): 112–21.

Bass, Bernard M., Dong I. Jung, Bruce J. Avolio, and Yair Berson. 2003. "Predicting Unit Performance by Assessing Transformational and Transactional Leadership." *Journal of Applied Psychology* 88 (2): 207–18.

Bennis, Warren G. 1990. "Managing the Dream: Leadership in the 21st century." *Training: The Magazine of Human Resource Development*, 44–46.

Blanchard, Kenneth H., and Paul Hersey. 1970. "A Leadership Theory for Educational Administrators." *Education* 90 (4): 303.

Buckingham, M. 2005. *The One Thing You Need to Know: . . . About Great Managing, Great Leading, and Sustained Individual Success.* New York: Free Press.

Buckingham, Marcus, and Curt Coffman. 1999. *First, Break All the Rules: What the World's Greatest Managers Do Differently.* New York: Simon & Schuster.

Burns, J. M. 1978. *Leadership.* New York: Harper & Row.

Collins, James C. 2001a. *Good to Great: Why Some Companies Make the Leap—and Others Don't.* Vol. 1. New York: HarperBusiness.

Collins, James C., and William C. Lazier. 1992. *Beyond Entrepreneurship: Turning Your Business into an Enduring Great Company.* Englewood Cliffs, NJ: Prentice Hall.

Collins, James C., and Jerry I. Porras. 1994. *Built to Last: Successful Habits of Visionary Companies.* Vol. 1. New York: HarperBusiness.

Collins, Jim. 2001b. "Level 5 Leadership." *Harvard Business Review* 79 (1): 66–76.

Collins, Jim. 2005. "Level 5 Leadership: The Triumph of Humility and Fierce Resolve [Cover Story]." *Harvard Business Review* 83 (7): 136–46.

Collins, Jim. 2009. *How the Mighty Fall: And Why Some Companies Never Give In*. New York: HarperCollins.

Collins, Jim, and Morten Hansen. 2011. *Great by Choice: Uncertainty, Chaos, and Luck—Why Some Thrive Despite Them All*. New York: HarperBusiness.

Conger, Jay A., and Robert M. Fulmer. 2003. "Developing Your Leadership Pipeline." *Harvard Business Review* 81 (12): 76–84.

Covey, Stephen R. 1992. *Principle Centered Leadership*. New York: Simon & Schuster.

Covey, Stephen R. 2005. *The 8th Habit: From Effectiveness to Greatness*. New York: Free Press.

Craig, Nick. 2009. *Visionary Leadership: Courageous Behavior Yields Big Payoffs*. Wharton@Work newsletter. Available at http://executiveeducation.wharton.upenn.edu/wharton-at-work/0906/visionary-leadership-0906.cfm. Accessed March 23, 2014.

Drucker, Peter F. 1987. *The Frontiers of Management: Where Tomorrow's Decisions Are Being Shaped Today*. Vol. 1. New York: Perennial Library.

Drucker, Peter F. 2001. *The Essential Drucker: Selections from the Management Works of Peter F. Drucker*. Vol. 1. New York: HarperBusiness.

Fiedler, Fred E. 1967. "The Effect of Inter-Group Competition on Group Member Adjustment." *Personnel Psychology* 20 (1): 33–44.

Fiedler, Fred E., Martin M. Chemers, and Linda Mahar. 1976. *Improving Leadership Effectiveness: The Leader Match Concept*. Vol. 23. Hoboken, NJ: John Wiley & Sons Inc.

Fleishman, E. A. 1957. "A Leader Behavior Description for Industry." In *Leader Behavior: Its Description and Measurement*, edited by R. M. Stogdill and A. E. Coons. Vol. 88. Columbus: The Ohio State University, Bureau of Business Research.

Fleishman, E. A., and E. F. Harris. 1998. "Patterns of Leadership Behavior Related to Employee Grievances and Turnover: Some Post Hoc Reflections." *Personnel Psychology* 51 (4): 825–34.

Fleishman, E. A., E. F. Harris, and H. E. and Burtt. 1956. *Leadership and Supervision in Industry*. Vol. 33. Columbus: The Ohio State University, Bureau of Educational Research.

Gardner, William L., and Bruce J. Avolio. 1998. "The Charismatic Relationship: a Dramaturgical Perspective." *Academy of Management Review* 23 (1): 32–58.

Gardner, William L., Bruce J. Avolio, Fred Luthans, Douglas R. May, and Fred Walumbwa. 2005. "'Can You See the Real Me?' A Self-based Model of Authentic Leader and Follower Development." *Leadership Quarterly* 16 (3): 343–72.

Goleman, Daniel. 1998. *Working with Emotional Intelligence*. New York: Bantam Books.

Halpin, A. W., and B. J. Winer. 1957. "A Factorial Study of the Leader Behavior Descriptions." In *Leader Behavior: Its Description and Measurement*, edited by

A. E. Coons and Ralph M. Stogdill. Vol. 88. Columbus: The Ohio State University, Bureau of Business Research.

Hammer, Michael. 1996. *Beyond Reengineering: How the Process-centered Organization Is Changing Our Work and Our Lives*. Vol. 1. New York: HarperBusiness.

Harrison, J. K., and M. W. Clough. 2006. "Characteristics of 'State of the Art' Leaders: Productive Narcissism Versus Emotional Intelligence and Level 5 Capabilities." *Social Science Journal* 43 (2): 287–92.

Hencley, S. P. 1973. "Situational Behavioral Approach to the Study of Educational Leadership." In *Leadership: The Science and Art Today*, edited by L. C. Cunningham and W. J. Gephart, 139–64. Itaska, IL: F.E. Peacock Publishers.

Hernez-Broome, Gina, and Richard J. Hughes. 2004. "Leadership Development: Past, Present, and Future." *Human Resource Planning* 27 (1): 24–32.

Hersey, Paul, and Kenneth H. Blanchard. 1969. "Life Cycle Theory of Leadership." *Training & Development Journal* 23 (5): 26.

Hersey, Paul, and Kenneth H. Blanchard. 1972. "The Management of Change." *Training & Development Journal* 26 (1): 6.

Hersey, Paul, and Kenneth H. Blanchard. 1981. "So You Want To Know Your Leadership Style?" *Training & Development Journal* 35 (6): 34.

Hersey, Paul, and Kenneth H. Blanchard. 1982. "Leadership Style: Attitudes and Behaviors." *Training & Development Journal* 36 (5): 50–52.

House, R. J. 1971. "A Path Goal Theory Effectiveness." *Administration Science Quarterly* 16 (1): 321–38.

Hoy, W. K., and C. G. Miskel. 1987. *Educational Administration: Theory, Research, and Practice*. Vol. 3. New York: Random House.

Hunt, J. G. 1967. "Fiedler's Leadership Contingency Model: An Empirical Test in Three Organizations." *Organizational Behavior & Human Performance* 2 (3): 290–308.

Hunt, Nancy P., and Roy M. Bohlin. 1993. "Teacher Education Students' Attitudes Toward Using Computers." *Journal of Research on Computing in Education* 25 (4): 487.

Jung, Dong I., and Bruce J. Avolio. 1999. "Effects of Leadership Style and Followers' Cultural Orientation on Performance in Group and Individual Task Conditions." *Academy of Management Journal* 42 (2): 208–18.

Lewin, K., R. Lippit, and R. K. White. 1939. "Patterns of Aggressive Behavior in Experimentally Created Social Climates." *Journal of Social Psychology* 10 (1): 271–301.

Likert, R. 1967. *The Human Organization: Its Management and Value*. New York: McGraw-Hill.

Maccoby, Michael. 1981. *The Leader: A New Face for American Management*. New York: Simon and Schuster.

Maccoby, Michael. 2000. "Narcissistic Leaders." *Harvard Business Review* 78 (1): 68–77.

Maccoby, Michael. 2001a. "Making Sense of the Leadership Literature." *Research Technology Management* 44 (5): 58–60.

Maccoby, Michael. 2001b. "The New New Boss." *Research Technology Management* 44 (1): 59–61.

Maccoby, Michael. 2002. "Learning from Jack." *Research Technology Management* 45 (2): 57–59.

Manasse, A. L. 1986. "Vision and Leadership: Paying Attention to Intention." *Peabody Journal of Education* 63 (1): 150–73.

Mayer, J. D., and P. Salovey. 1993. "The Intelligence of Emotional Intelligence." *Intelligence* 17 (4): 433–42.

McLaughlin, Corinne. 2001. *Visionary Leadership.* Available at http://www.visionarylead.org/articles/vislead.htm. Accessed March 23, 2014.

Mintzberg, Henry. 2004. *Enough Leadership.* Cambridge, MA: Harvard Business School Publication Corp.

Murphy, Mark. 2006. "Leadership IQ Study: Why New Hires Fail." *Public Management (00333611)* 88 (2): 33–34.

Musser, S. J. 1987. *The Determination of Positive and Negative Charismatic Leadership.* Grantham, PA: Messiah College.

Payne, Wayne. 1985. *A Study of Emotion: Developing Emotional Intelligence.* Cincinnati, OH: The Union Institute.

Peters, Thomas J., and Nancy Austin. 1986. *A Passion for Excellence: The Leadership Difference.* New York: Warner Books.

Porter, Michael E. 1991. "Towards a Dynamic Theory of Strategy." *Strategic Management Journal* 12 (Winter Special Issue): 95–117.

Porter, Michael E., and Victor E. Millar. 1985. "How Information Gives You Competitive Advantage." *Harvard Business Review* 63 (4): 149.

Ruderman, M. N., K. Hannum, J. B. Leslie, and J. Steed. 2001. "Making the Connection: Leadership Skills and Emotional Intelligence." *Leadership in Action* 21 (5): 3–7.

Shartle, Carroll L. 1956. *Executive Performance and Leadership.* Englewood Cliffs, NJ: Prentice-Hall.

Smith, Jan. 2008. "Now that You Have Achieved a Measure of Success, How Would You Like to Live the Next Phase of Your Life?" Center for Authentic Leadership. Available at http://www.authenticleadership.com/. Accessed March 23, 2014.

Stogdill, Ralph M. 1948. "Personal Factors Associated with Leadership: A Survey of the Literature." *Journal of Psychology* 25 (1): 35–71.

Stogdill, Ralph M. 1963. Manual for the Leader Behavior Description Questionnaire—Form XII. Columbus, OH: The Ohio State University, Bureau of Business Research.

Stogdill, Ralph M. 1972. "Group Productivity, Drive, and Cohesiveness." *Organizational Behavior & Human Performance* 8 (1): 26–43.

Stogdill, Ralph M. 1974. *Handbook of Leadership: A Survey of Theory and Research.* New York: The Free Press.

Tennant, Geoff. 2001. *SIX SIGMA: SPC and TQM in Manufacturing and Services.* Aldershot, UK: Gower Publishing, Ltd.

Vroom, Victor H., and Arthur G. Jago. 1988. *The New Leadership: Managing Participation in Organizations.* Englewood Cliffs, NJ: Prentice-Hall.

Vroom, Victor H., and Robert J. Sternberg. 2002. "Theoretical Letters: The Person Versus the Situation in Leadership." *The Leadership Quarterly* 13 (1): 301–23.

Vroom, Victor H., and P. W. Yetton. 1973. *Leadership and Decision-making.* Pittsburg, PA: University of Pittsburg Press.

Walumbwa, Fred O., Bruce J. Avolio, William L. Gardner, Tara S. Wernsing, and Suzanne J. Peterson. 2008. "Authentic Leadership: Development and Validation of a Theory-Based Measure." *Journal of Management* 34 (1): 89–126.

Walumbwa, Fred O., Bruce J. Avolio, and Weichun Zhu. 2008. "How Transformational Leadership Weaves Its Influence on Individual Job Performance: the Role of Identification and Efficacy Beliefs." *Personnel Psychology* 61 (4): 793–825.

Walumbwa, Fred O., John J. Lawler, and Bruce J. Avolio. 2007. "Leadership, Individual Differences, and Work-related Attitudes: A Cross-Culture Investigation." *Applied Psychology: An International Review* 56 (2): 212–30.

Yukl, Gary. 1971. "Toward a Behavioral Theory of Leadership." *Organizational Behavior & Human Performance* 6 (4): 414–40.

Yukl, Gary. 2008. "How Leaders Influence Organizational Effectiveness." *Leadership Quarterly* 19 (6): 708–22.

Yukl, Gary, Mark O'Donnell, and Thomas Taber. 2009. "Influence of Leader Behaviors on the Leader-Member Exchange Relationship." *Journal of Managerial Psychology* 24 (4): 289–99.

Yukl, Gary A., and David D. Van Fleet. 1982. "Cross-Situational, Multimethod Research on Military Leader Effectiveness." *Organizational Behavior & Human Performance* 30 (1): 87–108.

Zaleznik, Abraham. 2004. "Managers and Leaders: Are They Different?" *Harvard Business Review* 82 (1): 74–81.

Zhu, Weichun, Bruce J. Avolio, and Fred O. Walumbwa. 2009. "Moderating Role of Follower Characteristics with Transformational Leadership and Follower Work Engagement." *Group & Organization Management* 34 (5): 590–619.

Appendix C
Entrepreneurial Death Traps

25 ENTREPRENEURIAL DEATH TRAPS

How to Avoid the Classic Entrepreneurial Mistakes

Frederick J. Beste III
Mid-Atlantic Venture Funds

116 Research Drive Drive
Bethlehem, PA 18015
(610) 865–6550

Delivered to Lehigh University "V-Series" students
Bethlehem, Pennsylvania
March 16, 2007

A few years ago, a friend of mine, a successful entrepreneur, was crying on my shoulder. "Fred," he said to me, "when I started my company I knew I needed a Mr. Inside, and I knew a good one, my friend George. I offered him 50% of the company. He'd have jumped just as quickly for 20%, but I liked the **fairness** feeling of being 50–50 partners.

Today, after five years of hard work, we're nicely profitable on $10 million of sales. We're pulling really good money out in salaries. We have every fringe benefit we can think of. Best of all, we've only scratched the surface. I can *taste* $25 million in sales in two to three years. At that level, we'll be the undisputed king of the mountain in our industry, and making so much money we won't know what to do with it."

"Gee, Lee" I said, "I'd like to be of help, but I'm having a hard time figuring out where the problem lies."

"It's George" he said. "I went into his office last week and said to him, George, we need to get away from here for a couple of days and map out a new business plan designed to triple our size by 2008."

"And what did he say" I asked.

He said, "Gee Lee, that's nice. Right now I've got to leave for my golf lesson. I'll be back by two, however, and we can talk about this. Quite frankly, though, it sounds like a helluva lot of work to me."

"Fred", Lee said to me, "George hasn't been in here on a weekend in almost a year. He's never in before 8:00 A.M. anymore and never here after 5:30. We're losing momentum and I can't carry this company by myself. Also, he doesn't want to risk the investment that would be required to pull the thing off. And being exactly a one-half owner of the company, he can and does veto anything he wants. I'm going absolutely nuts."

I didn't have a good answer for him. As I was driving to a board meeting right afterwards though, I thought to myself, I'll bet that that's the tenth time in my career that I've heard this 50–50 partnership tale of woe. Why do such otherwise smart people keep doing this to themselves? After no more than an instant's reflection, I *knew* the answer. Because they've never been there before. Because "equal partners" seems so human-naturally fair. Boy, what a beguiling trap, even deathtrap, this has been for countless entrepreneurs, I thought.

But wait, I reflected, there's more! What about the three (or four) (or five) musketeer's death trap? Although in one sense it's a corollary of the 50–50 partnership deathtrap, in some ways it's even more insidious. You know the story. Three friends decide to start a company. They split the ownership absolutely equally, they draw identical salaries, they're going to make decisions "by consensus." It's the logical, "fair" thing to do. One of them (perhaps the oldest or the one whose idea it was originally) reluctantly assumes the presidency because state law requires there to be one.

What a recipe for failure! There are three primary problems with this set-up. First, this company has no leader, no one ultimately responsible for its success or failure. Second, sooner or later a major, honest difference of opinions will arise. What do they do then? Third, the reluctant president will almost inevitably come to see himself as "a little more than equal." If they have *any* success, for example, and get written up in the local or trade press, guess whose picture the reporter will want? Guess whose quotes will be plastered all through the story? Guess which other two people are going to hang the article on their family room dartboard?

The solution? Pick a CEO and treat him like one. Give him the largest equity position and salary, even if they are only symbolically larger. *Somebody* has to sit where the buck stops.

By now I was on a roll. There was a cardboard box lying on the passenger seat of my car. I flipped it over to reveal its blank bottom and started scribbling notes relating to other deathtraps all over it. By the time

I reached my destination, it was covered up. I counted them. There were exactly 25. Wow, I thought. I could turn this into a speech and get invitations to deliver it in places like Bethlehem in March! And the rest, as they say, is history.

Sadly, so are thousands of otherwise good little companies history. Entrepreneurs face all kinds of potential adversity—some kinds can kill them, some kinds merely set them back a little. Some kinds are unpredictable, others much more so. The saddest failures that I have witnessed are the conceivably predictable, lethal ones, the ones that could and should have been avoided.

Now, as senseless as small business deaths are which fall prey to the many-times-tripped death traps, they can be damnably difficult to avoid. Many of them appear in the form of beautiful, well-worn paths which logic, greed and even common sense might suggest taking. How tragic that they take entrepreneurs over cliffs time and time again.

To compound the challenge of avoiding such a demise, *none* of these paths is *assuredly* fatal. The important point is that they *can* be, and *have* been for many others. Each should be avoided or tempered if at all possible.

We've already covered two, the 50–50 partnership deathtrap and the three musketeers' deathtrap. Although I have put the lot of them in no particular order, the third is potentially the ugliest, because when it strikes, it is only *after* a long run of euphoric success. For lack of a better term, I call it the One or Two Customer Over-reliance deathtrap.

Let's say that you own a small, recently established machine shop. You're limping along, hand-to-mouth, at about $50,000 of sales/month. Then one day you get a call from a buyer at the largest industrial company in the county. He's in a jam. He needs $100,000 worth of aluminum housings in two weeks and his regular vendors are backed up for a month of Sundays. You meet with your four machinists. You know you're crazy but you take the job. You man a milling machine yourself and the five of you work 'round the clock and deliver the last of the housings at 7:00 A.M. on the deadline date. You've saved the guy's bacon. He's appreciative. Two years later you're doing $5 million in sales, $4 million of it from this one customer. You're personally pulling $300,000/year out of the company and there's enough left over to fund your working capital needs. Your bank is only too happy to finance your new equipment needs and your new, expanded building. (Back in the *old* days when you were a banker's pariah, you had to *buy* your original equipment *used*, out of your savings.)

What do you think this guy's thinking? That this is risky? Hell, no! I'll tell you what he's thinking! He's thinking he's a genius, a role model, the envy of his friends. He's thinking that his major customer is mighty lucky to have found him. In fact, he's thinking that their continued success is due in no small part to his talent and hard work

I mean, is this an accident waiting to happen or what? How many times in situations like this has such a buyer ultimately called and said something like, "Gee, Bob, 'fraid I've got a bit of bad news. As you probably knew (he didn't), our union contract has a no-layoff clause, and what with the recession and all, we've re-assigned 60 employees to our machine shop. We're bringing all of our machine shop work back in-house."

Bam! In one fell stroke this guy's running a million dollar company with a $3 million break-even.

Now, I am not necessarily suggesting that this poor slob should have turned any of this juicy business down. What I *am* suggesting is that he should have been working like mad to build the rest of his business, and thereby reduce his dependence on this customer. What I *am* suggesting is that in situations like this he should have been *renting used* equipment, not *borrowing* for *new*, etc., etc.

How could he have been so dumb?! Simple. It surely didn't feel threatening to him while it was happening, and he had never passed that way before.

Picking up the pace a bit, here are the remaining 22.

4. "Mousetrap" Teams

A handful of brilliant scientists or engineers disappear into a basement and emerge six months later with an absolutely gee-whiz prototype that by all rights should run circles around the competition in the marketplace.

They have, in short, invented a "better mousetrap." The world, though, to their great frustration and confusion, does not beat a path to their door.

This should not be a surprise—no one on this team has ever commercialized technology before. Doing this well is every bit as difficult and specialized as coming up with the product itself. It is absolutely critical that this talent be found in at least one key member of the team, and preferably the CEO.

5. Inadequate Pricing

In my friend Bill Stolze's marvelous book *Start-Up*, he notes that "there is no start-up strategy more likely to fail than one predicated on being the lowest price competitor." Adopting such a strategy is roughly equivalent to Luxembourg insisting on settling a dispute with the U.S. with cruise missiles. I would add that the start-up company statement that causes me to lose my last meal the quickest (*always* accompanied by big smiles, no less) is: "We're going to have the *best* product at the *lowest* price!"

The message: Price to market. Gross margin is your best friend. It can absorb all manner of adversity with two exceptions: philanthropy or pricing stupidity (and actually, in this case, the two are synonymous).

6. *Insufficient Start-Up Capital*

Let's give our hypothetical founders credit and assume that they prepared a cash flow projection before their launch. History shows that 90% of the time, first year sales and gross margin do not reach expectations for whatever perverse, Murphyish reason. Both affect cash needs negatively. If each founder originally chipped in the limit of his second mortgage potential, it might already be time for the fat lady to sing.

Don't start a company if you cannot assuredly come up with more capital than you think you'll need. It's almost certain that you'll have to.

7. *Failure to Look at the Downside*

Some have called "spreadsheet spread" a plague. Even if it is, it doesn't often feature the forecasting of downside scenarios.

Consider, for example, the case of a manufacturing start-up. Three critical assumptions drive the cash flow projection—product development time, sales and gross margin. Most entrepreneurs tend to be overly optimistic with respect to all three. If the assumptions for the three are six months development time, sales of $20,000/month growing at 25% per month and 60% gross margin, but the truth turns out to be **nine** months, **$10,000**/month growing at **25%** per month and **50%**, the effect on cash needed would be substantial.

Looking at the downside possibilities in advance, monitoring actual performance against budget and developing fallback plans is just about the only effective medicine for failed fundamental assumptions.

8. *Failure to Look at Industry Norms*

Most failed entrepreneurs claim "undercapitalization" as the culprit. More often the truth is that performance did not match the capitalization available. Over-optimism in a different form is the villain again.

With minimal effort you can learn (via trade journals, annual reports, *Robert Morris Associates' Annual Statement Studies,* etc.) whether your industry is closer to a 30% or a 55% gross margin business; or whether its top performers earn 4% or 18% pre-tax. Counting on industry-unrealistic performance has drained many an initial capitalization.

9. Lack of Focus

A new venture's most precious resource is talent. Doing one thing well from scratch is an enormous challenge. Tackling three or four at once is inviting across-the-board mediocrity or worse.

Carefully sort through your opportunities before you start. Focus on the marketplace and the competitive environment. Then pursue the daylights out of the best of them.

10. *Bringing on the Vulture*

The *bad* news is that, while all money is green, it is not all equal. There really are vulture capitalists out there, and they don't all work for venture capital firms. They're obstructive, controlling, heavy-handed and mistrustful.

The *good* news is, there are also investors out there who are *gems*—experienced, connected, constructive, supportive—and they don't all work for venture capital firms, either.

How can you tell a jerk from a gem, *before the fact*? Do two things. One, ask around among the service providers—the lawyers, the accountants, the bankers. They know who the good guys and the bad guys are. Two, ask for as long a list as exists of references of CEO's of companies that firm or individual has backed, after which, call them and grill them mercilessly.

11. *First Class from the Start*

Show me a start-up in fancy space with lots of glass and chrome, all new furniture and equipment, and a management team drawing salaries at least equal to their old ones, and I will show you a prescription for failure. This is analogous to throwing a graduation party for **yourself** in the first semester of your freshman year.

Most of the best entrepreneurs I've seen have had an uncanny ability to spend a nickel in six places. They not only know that cash is, to use my favorite cash flow phrase, **more important than their mother,** they also realize that *lack* of cash is *death.* They part with it only when it makes a true difference, only when it stands to directly impact their objectives.

12. *Inappropriate Distribution Path to Market*

Sales reps are the most appropriate distribution path for start-ups, because there are no costs until and **unless** they sell something, right? Maybe they are, and maybe they aren't, but certainly not for the reason cited. And the real danger is that word "unless," as there is nothing more expensive than no commissions owed because no sales were made. There are dozens of nuances to using reps, and for some products (big ticket, high-tech products, for example), sales reps are flat-out ineffectual.

In a similar vein, I have hardly ever seen a business plan which did not highlight how trade show attendance and trade journal advertising would lead to worryingly high backlog (this is the "if they see it, they will buy" theory of sales). Short of Microsoft-sized budgets for these, I have *never* seen them meet expectations. The *keys* to the marketplace almost always lie elsewhere, and are usually nowhere near as expensive.

13. *Emotional Litigation*

It has been said that a lawsuit is a machine which you go into as a pig and come out of as a sausage. I am virtually allergic to litigation, and especially small business litigation. Just for starters, justice is all too often not done. Also, I have seen too many, multi-year, multi-hundreds of thousands of dollars, bile-producing, emotionally straining, outrageously distracting lawsuits end up with all parties agreeing to drop all actions out of acute, mutual frustration.

I am not suggesting that there aren't circumstances where litigation should be pursued. What I *am* suggesting is that the *vast* majority of the time entrepreneurs would be better served by biting their tongues hard, settling out of court and getting on with building their businesses. *This is not easy to do when you've been wronged!* But before you decide to bring a legal action, talk to some peers who have been through the experience. The horror stories are out there in abundance.

14. *Product Never "Ready" for Market*

It's time to pick on the scientists and engineers again. Some just won't show their baby to the world until it's perfection itself.

This is an unattainable goal. Technology evolves. There is always an improvement that can be made, a bell or whistle that can be added. When you've developed your product to the point where it represents a clearly superior marketplace choice, freeze the design and hand it over to the sales force.

15. *"Going Direct" When Raising Capital*

Deal flow may be the sine qua non of the venture capital business, but it's also Chinese water torture. Given the never-ending stream of opportunities which come into any venture capital firm, even the most extreme deal junkie can't help but get to the point where any deal which comes in cold is viewed as guilty until proven innocent.

Use a well-connected and respected law firm or accounting firm to make the introduction, however, and you instantly become innocent until proven guilty. There are firms in this business which are decades old which pride themselves on never having done a deal which came in "over the transom." So don't.

16. *Inadequate Market Research*

A book could be written on this phenomenon alone. Suffice it to say that a failure to do adequate market research, *including getting out into the marketplace and talking to at least a dozen prime customer targets before committing to a product strategy*, is asking for trouble.

17. *Failure to Segment Market*

The U.S. tent market is $100 million. You plan to sell high-end backpacking tents and expect to be shipping $5 million worth of them in five years. All you have to get is 5% of the tent market, right? No sweat, piece of cake.

Wrong. On closer inspection, one discovers that circus, funeral and special event tents make up 30% of the tent market; moreover, the military represents 20% and backyard family tents 20%. Finally, the two largest backpacking retailers, representing 20% of the market, own captive suppliers. That leaves 10% of the $100 million. The truth is that your falling-off-a-log $5 million sales objective represents 50% of the actual, segmented market.

18. *No Reason for Customer to Change*

The best entrepreneurial efforts I've seen have flowed from the development of a competitive matrix, i.e., a comparison by vendor (competitor) of all of the major factors which buyers consider when making a purchase decision. If, in reviewing such a matrix, you cannot reach the conclusion that any fully informed buyer would be crazy not to seriously consider purchasing your product, the buyer has no reason to switch to you . . . and probably won't.

19. *Payback Can't Be Calculated*

If you intend to sell your product on the basis of cost savings, make sure that these savings are *clearly* calculable. A claim of raw material scrap reduction can be demonstrated up front; one that promises to reduce employee back injuries probably cannot. The latter is a *much* tougher sale than the former.

20. *Failure to Admit a Mistake*

Psychologically, one of the most insidious death traps is the one which might be titled "we have too much invested in this initiative to walk away from it now"—in other words, the good money after bad judgment. For all kinds of reasons (fear, ego, etc.), these judgments are *tough* to make objectively.

I would suggest to you that the appropriate mind-set for looking at such situations is as follows:

- To date, this has been a major disappointment.
- At some point, the level of exposure could become so large as to threaten to take down with it the whole business.
- *Most importantly, the money invested to date is gone—our cost basis is zero! There is nothing to protect!*
- The appropriate question to ask yourself is, **"Would we invest the needed funds in this project today if it was presented to us as a fresh opportunity?"**

21. *Step Function Growth*

Every once in a while I see a venture which is doing so well that sales grow by leaps and bounds for long periods of time. When such a happy event occurs, it is altogether too easy to succeed oneself into bankruptcy. So many things can get out of control—credit checks, hiring, customer service, quality control, etc.

If business ever gets so good that you feel out of control, you probably are. Step back, take an objective look at things and adjust accordingly.

22. *Betting the Ranch*

Contrary to legend, great entrepreneurs are not high risk takers. They are not afraid to take a moderated risk which is largely within their control, but they would never bet the ranch, whether on an acquisition, new product or anything else. They will not risk all that they have, even for what appears to be a "sure thing." It is amazing and frightening how a "great opportunity" can quickly grow to need three times the cash flow generated by an old, "cash cow" line of products.

23. *Ignoring the Handwriting on the Wall*

Holding on to old ways, continuing to rely on original, bedrock assumptions in the face of mounting evidence to the contrary, can take a healthy company down in an amazingly short period of time.

Some years ago the stuffed toy industry began to quickly shift to off-shore production in order to reap the benefits of low wage rates. A previously successful domestic manufacturer reacted to its eroding market share by cheapening its line, thereby reducing product quality and image, while addressing the wage cost differential only marginally. Needless to say, this did not produce the desired results. Ultimately the firm admitted the inevitable and redirected its efforts into other areas, abandoning stuffed toys for good.

24. *Spiraling Costs*

As you expand from garage-quality space to an industrial park, as you finally hire that chief financial officer, as you install the new computer system, as you bring on additional production equipment, your break-even level will creep, maybe even gallop, inexorably higher and higher. While none of the above is frivolous, any or all of them could subject you to the risk of losses in the event of a downturn.

Particularly if you are in a cyclical and/or recession-sensitive industry, build your various infrastructures very calculatingly. Develop fallback plans well before you need to implement them.

25. *Silliness Phase*

Now we come to the frivolous! While few small companies ever get to the far (company jet) edge of the silliness phase, lesser gluttonies can produce the same effect. "I really need my own secretary now that we're on top of the heap." "If ABC Corporation can afford leased Mercedes and country club memberships for their execs, *we* surely can." "This place needs some decent art on the walls—in fact, it needs some serious interior decoration attention."

Beyond the obvious non-productive costs of this disease, its most insidious characteristic is its primary side effect—it inflicts major damage to workforce morale and management energy, sharpness and desire.

So . . . as you go about building your business, keep this list in mind. *It may sound strange, but you can't succeed if you don't avoid failure.* Entrepreneurial human nature is to just play offense; but even in business building, defense is critically important. Avoid making these classic mistakes and you can be assured that you have substantially increased your chances of winning the game.

Appendix D
Website Resources

List is compiled and copyrighted (2014) by HPL Consortium, Inc. Used by permission. Company websites listed retain their own trademarks, service marks and copyrights. Please remember that printed lists of websites are not reliable due to the dynamic nature of the world wide web.

Website	Primary Purpose	Supporting Details
ETTP.org HPL Consortium.com HPL501c3.org	Connecting people and groups with each other. Entrepreneurs Traveling to Prosperity Health, Prosperity, and Leadership Consortium and Institute.	Online support group for entrepreneurs and small business owners. Technology tools and resources.
GoDaddy.com Hover.com Namecheap.com Gandi.net iPage.com	Domain name registration and hosting	Domain name registration and hosting for both personal and professional websites
InfusionSoft.com OfficeAutoPilot.com	Customer relationship management, e-mail, e-commerce	Primary platform for profiles, contact lists, events, products, services, etc.
Quickbooks.com	Financial accounting	Sync with contact list Sync with product list Sync with sales/ e-commerce

(*Continued*)

Website	Primary Purpose	Supporting Details
Nefsis.com GoToMeeting.com WebEx.com Skype.com Google+ Hangouts	Sets up videoconferences between one or more people	Provide connection through videoconferencing technologies to people (complicated)
Staples.com Kinkos.com (FedEx .com) OnDemandPrinting .com	Printing services	Provide the ability to print a document on demand
BarnesAndNoble.com Amazon.com	Retail sales	Sell Books, DVDs, other products
Archives.com Intelius.com	Vital records (birth, death, marriage)	Sync with contact list
Asuresoftware.com	Meeting Room Scheduling	Sync event items Sync with calendar
CompanionLink.com	Synchronization software	Sync with multiple devices and databases
ConstantContact	Newsletter and contact list management	Sync with contact list Use to send news-letters
DialMyCalls.com	Robocalls	Robocalls to contact list (or sync to contact list)
FindASeminar.com	Site to connect people to workshops and seminars	Sync with contact list Sync with event list Sync with calendar
FlagshipMerchantSer vice.com IntuitPayments.com LeadersMerchant Services.com	Credit card merchant services	Provide merchant account to accept credit cards for purchases Sync with Quickbooks
FreeConference.com FreeConferencing.com FreeConference Calling.com	Sets up audio conferences (bridge calls)	Provide telephone bridge calls for group meetings
ISBN.org	Provide ISBN numbers	Provide ISBN numbers for new books and DVDs

(Continued)

Website	Primary Purpose	Supporting Details
Join.me screenleap.com	Screen sharing software	Provide the ability to share a computer screen in a group meeting to others (easily)
Maps.google.com	Provide directions	Provide directions from home or work address to any address in database
Paypal.com	Payment services	Provide the ability to accept credit cards or direct payment through e-mail without a merchant account
ProHealth.com	Retail for integrative health products	Sync with product lists
Reputation.com MarkMonitor.com	Monitors reputation and privacy online	Provide online reputation and privacy controls to members
SurveyMonkey.com	Conduct and analyze surveys	Conduct polls and surveys
SendOutCards.com	Send out handwritten cards	Send out handwritten notes and cards to contact list
HighTail.com	Send large files	Send large files to contact list (or sync to contact list)
YouTube.google.com	Video sharing	Link to free teaser videos
Lulu.com Scribd.com DiggyPod.com TheBookPatch.com	Book publishing	Create, Edit, Print, Publish books both on and offline
	Site to manage projects	
cEvent.com Eventbrite.com	Registration for events	Online registrations for events
ClubExpress.com YourMembership.com WildApricot.com	Club management, credit card processing, donations	Manage membership lists and websites

(*Continued*)

Website	Primary Purpose	Supporting Details
Convos.com	Mobile application to plan and promote events	Manage event planning
Craigslist.com	Apartment and personal ads	Personal activities
DonorPerfect.com	Site to manage fundraising campaigns	
Phonesheet.com UnifiedInBox.com	Site to manage messages from a myriad of sources	
Bluetracker.com Wiggio.com	Site to manage groups of people working on a project together	Manage virtual teams
Yahoogroups.com	Groupware	E-mail distribution lists
411.com or Whitepages .com	Find people	
Academia.edu	Site to connect to top faculty	
Authorize.net	Credit card authentication	Provide authentication for online merchant account. (Service provided through merchant account)
Blogger.com	Blogging site	Sync with website
Brickworkindia.com DoMyStuff.com Freelance.com ELance.com AngiesList.com ServiceMagic.com	Site to connect to virtual assistance and short-term project workers. Sites often also provide places to review services.	Provide people to do projects and tasks
BusinessEducators .com	Site to connect to top business educators	Sync with profile
DiscMakers.com	Duplicates DVDs	Provide DVDs and packaging for DVDs

(*Continued*)

Website	Primary Purpose	Supporting Details
Experian.com Equifax.com TransUnion.com	Credit scoring bureaus	Provide credit scoring data for potential contacts (Services provided through credit card authentication and directly)
ExpertClick.com Guru.com	Site to connect to top experts in various domains	
Facebook.com Twitter.com	Social Media—connect with people (friends and family oriented)	Marketing output
Facetimescheduler.com	Site to connect vendors to buyers	
Google.com	Search webpages	Search analysis data
IMCusa.org	Site to connect to top consultants	Sync with profile
JustAnswer.com	Site to connect to people with expertise in different domains who can answer quick questions	Provide individualized expertise in various fields
LinkedIn.com	Connect with other people (business oriented)	Online relationships and tools
Mail.Google.com	Contact list and e-mail	Sync with contact list and e-mail
ORCID.org	Site to connect to top researchers	Sync with profile
SBA.gov/content/small-businessdevelopment-centers-sbdcs Kauffman.org HarvardBusinessServices.com Business-in-a-Box.com IRS.gov	Help in starting a business	Provide support to for people starting their businesses

(*Continued*)

Website	Primary Purpose	Supporting Details
Travelocity.com Expedia.com Priceline.com Orbitz.com	Site to make travel arrangements and review airlines, hotels, car rentals, vacation packages, etc.	Provide people with an easy to use travel planning tool
USPS.com	US Postal Service	Send documents and letters, look up zip codes, Purchase stamps
Webmd.com/phr	Personal health record	
Wikipedia.com	Site to provide information on any topic	Provide bulk written expertise in various fields
YP.com Manta FindTheData.com FindTheCompany.com FindTheBest.com	Find businesses	

Appendix E
Goal Seek and Break-Even Analysis

USING GOAL SEEK TO
CALCULATE PROFITABLE PRICING

Using the fictional book example from Chapter 8, we can use the Goal Seek function of Excel in order to figure out at what price we would have to sell the first book if we equally apportioned the fixed costs.[1] In this case, we want to know what price we would need to establish in order to get $100,000 in profit on the first book based upon $333,333 (one-third of the million) in fixed costs and per book variable costs of $18. We can see the formulas in Figure E.1.

Figure E.1. The Formulas for the Goal Seek Example

	A	B
1		EGT Selling
2	**Number of Units Sold**	10,000
3	**Price per Unit**	61.3333333333333
4	**Sales (# units * Price per unit)**	=B3*B2
5	**Variable Costs**	=18*B2
6	**Gross Profit**	=B4-B5
7	**Fixed Costs**	=1,000,000/3
8	**Net Profit**	=B6-B7

Source: HPL Consortium, Inc., copyright 2014, used with permission.

Notice that most of the cells (except B3, the number we want Excel to tell us), have formulas in them. In Figure E.2 we can see how the Goal Seek function works. We set the Net Profit cell (B8) to 100000 in the Goal Seek dialog box, and ask Excel to calculate the price (B3).[2]

Figure E.2. Goal Seek to Calculate Price

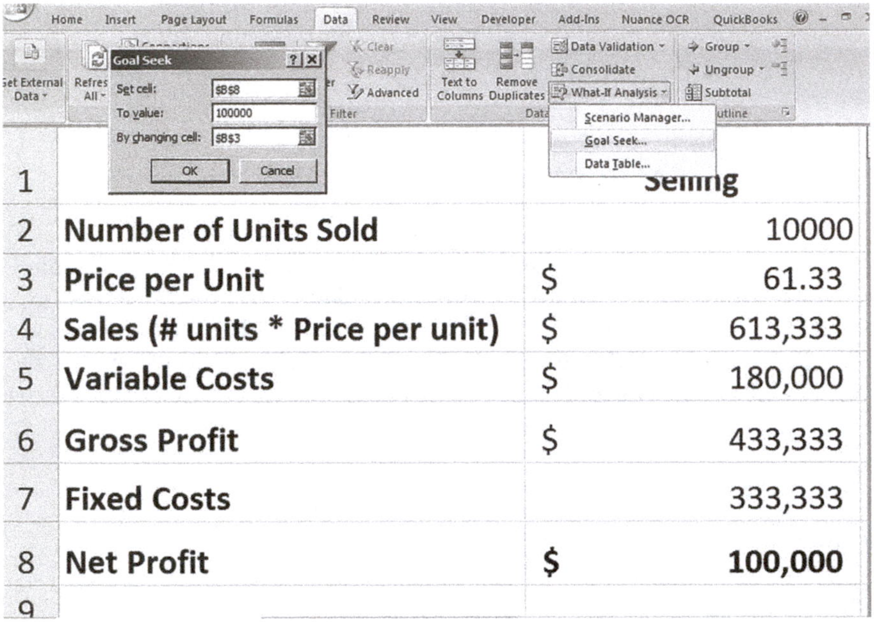

1			Selling
2	Number of Units Sold		10000
3	Price per Unit	$	61.33
4	Sales (# units * Price per unit)	$	613,333
5	Variable Costs	$	180,000
6	Gross Profit	$	433,333
7	Fixed Costs		333,333
8	Net Profit	$	100,000
9			

Source: HPL Consortium, Inc., copyright 2014, used with permission.

Notes

INTRODUCTION

1. If you read carefully, you might note that we attempt, both in this book and in the series, to use gender-ambiguous names so that the reader can envision the gender of the protagonist of the story. We've found that given a gender-ambiguous name, women tend to envision women and men tend to envision men. That helps us overcome the cultural bias that business owners are male and underlings are female.

CHAPTER 1

1. That's not to devalue the power of common sense. As Alan Weiss, a management consulting guru and one of my mentors, says: *The value of common sense is always rising.*

2. If you said "all of them," you are correct. Many of the largest businesses today were started during a recession.

3. You can read the article in the journal published in 2012, but truth be told, the academic research really doesn't have much practical value. I'd save your time, if I were you, and focus on reading Collins or the other books in the series.

4. If you don't recognize what these factors are, several of them are explained in Chapter 9 on Financials. The rest can be found in *The Entrepreneur's Guide to Understanding Financial Statements* by David Worrell.

5. This point is discussed in more detail in the chapter on Financials, along with the description of the workshop by Carl Forssen, and how the break-even point can be used to transfer fixed expenses to variable expenses.

6. A lot more on this topic can be found in *The Entrepreneur's Guide to Managing Information Technology.*

7. The same lessons that Dave Bosler taught me about sales appear in *The Entrepreneur's Guide to Selling* by Jonathan London. Dave can be contacted by phoning 610–207–2265 or by e-mailing him at DavidBosler@gmail.com. As of publication, Dave was still helping clients.

CHAPTER 2

1. There are many situations in this book where the advice given is to "soften up," give away credit, or be less assertive. Please note that this advice is context and gender sensitive. Women typically need to be more assertive, not less. In that case, softening up even more would be detrimental, especially if the woman is competing with aggressive men. Additionally, giving away credit doesn't work for someone not yet in a leadership role. The advice to give away credit is intended for people who are already in a leadership position. People in a subordinate role will not get the deserved respect or recognition without becoming more assertive and open about their accomplishments, especially if their boss is not a good leader and takes credit for their work. In those cases, they should seek others who will give them credit for their own work until they rise to a leadership level themselves.

CHAPTER 3

1. *Pitch Then Plan* is available at http://www.kutztownsbdc.org/business_planning_tool.asp.

2. After re-reading this advice, I did a search-and-replace for all instances of "very" in this book, only to discover several dozen! I had no idea I'd used the term so often since I already knew that the term "very" takes away power from the statement. The next time you encounter a statement with the word "very" in it, read the statement again without the "very." Did the "very" add or take away from the power?

3. Since a cliché is in the eye of the beholder, we need to consider what the reader might consider cliché.

CHAPTER 4

1. This was one of those occasions where the computer installation and maintenance were handled by an outsourced firm with a service agreement that said that computer problems reported to the help desk will be responded to within 24 hours. The help desk always responded within minutes, but only to say that someone would solve the problem as soon as possible. The problem was often not solved for days or weeks (depending upon the difficulties encountered). In my case, it took them more than a week to determine the problem was the mouse driver (not the mouse, which they replaced four times before they would look further).

2. These losses were, for many years, inconsequential as we were gaining more than a million customers a month. It was only when the industry became completely saturated and new customers were becoming harder to find that anyone started taking notice of how many customers we were losing.

3. Disney does not use the term "Employees" to refer to the people who work there. They use the term "Cast Members." Similarly, the financial firm for which I worked used the term "People" instead of the term "Employee."

4. Keep in mind that web resources are changing constantly, so there is no telling whether or not the websites listed in Appendix C will be active by the time you read this book. Indeed, even during the few months of time that this book was in final edit, several of the websites I had originally listed either went out of business or changed their name.

5. Can you tell that I worked in a matrixed organization? It is horrendous, and I would highly recommend staying away from the concept. NASA and a few other organizations I know are still using this idiotic management method, but most have seen the light and have dropped it.

CHAPTER 5

1. You can read many of Jim Collins articles on this topic from his website: http://www.jimcollins.com/article_topics/articles-technology.html.

2. Graph can be found on http://www.ustelecom.org/broadband-indus try/broadband-industry-stats/connections/us-fixed-broadband-connec tions. Used with permission of US Telecom Associates.

3. When talking about network or Internet speeds, we really don't mean speed. Packets travel at the speed of light, as does electricity. What we are really talking about is "how big is the pipe"—that is, how many people can send and receive data transmissions at the same time. The faster the speed, the more devices and the larger the data transmissions can be. In the old days, when transmissions were just text, there was no problem with small pipes. These days, with graphics, colors, sound, video—those pipes must be huge. Each videostream or videoconference, for example, requires an open pipe of at least 10 megabits per second. Two videos would require 20 megabits per second. And so on.

4. If you are wondering about my research project, DSL won as the pre-ferred method because it isn't a shared service, and therefore, was more re-liable than cable modem. There were still many technical problems at the time with our cable modem service provider, all of which I'm sure have been cleared up by now, but at the time, it was enough to make me stick with DSL.

5. Ned Lilly's ERP Graveyard (http://www2.erpgraveyard.com/tombs .html) is the behind-the-scenes tell-it-like-it-is place for the machinations and vagaries of the financial software company's moves.

6. Quickbooks is still the financial system of choice for small companies. Business Dynamic is still the financial system of choice for slightly larger com-panies with a strong Microsoft base. Oracle's JD Edwards is still the choice for manufacturing, People Soft for services, Oracle Financials for in between. SAP is the clear leaders for really large worldwide organizations, and has made

strong inroads into other industries, such as education and healthcare as well. Sage and Infor are both still trying to manage their dozens of acquisitions, and not doing so very successfully.

7. If you didn't know, the original term googol (which is the basis for name Google) is a number equal to 10000000000000000000000000000000000000000 00000000000000000000000000000000000000000000000000000000000000000 (10 to the power of 100).

8. At least for a short time. Like many addictions, social media actually hurts those who depend upon it; a recent study revealed that youth who use Facebook are not as happy and satisfied with their lives as those who do not use Facebook. http://www.plosone.org/article/info%3Adoi%2F10.1371% 2Fjournal.pone.0069841.

9. Antonio Regalado. *Who Coined 'Cloud Computing'?* October 31, 2011, http://www.technologyreview.com/business/38987/ (Retrieved December 28, 2011).

10. Those who manage Internet technology (the World Wide Web Consortium) have been talking about the need for IPv6 (which is a 64 bit IP address rather than a 32 bit IP address) since 1994. On June 6, 2012, world-shattering progress toward universal adoption of IPv6 occurred. On that day, known in technology circles as IPv6 day, the newer IPv6 was installed on all the backbone routers transferring packets of data across the Internet. That will lay the groundwork for Quality of Service (QOS) to be implemented. QOS is a misnomer because it has nothing to do with quality of service, but rather with the prioritization of certain packets of information, such as allowing video traffic through while holding back e-mail traffic.

11. Wii is a hands-on video game technology that enables you to play physical games like golf and tennis virtually.

CHAPTER 6

1. A full description of how to use each one of these tools, along with examples and detailed uses, can be found in *The Entrepreneur's Guide to Market Research.*

2. Two Apple mobile devices based on ARM processors. 162MHz on the Newton, 412MHz on the iPhone. Posted July 7, 2007. Licensed under the Creative Commons Attribution 2.0. Found via Wikimedia Common, a freely licensed media file repository. Source: Newton and iPhone: ARM and ARM (http://www.flickr.com/photos/35448539@N00/2379207825/) Photo owned by Blake Patterson (http://www.flickr.com/people/35448539@N00) from Alexandria, VA. Used by permission.

3. The concept that a business cannot convince the buying public to purchase a technology for which they are not yet ready is encapsulated in Loewy's Law: *Most Advanced Yet Most Acceptable.*

CHAPTER 7

1. Jakob Nielsen, the world's top expert in Computer Human Interface Design has published Jakob's Law: **Users spend most of their time on** *other* **sites.** The bottom line is—do navigation like everyone else. Don't get fancy. Stick with the basics, and make absolutely sure the site comes up quick—no bloated graphics to slow down the user experience or people will leave the site before reading it. The original publication can be found on http://www.nngroup.com/articles/end-of-web-design

2. Co-opetition is the friendly cooperation between companies typically considered competitors. The term is related to frenemies, when two people who would typically be considered enemies become friends (or vice versa).

3. More details on how the Google search engine works (and why we should avoid SEO services) can be found in *The Entrepreneur's Guide to Managing Information Technology* book.

4. You can find Google's full list of best practices at https://static.google usercontent.com/external_content/untrusted_dlcp/www.google.com/en/us/webmasters/docs/search-engine-optimization-starter-guide.pdf.

CHAPTER 8

1. Note that the culture identifies whether or not a certain brand carries a certain meaning. At one job where I was vice president, it was expected for people to wear expensive suits, carry Mont Blanc pens, and wear Rolex (or men) or Movado (for women) watches. When I switched to another corporation, also as vice president, they didn't even know what a Mont Blanc pen was, and couldn't care less what kind of watch you wore.

2. One of the most important sales lessons I learned was how to create a need that was not previously there. The secret is the same—listen to the client to find out what is of interest to the client. Once you've established what is of most concern to the client, find a way to hook your products or services onto that concern so that it solves a need for the client. Obviously, if there are no hooks at all, then the idea is to extricate yourself as quickly as possible so that you can move on to find someone who has concerns that are solved by your products and services. In writing, you have to rely upon the reader to self-impose the time limit (by abandoning the book or article) if your advice is not dealing with the reader's concerns.

CHAPTER 9

1. Have you noticed how similar the selling skills are to leadership skills? There is quite a bit of overlap.

CHAPTER 10

1. Quickbooks has *classes,* which allows us to track each expense by two different attributes. You can also accomplish the same thing by setting up two different accounts for each expense, for example, direct advertising and indirect advertising. The important thing is to get the bookkeeper to enter specifically what the expense is for at the time of entering the order or invoice. This is not easy because though a bookkeeper can tell an advertising expense because the invoice is for an ad, a bookkeeper cannot tell if the advertising was direct or indirect, so the process must find a way to include that information in the forms entered by the bookkeeper.

2. Even large public companies sometimes book too little depreciation. Ever wonder how companies such as Facebook can appear to show a profit when their income is so much lower than the cost of running the business? They capitalize the majority of the costs over a very long time frame, so each period appears profitable. If they do well in the future, they can make up for the difference because most of their costs are fixed, and their variable costs are negligible. If they don't do well in the future, since they can't really sell the assets they booked that are depreciating, they can quickly lose all their value. Sometimes, the gamble pays off (as in Google), and sometimes, it doesn't (as in MySpace).

3. Essentially, Section 179 of the IRS tax code allows businesses to deduct the full purchase price of qualifying equipment and/or software purchased or financed during the tax year as an incentive to encourage businesses to buy equipment and invest in themselves. (Source: http://www.section179.org/section_179_deduction.html). That means that if you buy (or lease) a piece of qualifying equipment, you can deduct the full purchase price from your gross income. There are limits on what you can deduct ($500,000 in 2013) and limits on where it can be applied. There's also the first-year bonus depreciation that can be applied to Section 179 eligible property and MACRS rules for depreciable lives. None of this should matter for purposes of either financial or managerial pictures of the business.

CHAPTER 12

1. In case you didn't know, the term "boutique firm" usually means a one-person shop with lots of help (of the 1099, not W-2, variety). It's a nice way of saying "tiny but powerful."

2. Kathleen Passanisi was great and I highly recommend her as a lunch or dinner speaker. You can contact her via http://www.kathleenpassanisi.com/, or by calling 636 561–2516 or e-mailing kathleen@kathleenpassanisi.com

3. If you see the videoconferencing revolution as I see it, and you want to charge forward (think Telehealth!), then feel free to borrow freely from my initial efforts. I'll even send you my business plan if you wish.

APPENDIX E

1. If you have never learned how to use the Goal Seek function of Excel, now is a great time to learn. Given any formula, it will calculate what one value must be, based upon another given value. If you would like further details than the simple explanation in this chapter, contact CJ Rhoads for access to a video tutorial on the topic.

2. Goal Seek can be found under the **Data ribbon**, under the **What If Analysis** button in Excel 2010 version. In the example, don't worry about the dollar signs appearing in the cell addresses (B8 and B3). Dollar signs indicate that the cell address is *absolute*. If absolute cell addresses were used in a formula, they would not adjust relative to a new location if they were copied. Since we are not copying, it makes no difference at all if the cell address says B8 or B8.

References

Benson, Herbert, and William Proctor. 2003. *The Breakout Principle: How to Activate the Natural Trigger That Maximizes Creativity, Athletic Performance, Productivity, and Personal Well-Being*. New York: Scribner.

Beste, Frederick. 1996. *Entrepreneurial Death Traps*. New Haven, CT: Yale School of Management.

Blank, Steve. 2013. "Why the Lean Start-Up Changes Everything." *Harvard Business Review* 91 (5): 63–72.

Bradley, Tony. 2011. *Apple iPad, Day 30: The Verdict—Can an iPad Replace a PC?* PCWorld, July 31, 2011. Available at http://www.pcworld.com/article/236995/apple_ipad_day_30_the_verdict_can_an_ipad_replace_a_pc.html?page=2. Accessed May 1, 2013.

Brenda. 2013. *What Is the Disney Vault? What Is Disney Releasing from the Vault in 2013?* Squidoo.com, January 24, 2013. Available at http://www.squidoo.com/disney-vault. Accessed June 12, 2013.

Buckingham, M. 2005. *The One Thing You Need to Know: . . . About Great Managing, Great Leading, and Sustained Individual Success*. New York: Free Press.

Byrne, Rhonda. 2007. *The Secret*. Hillsboro, OR: Atria Books/Beyond Words.

Center for Internal Change Inc. 2013. *What Is DiSC? Which Should I Use Everything DiSC Or DiSC Classic?* Center for Internal Change, Inc. 2013. Available at http://www.internalchange.com/which-disc-to-use.html. Accessed July 20, 2013.

Chan, James. 2000. *Spare Room Tycoon: Succeeding Independently: The 70 Lessons of Sane-Self-employment*. Naperville, IL: Nicholas Brealey Pub.

Collins, James C. 2001. *Good to Great: Why Some Companies Make the Leap—And Others Don't*. Vol. 1. New York: Harper Business.

Collins, James C., and William C. Lazier. 1992. *Beyond Entrepreneurship: Turning Your Business into an Enduring Great Company*. Englewood Cliffs, NJ: Prentice Hall.

Collins, James C., and Jerry I. Porras. 1994. *Built to Last: Successful Habits of Visionary Companies*. Vol. 1. New York: Harper Business.

Collins, Jim. 2005. "Level 5 Leadership: The Triumph of Humility and Fierce Resolve [Cover Story]." *Harvard Business Review* 83 (7): 136–46.

Collins, Jim. 2009. *How the Mighty Fall: And Why Some Companies Never Give In.* New York: HarperCollins.

Collins, Jim, and Morten Hansen. 2011. *Great by Choice: Uncertainty, Chaos, and Luck—Why Some Thrive Despite Them All.* New York: Harper Business.

Conlin, Michelle. 2004. "Meditation." *Business Week* (3897): 136–37.

Conner, Cheryl. 2013. *The Biggest Mistake an Entrepreneur Can Make.* Forbes, October 16, 2012. Available at http://www.forbes.com/sites/cherylsnappconner/2012/10/16/the-biggest-mistake-an-entrepreneur-can-make/. Accessed May 30, 2013.

Covey, Stephen R. 2005. *The 8th Habit: From Effectiveness to Greatness.* New York: Free Press.

DesMarais, Christina. 2013. *9 Insanely Successful Kickstarter Campaigns.* Inc.com, August 2, 2013. Available at http://www.inc.com/ss/christina-desmarais/10-insanely-successful-kickstarter-campaigns. Accessed August 14, 2013.

Dobbs, Richard, Tomas Karakolev, and Rishi Raj. 2007. "Preparing for the Next Downturn." *McKinsey Quarterly* (3): 81–83.

Ferriss, Timothy. 2007. *The 4-Hour Workweek.* New York: Crowne Publishing.

Frampton, Jez. 2013. *The Top 100 Brands.* Interbrand, June 19, 2013. Available at http://www.interbrand.com/en/best-global-brands/2012/Best-Global-Brands-2012-Brand-View.aspx. Accessed June 19, 2013.

Frankl, V.E., I. Lasch, H. S. Kushner, and W. J. Winslade. 2006. *Man's Search for Meaning.* Boston: Beacon Press.

Henderson, John C., and Paul C. Nutt. 1980. "The Influence of Decision Style on Decision Making Behavior." *Management Science* 26 (4): 371.

Herzberg, Frederick. 2008. *One More Time: How Do You Motivate Employees?* Cambridge, MA: Harvard Press.

Johnson, Scott D., Chanidprapa Suriya, Seung Won Yoon, Jared V. Berrett, and Jason La Fleur. 2002. "Team Development and Group Processes of Virtual Learning Teams." *Computers & Education* 39 (4): 379.

Katzenbach, Jon R. 1998. *Teams at the Top: Unleashing the Potential of Both Teams and Individual Leaders.* Boston: Harvard Business School Press.

Katzenbach, Jon R., and Douglas K. Smith. 1994. *The Wisdom of Teams: Creating the High-Performance Organization.* Vol. 1. New York: Harper Business.

Kiisel, Ty. 2013. *65% of Americans Choose a Better Boss Over a Raise—Here's Why.* Forbes, October 16, 2012. Available at http://www.forbes.com/sites/tykiisel/2012/10/16/65-of-americans-choose-a-better-boss-over-a-raise-heres-why/. Accessed May 30, 2013.

Knorr, Eric. 2013. "Protect Yourself from the Coming Cloud Crack-up." *Info World.* Available at http://www.infoworld.com/t/cloud-computing/protect-yourself-the-coming-cloud-crack-218872. Accessed May 20, 2013.

Kwoh, L. 2010. Economic Slump Called "Great Recession" by Associated Press Manual [Homepage of Star Ledger]. Available at http://www.nj.com/business/index.ssf/2010/02/from_now_lets_call_it_the_grea.html Accessed June 27, 2010.

Lee, Fiona, Christopher Peterson, and Larissa Z. Tiedens. 2004. "Mea Culpa: Predicting Stock Prices from Organizational Attributions." *Personality and Social Psychology Bulletin* 30 (12): 1636–49. doi: 10.1177/0146167204266654.

Levine, Stuart R., Michael A. Crom, Carnegie Dale, and Associates. 1993. *The Leader in You: How to Win Friends, Influence People, and Succeed in a Changing World*. New York: Simon & Schuster.

Luzar, Charles. 2013. *SEC Chairman White: Crowdfunding Rules Coming in Fall. Crowdfund Insider*, July 31, 2013. Available at http://www.crowdfundinsider.com/2013/07/19778-sec-chairman-white-crowdfunding-rules-coming-in-fall/. Accessed August 14, 2013.

McGovern, Joy, Michael Lindemann, Monica Vergara, Stacey Murphy, Linda Barker, and Rodney Warrenfeltz. 2001. "Maximizing the Impact of Executive Coaching: Behavioral Change, Organizational Outcomes, and Return on Investment." *The Manchester Review* 6 (1): 1–9.

Müller, Günter F., and Cathrin Gappisch. 2005. "Personality Types of Entrepreneurs." *Psychological Reports* 96 (3): 737–46.

Rhoads, CJ, and Keshav Gupta. 2012. "*Leadership Lessons for the Business Community: Strategies to Maintain Prosperity during a Recession.*" *International Journal of Society Systems Science* 4 (1): 28–54.

Ryan, Oliver. 2007. "Om Work." *Fortune* 156 (2): 193–94.

Sandler, David H. 1995. *You Can't Teach a Kid to Ride a Bike at a Seminar.* New York: Dutton.

Scheid, Lisa. 2013. "The Crowd Comes to Funding." *Reading Eagle*, August 4, p. 1.

Shane, Scott Andrew. 2005. *Finding Fertile Ground: Identifying Extraordinary Opportunities for New Ventures.* Upper Saddle River, NJ: Wharton School Pub.

Stangler, Dane. 2009. *The Economic Future Just Happened.* Kansas City, MO: Ewing Marion Kauffman Foundation.

Stanko, J. 2000. *So Many Leaders So Little Leadership:* Mobile, AL: Evergreen Press.

Steinberg, Marc. *ROI—Executive Coaching.* Consciousness Coaching Academy. Available at http://smartrevolution.org/consciousness-coaching/.

Tannen, Deborah. 2001. *Talking from 9 to 5: Women and Men at Work.* New York: William Morrow Paperbacks. Original edition, 1995.

U.S. Census Bureau. 2012. *Statistics about Business Size (including Small Business) from the U.S. Census Bureau.* (Last revised May 21, 2012). U.S. Census Bureau. Available at http://www.census.gov/econ/smallbus.html. Accessed July 7, 2013.

Walton, Alice G. 2013. *How Yoga Might Save the U.S. Trillions of Dollars, And A Lot of Lives*. Forbes, July 24, 2013. Available at http://www.forbes.com/sites/alicegwalton/2013/07/24/how-yoga-might-save-the-u-s-trillions-of-dollars-and-a-lot-of-lives/. Accessed July 24, 2013.

Yihan, Lin. 2013. *Sam Walton Leadership Case Study*. Leadership with You 2013. Available at http://www.leadership-with-you.com/sam-walton-leadership.html. Accessed July 7, 2013.

Index

About the Author

CJ RHOADS, M.Ed., D.Ed., is founder and CEO of HPL Consortium, Inc., a business that develops technology tools to help people and groups connect towards health, prosperity, and leadership. She speaks and writes about entrepreneurship, business strategy, leadership development, information technology, and the economics of healthcare and integrative health practices. In 2009, she was honored as one of Pennsylvania's Best 50 Women in Business. She received the Athena Leadership award in 2011 and was named one of the 25 Women of Influence by Lehigh Valley Business in 2013. Rhoads is an associate professor in the College of Business at Kutztown University and a prolific writer, authoring over 165 articles and six books. In 2014 she was named Top Faculty Researcher of the Year by the scholarly activity committee in the College of Business at Kutztown University. She is the editor of ABC-CLIO's *The Entrepreneur's Guide* series and author of *The Entrepreneur's Guide to Managing Information Technology*. She received her D.Ed. in Educational Technology with a minor in Business Administration from Lehigh University, and her M.Ed. from Temple University in Educational Psychology focusing on Instructional Design. She is also well known in the Integrative Health Practices world, having recovered from a devastating brain injury as the result of a car accident in 2002. She manages her chronic pain through a combination of good nutrition and several daily activities such as Tai Chi, Qigong, and Pilates (rather than pain management drugs). She can be reached at CJRhoads@HPLConsortium.com.